C000255732

JAPAN'S BLITZKRIEG

WITHDRAWN FROM STOCK

JAPAN'S BLITZKRIEG

*The Rout of Allied Forces
in the Far East 1941–2*

by

Bernard Edwards

Pen & Sword
MARITIME

First published in Great Britain in 2006 by
Pen & Sword Maritime
an imprint of
Pen & Sword Books Ltd
47 Church Street
Barnsley
South Yorkshire
S70 2AS

Copyright © Bernard Edwards, 2006

ISBN 1 84415 442 4
978 1 84415 442 5

The right of Bernard Edwards to be identified as Author of this Work
has been asserted by him in accordance with the Copyright,
Designs and Patents Act 1988.

A CIP catalogue record for this book is
available from the British Library.

All rights reserved. No part of this book may be reproduced or
transmitted in any form or by any means, electronic or mechanical
including photocopying, recording or by any information storage and
retrieval system, without permission from the Publisher in writing.

Typeset in Sabon by
Phoenix Typesetting, Auldgirth, Dumfriesshire

Printed and bound in England by
Biddles Ltd., King's Lynn

Pen & Sword Books Ltd incorporates the Imprints of Pen & Sword
Aviation, Pen & Sword Maritime, Pen & Sword Military, Wharncliffe
Local History, Pen & Sword Select, Pen & Sword Military Classics and
Leo Cooper.

For a complete list of Pen & Sword titles please contact
PEN & SWORD BOOKS LIMITED
47 Church Street, Barnsley, South Yorkshire, S70 2AS, England
E-mail: enquiries@pen-and-sword.co.uk
Website: www.pen-and-sword.co.uk

This is for my first ship, the dear old *Clan Murdoch*.
She sailed serenely through it all.

Painting her shapely shadows from the dawn
An image tumbled on a rose-swept bay,
A drowsy ship of some yet older day.

JAMES ELROY FLECKER

LEICESTERSHIRE LIBRARY SERVICES	
4055230	
Bertrams	31.10.06
940.5425	£19.99
SW	

Contents

Acknowledgements

The author wishes to thank the following for their help in researching for this book:

Royal Naval Association, Swindon Branch; Instituut voor Maritieme Historie; US Naval Historical Center; National Archives, Kew; and Willem Hage, Albert Kelder, George Monk, Bernard De Neumann, Frits Norbergen and Ken Williams.

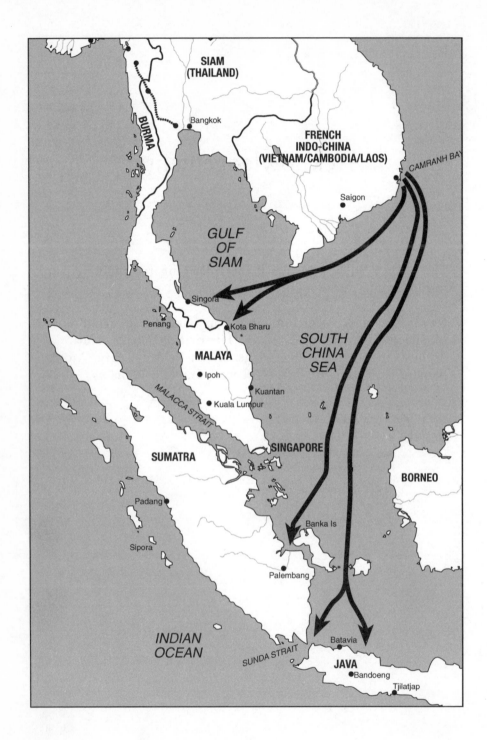

SIAM
(THAILAND)

BURMA

Bangkok

FRENCH
INDO-CHINA
(VIETNAM/CAMBODIA/LAOS)

CAMRANH BAY

Saigon

GULF
OF
SIAM

Singora

Penang

Kota Bharu

SOUTH
CHINA
SEA

MALAYA

Ipoh

Kuantan

Kuala Lumpur

SINGAPORE

SUMATRA

BORNEO

MALACCA STRAIT

Padang

Banka Is

Sipora

Palembang

INDIAN
OCEAN

Batavia

SUNDA STRAIT

JAVA

Bandoeng

Tjilatjap

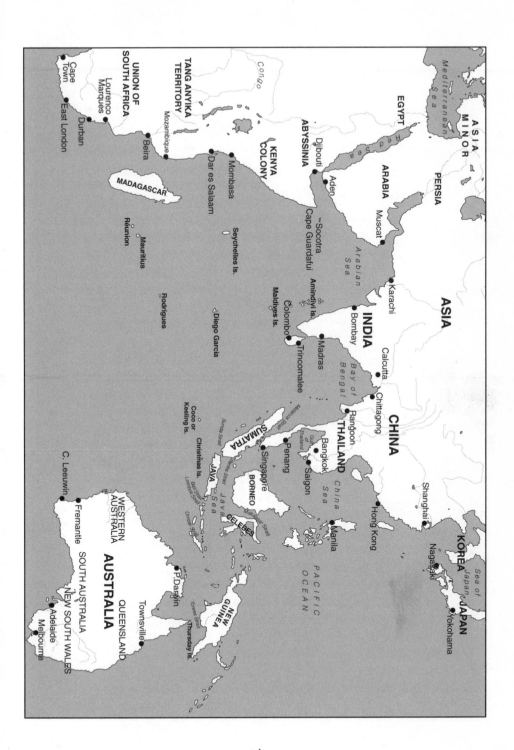

JAPAN'S
BLITZKRIEG

Chapter One

Prelude to War

The evacuation of the remnants of the British Army from the beaches of Dunkirk in June 1940 has always been seen as snatching victory from the jaws of defeat. Britain then stood alone, and in the months that followed her cities suffered intense bombing, and the threat of invasion from across the Channel was ever imminent. Yet in the midst of all this adversity thoughts were turned towards the defence of the Empire in the East. On 11 August 1940, Winston Churchill wrote to the Prime Ministers of Australia and New Zealand:

> The combined Staffs are preparing a paper on the Pacific situation, but I venture to send you in advance a brief fore-word. We are trying our best to avoid war with Japan . . . I do not myself think that Japan will declare war unless Germany can make a successful invasion of Britain . . . Should Japan nevertheless declare war on us her first objective outside the Yellow Sea would probably be the Dutch East Indies . . . In the first phase of an Anglo-Japanese war we should of course defend Singapore, which if attacked – which is unlikely – ought to stand a long siege. We should also be able to base on Ceylon a battle-cruiser and a fast aircraft carrier, which, with all the Australian and New Zealand cruisers and destroyers, which would return to you, would act as a very powerful deterrent upon the hostile raiding cruisers . . .

Churchill's defiant words were characteristic of British thinking in those early days, but with regard to Singapore his optimism was unfounded. It had been said many years before the outbreak of war that the 'impregnable fortress' of Singapore was a myth, and it was in reality 'a £60 million floating dock whose sole defence was six 15-inch naval guns pointing mutely out to sea'. As for basing a powerful naval force on Ceylon, with the Royal Navy needing all its strength merely to keep open Britain's vital sea lanes in the Atlantic, this was a fantasy that could in no way become reality.

The defence of the Eastern sphere was discussed at a meeting of the War Cabinet in Whitehall in late August 1940 with Ministers and Chiefs of Staff present. It was the opinion of the Chiefs of Staff that Britain was in no position to face war with Japan, and following the meeting a top-secret twenty-eight-page report on the true situation was compiled. A copy of this report was to be sent to the C-in-C Far East without delay, and by as secure a means as possible.

Monday, 11 November 1940. As the sun rose in the east, turning the gently undulating waters of the Indian Ocean from steel-grey to a rich blue, the memories came flooding back to Captain William Ewan; memories of that other war, ended twenty-two years ago this day. So many men had died, amongst them men with whom he had sailed and whom he had known so well. Shipmates. Now, here he was once again pacing the bridge of a merchantman, her distinctive company colours hidden under a coat of drab Admiralty grey. He stopped in his stride and turned to look aft, to where the long barrel of the recently fitted 4-inch gun – another relic of that distant war – dominated the poop deck. He wondered if this gun would ever be fired again in anger. Looking back on the events of the night just past, he concluded that this might well be so.

Captain Ewan's command, the 7528-ton *Automedon*, was one of Alfred Holt's prestigious Blue Funnel Line, a regular Far East trader. Built on the Tyne in 1922, she was too young to have seen that other war, but had given a lifetime of exemplary service on the road to the East, and looked set to go on for another twenty years or so. Like most British cargo liners of her day, she had no pretensions to luxury, but was solid and dependable, her double-reduction turbines, even after so many thousands of miles steamed, still turning out a consistent 14 knots. She was manned by British officers and Chinese ratings, a total complement of ninety-three, and had accommodation for twelve passengers, although on the current voyage only one of her cabins was occupied, by Mr Alan Ferguson and his wife, newly-weds on their way back to Singapore. In her holds, the *Automedon* carried a cargo of cased aircraft, vehicles, machinery spares, bicycles, microscopes, service uniforms, cameras, sewing machines, steel and copper sheets, whisky, beer, cigarettes, food supplies, and 120 bags of mail, a bizarre mélange of the necessities of war and peace.

The *Automedon*'s long outward passage, beginning in Liverpool in late September and taking her south to Freetown, around the Cape of Good Hope to Durban, and thence across the wide reaches of the Indian Ocean, had been uneventful. Once past Finisterre, the long lazy days at sea under untroubled blue skies, when the watches came and went by the bridge bell, and gins and tonics and steamer chairs at sunset signalled the end of another day, had lulled all on board into a false sense of security. The war was far away – until, on the evening of 10 November, when the ship was forty-seven days out from Liverpool and approaching the north-western tip of the island of Sumatra, the idyll came to a sudden end.

Dinner was over, and the night was quiet, the *Automedon* carving out a long furrow of phosphorescence as she steamed north-easterly under a black sky studded with a million twinkling stars. From her wireless room, immediately abaft the bridge, came occasional muted bursts of morse as the operator on watch trawled the wavelengths in search of something to enliven the boredom of the long hours. Then, suddenly, loud and clear came an urgent signal, 'QQQ, QQQ, QQQ', followed by 'POSITION 2 DEGREES 34 N 70 DEGREES 56 E OLE JACOB. UNKNOWN SHIP HAS TURNED AND NOW COMING AFTER US'. And a few minutes later, 'QQQ STOPPED BY UNKNOWN SHIP'. Then there was silence, broken only by the faint crackle of atmospherics.

When the Radio Officer handed him the signals form with its scribbled message, Bill Ewan felt a trickle of cold sweat run down his spine. 'QQQ' was code for 'I am being attacked by an enemy merchant raider', and the call for help had come from the Norwegian tanker *Ole Jacob*. Before sailing from Durban, bound for Malaya, Ewan had been warned that at least two German surface raiders were operating in the Indian Ocean. The Norwegian ship had obviously met up with one of these. However, he drew comfort from the fact that when the *Ole Jacob*'s position was plotted on the chart it put her at least 600 miles to the west of the *Automedon*, and at her present speed of 14 knots she would reach Penang, her first port of discharge, long before any harm came her way. Unfortunately for Captain Ewan, someone aboard the *Ole Jacob* had got their calculations very wrong. When the tanker came under attack, she was actually only 200 miles north of the *Automedon*, less than twelve hours steaming in a fast ship – and the German raider would undoubtedly be fast.

The first sign of danger for the *Automedon* came at 0700 on the 11th, when a ship was sighted at three points on the port bow, hull down on the horizon. Fifteen minutes later she was clearly visible, and on a converging course. Ewan, who was on the bridge with Second Officer Donald Stewart, immediately became suspicious, but when he examined the stranger through his binoculars he decided she was probably a Dutchman, one of the Royal Dutch Mail Line's regular traders, a common enough sight in these waters. Instructing Stewart to keep his eye on the approaching ship, Ewan went below, where his morning tea and toast awaited him.

At 0820, Captain Ewan was called to the bridge by Second Officer Stewart, who was concerned that the 'Dutchman' was now only 2½ miles off and still converging. Under the International Collision Regulations, which govern the conduct of ships at sea, the stranger was the 'giving-way' ship, and as such should have by now altered course to avoid the *Automedon*. Ewan examined her again through his binoculars, and was about to tell Stewart to contact her using the Aldis lamp, when he saw a puff of smoke drift away from the other ship's bow. This was followed by a bang, and seconds later a fountain of water appeared off the *Automedon*'s starboard bow. They were being fired on.

The *Automedon*'s assailant was the German surface raider *Atlantis*, ex-*Goldenfels* of the Hansa Line, a 7800-ton cargo liner, which in the far-off days of peace had sailed these waters side by side with Blue Funnel ships. On the outbreak of war she had been taken into a naval dockyard in Kiel, and re-emerged in March 1940 flying the battle ensign of the *Kriegsmarine*, and armed with six 5.9-inch guns, a 75mm in the bows, two twin 37mm and four

20mm AA guns, and four 21-inch torpedo tubes. All these guns, and her Arado seaplane were hidden behind portable shutters or below decks, so that to all but the most critical observer she looked like a run-of-the-mill merchantman going about her legitimate business. But manned by 347 trained men, and commanded by Kapitän-zur-See Bernhard Rogge, she was a formidable warship, already with an impressive record of ships captured and sunk.

Having put a warning shot across the *Automedon*'s bows, the *Atlantis* broke out her battle ensign, cleared away her guns, and ordered the British ship to stop. This was a challenge that few British shipmasters were prepared to accept in this war, and Bill Ewan was no exception to that rule. Swinging his ship under full helm until she was stern-on to the raider, he called for full emergency speed, and ordered his gunners to man the 4-inch.

Quartermaster Stan Hughill, who was at the wheel recalled vividly the next hectic moments:

> Next minute, bang over the bows with a warning shot, up went the German battle flag. So that was it. The Old Man said to me 'hard a'starboard', you see, so that meant the ship's bows went that way [he points] and the stern went that way, next minute we were at right angles to the raider, the one we thought was the Dutchman. Next minute, bang, bang, bang, 'cos our captain was the stuff Nelson was made of – they don't exist any more, people like this – shouts 'We'll fight 'em, you know!' and turned his pea shooter towards this chap, who could have blown us out of the water in no time.

The *Automedon*'s gun crew got off three rounds in quick succession, but meanwhile Rogge had swung his ship to put her beam-on to the fleeing merchantman, and opened up with a full broadside from his 5.9s, followed by a second broadside and then a third. When the smoke cleared, the effect on the *Automedon* of the heavy German shells was seen to be devastating. Her bridge had been almost completely demolished, the boat deck was a smoking shambles with all four lifeboats blown over the side, the officers' accommodation below the bridge was also wrecked, and all around men lay dead and wounded. Captain Ewan was dead, Second

Officer Stewart was dead, as were four other officers, while twelve of the crew were wounded, some of them seriously.

The engagement – if it could be called that – lasted exactly three minutes, during which time the *Automedon* had been brought to a standstill and reduced to a drifting wreck. Rogge now sent over an armed boarding party, led by Leutnant Ulrich Mohr, the *Atlantis*'s first lieutenant. Mohr wasted no time, going straight to the master's safe, which when broken open was found to contain only a small amount of petty cash. The mail room, on the other hand, proved to be much more rewarding. In Mohr's words: 'In the mail room we found a number of bags marked "Safe hand. By British Master only". This contained, passing all our expectations, the whole of the Top Secret mail for the High Command Far East, new code tables for the fleet, secret Notices to Mariners: information about minefields and swept areas, plans and maps and many other documents.' And there was more to come. Making his way through the smoking ruins that had once been the *Automedon*'s bridge, Mohr entered the chartroom, where a quick search of the drawers revealed a find that left the first lieutenant open-mouthed. He later wrote:

> Our prize was a long narrow envelope enclosed in a green bag equipped with brass eyelets to let the water in to facilitate its sinking. The bag was marked 'Highly confidential. To be destroyed', and the envelope addressed to the 'C-in-C Far East . . . To be opened personally'. The documents had been drawn up by no less an authority than the Planning Division of the War Cabinet and contained the latest appreciation of the military strength of the Empire in the Far East. There were details of RAF units, details of naval strength, an assessment of the role of Australia and New Zealand, and most piquant of all, a long paragraph regarding the possibility of Japan entering the war, a paragraph accompanied by copious notes on the fortifications of Singapore. What the devil were the British about, sending such material by a slow old tub like the *Automedon*, I puzzled? Surely a warship would have been a worthier repository? We could not understand it.

Little wonder Mohr failed to understand the appalling lack of security in sending such a sensitive document by a merchant ship which was sailing unescorted and with nothing more to defend herself than a single First World War vintage 4-inch gun manned by one trained naval gunner and a scratch crew of merchant seamen. The document in question resulted from a War Cabinet meeting in London on 8 August 1940, and was addressed to Air Chief Marshal Sir Robert Brooke-Popham, C-in-C Far East. It ran to twenty-eight pages, and contained the most damning evidence of Britain's inability to confront Japan should she decide to attack in the East. The Cabinet was of the opinion – and this was stated in no uncertain terms – that British forces were too far stretched in other theatres to mount a credible defence of Hong Kong, Malaya, Singapore or the Dutch East Indies should they be threatened.

It seems likely that Captain Ewan, who must have been aware of the importance of this report, had kept the weighted bag in the chartroom so that it could be quickly thrown overboard should the ship be stopped. In the event, the ruthless shelling of the *Automedon* – the *Atlantis* had fired twenty-eight shells, eleven of which were direct hits – had wrecked the bridge of the British ship, killing Captain Ewan and Second Officer Stewart before they had the opportunity to get rid of the top secret document.

Kapitän Rogge, who was fluent in English, was quick to realize the importance of the Cabinet report when Mohr handed it to him on returning to the *Atlantis* after placing scuttling charges aboard the *Automedon*. Subsequently Rogge transferred the document to the *Ole Jacob*, which had been taken as a prize, and instructed Leutnant Paul Kamenz to take the tanker, along with her cargo of 10,000 tons of aviation fuel, to Japan.

The *Ole Jacob* arrived in Kobe on 4 December, where Leutnant Kamenz handed over the top secret Cabinet report to a courier, who delivered it to Admiral Paul Wenneker, the German Naval Attaché in Tokyo. Having read through the document, Wenneker telegraphed a summary to Berlin, and then entrusted the original to a courier, who travelled by train across the length of the still neutral USSR to deliver it to Naval Intelligence in Berlin. Eventually, a copy was handed over to Captain Yokai, the Japanese Naval Attaché in that city, who in turn despatched a summary of the contents to the Naval Staff in Tokyo. To complete the long, complicated diplomatic round, the original document was returned to Tokyo, where Admiral Wenneker handed it over to Vice Admiral Kondo.

It seems that the Japanese were initially suspicious of the report. They could not believe that the Great Britain which had carved out and held for a hundred years a huge Empire in the East was so weak as to be unable to defend that Empire. And if it was so, then no government would be foolish enough to commit such sensitive material to paper, let alone despatch it across the world by a slow, vulnerable merchant ship. It began to look very much like a German plot to bring Japan into the war on their side. However, a closer examination of the defences of the British bases eventually convinced the Japanese of the validity of the *Automedon* document, and they decided to act.

In the opinion of Professor J. W. M. Chapman, a leading expert on the conduct of the war in the Far East, the loss of the *Automedon*, and in particular the unforeseen sudden deaths of Captain William Ewan and Second Officer Donald Stewart, led to a dramatic turn of events. He writes:

> This fact [the handing over of the top level British Cabinet papers by the Germans] enabled the Japanese Combined Fleet to concentrate single-mindedly on the attack on Pearl Harbor in the certain knowledge that Britain could not provide strong enough forces to compel the Japanese to divide the Combined Fleet more evenly between the British and American Fleets. It also accounts for one of the reasons for the British Authorities, who had the original War Diary [Wenneker's] in their possession since 1945, being reluctant to reveal fuller details of the incident and its background. This knowledge is quite indispensable for an understanding of the reasons why the European War was transformed into a global conflict.

The extent to which the British Government was embarrassed by the loss of the *Automedon* papers may be judged by its reluctance to divulge details of the incident. In fact, to this day there is no reference to the incident in the very comprehensive files concerning the Second World War held in the National Archives at Kew. It was not until 1980 that the capture of these sensitive Cabinet papers came to light, and then only through the US National Security

Agency, which in that year declassified 130,000 pages of wartime decrypts. Among them was Captain Yokai's summary of the contents of the papers sent to the Naval Staff in Tokyo. As so many years had then passed since the capture of the *Automedon* in 1941, the matter received little or no publicity at the time.

Chapter Two

Japan Attacks

In December 1941, the US Pacific Fleet, under the command of Admiral Husband E. Kimmel, was based at Pearl Harbor on the south coast of Oahu, in the Hawaiian Islands. Situated in mid-Pacific, 21 degrees north of the Equator, 2000 miles from America's west coast and 3000 miles from the nearest foreign shore, Pearl Harbor was a huge natural harbour, capable of holding the entire fleet safe from surprise attack. The approach was by a narrow, winding channel, 40 feet deep and fully protected by anti-submarine nets. Coastal gun batteries gave the harbour all-round protection, and nearly 300 fighter and bomber aircraft based at six airfields on the island gave comprehensive air cover. On shore, the base was a Little America set down in mid-Pacific. With schools, hospitals, shopping centres, cinemas and sports facilities, the servicemen and their families stationed there wanted for nothing. Even the weather on Oahu, with the exception of the occasional tropical cyclone, was out of an exotic holiday brochure. Little wonder that Pearl Harbor, Hawaii was a very much sought after posting.

The idyllic life of Pearl Harbor and its seemingly impregnable defences inevitably bred complacency not only amongst its American inhabitants, but also in Washington. In the closing months of 1941, war with Japan was an odds-on certainty, yet when Richard Sorge, a Soviet spy in Tokyo, obtained information of a planned attack on Pearl Harbor and passed this information on to Washington, it was ignored. American crypto-analysts, who were reading the Japanese codes, later confirmed

Sorge's warning, but still no action appears to have been taken.

Starved of the oil and raw materials needed to develop her economy by international sanctions imposed on her in retaliation for her invasion of China, Japan had long cast an avaricious eye on other territories in the East. Oil she needed desperately, her annual domestic production yielding less than half a million tons, while her annual consumption was five million tons. To the south lay the Netherlands East Indies, which produced eight million tons of oil a year, not one barrel of which came Japan's way. To the west was the British controlled Malay Peninsula, the world's chief source of rubber and tin, with its great port of Singapore, gateway to the Far East, all of which was denied to Japan. To Japan's leaders, backed by a growing military might, the temptation to gain access to their country's needs by force was proving irresistible. Only one thing stood in their way, and that was the huge American Pacific Fleet based at Pearl Harbor.

The idea for a surprise attack on Pearl Harbor was the brainchild of Admiral Isoroku Yamamoto, Commander-in-Chief of Japan's Navy. He was of the opinion that if the powerful US Pacific Fleet could be paralyzed by one surprise blow the Americans would be unable to interfere with Japan's expansion in the Pacific. Vice-Admiral Chuichi Nagumo was appointed to command, and by 22 November he had assembled his striking force at Tanakan Bay, an isolated anchorage in the remote Kurile Islands at the northern extremity of Japan. When complete, Nagumo's force consisted of two battleships, six aircraft carriers with 423 aircraft on board, two cruisers and nine destroyers, with eight fleet tankers and supply ships in support. With three I-class submarines scouting ahead, the ships sailed from Tanakan Bay on the night of the 26th, and set course for Pearl Harbor, over 3,000 miles to the south-east. A submarine force consisting of twenty-five I-class boats, five of which were carrying two-man midget submarines, had already sailed from Japanese ports. Their task was to lie off the entrance to Pearl Harbor and sink any American ships trying to escape.

The weather in the North Pacific was in Nagumo's favour, fog and gales hiding the movement of his armada for much of the way, enabling it to arrive at a position 275 miles north of Pearl Harbor completely undetected eleven days later, on 7 December. The first wave of aircraft, led by Commander Mitsuo Fuchida, and consisting of 183 dive bombers, torpedo-carrying planes and fighters, took off shortly before sunrise. A second wave of 170 aircraft took to the air soon afterwards.

Meanwhile, Pearl Harbor was settling down to a normal peace-time Sunday morning routine. Alongside the wharves and in the anchorage ninety-four ships, including eight battleships, of the United States Pacific fleet lay with white awnings spread antici-pating the coming heat of the day, and decks were being scrubbed ready for Captain's inspection and Divisions. As a concession to the uncertainty of the situation regarding Japan, orders had been issued to man every fourth gun aboard ship, but the likelihood of the peace of America's Pacific outpost being disturbed on such a tranquil Sunday seemed so remote that blind eyes were being turned. In fact, none of the main anti-aircraft guns were manned, and the ammunition for the machine-guns was under lock and key. The only warlike activity had been left to the fleet aircraft carriers and their cruiser escort, who, providentially for them as it turned out, were at sea on manoeuvres.

The first sign that anything might be amiss had come very early on that December Sunday morning, when at 0300 the destroyer USS *Ford* radioed that she had sighted a number of Japanese submarines in the waters around Oahu. She repeated this report at 0500, but on both occasions she was told to 'Reinvestigate and report'. At about the time of the *Ford*'s second report, two radar operators stationed at the north end of the island were surprised to see a large concentration of aircraft on their screen. They tele-phoned Pearl Harbor to report their sighting, but were told to ignore the sighting, as a force of B-17 bombers was expected to be flying in to the island. At 0645, another destroyer, USS *Ward*, on patrol off Pearl, radioed in that she had sunk a midget submarine off the entrance to the harbour. All these disturbing reports failed to alert Pearl Harbor to the danger approaching, and the base continued its normal Sunday morning routine. And all the while the first wave of Japanese aircraft, led by Commander Fuchida, was drawing nearer to its target.

The first visual sighting of Fuchida's planes is believed to have been made at 0730 by a boatswain's mate stationed somewhere in the north of Oahu, who reported twenty to twenty-five un-identified aircraft approaching the coast. What the observer had

12

seen was the vanguard of the Japanese attack, which was homing in on a tall radio mast near Pearl Harbor. Once again, presumably because of the expected arrival of the B-17s, this report was also ignored. Twenty-five minutes later, the bombs began to fall on the totally unsuspecting base.

The leading Japanese pilots, hardly able to believe their luck in being able to fly the length of Oahu without being fired on, swooped on the Army Air Force's Hickham Field near the seaward end of Pearl Harbor. Bombs and machine-gun fire cut a swathe of destruction through fighter planes standing unattended on the aprons, and a 500lb bomb landed on the mess hall, killing thirty-five airmen who were enjoying a leisurely breakfast.

With only sporadic bursts of anti-aircraft fire to deter them, bombers and torpedo planes flew low over the harbour, concentrating on the eight American battleships, which were conveniently moored in a north and south line in what was known as 'Battleship Row'. The big ships, their guns largely silent, were helpless. The *Arizona* (32,600 tons), hit by a torpedo and eight bombs, blew up and broke her back. She sank, taking 1,177 men with her. The *Oklahoma* (29,000 tons) was hit by three torpedoes, and immediately capsized. Only thirty-two of her crew survived. The *West Virginia* (31,800 tons), hit by four torpedoes and one bomb, also sank, while the *California* (36,600 tons), was set on fire and abandoned. The *Nevada* (29,000 tons) had steam up, and made a dash for the open sea, but she was bombed on her way down the channel and ran aground with heavy damage. The remaining three battleships in port were relatively unscathed: the *Pennsylvania* (33,100 tons) was in dry dock and escaped the attentions of the Japanese planes, while the *Maryland* (31,500 tons) and the *Tennessee* (32,300 tons) suffered only minor damage.

On the northern side of the harbour, the seaplane tender *Curtiss* and the 6-inch gun cruisers *Helena* and *Honolulu* were both hit by bombs, but would sail again, while another light cruiser, USS *Raleigh*, was put out of action for many months to come. Of the smaller ships in harbour, the minelayer *Oglala* was sunk, and the destroyers *Cassin*, *Downes* and *Shaw* were heavily damaged, as was the repair ship *Vestal*.

While most of the Japanese planes concentrated on knocking out the American capital ships, others bombed and strafed the island's airfields, destroying 164 aircraft on the ground. Only thirty-eight American planes succeeded in getting airborne, and ten of these were shot down.

Having laid waste to the US Pacific Fleet and much of its air support in less than thirty minutes, and at the cost of only nine of his aircraft, Mitsuo Fuchida rounded up his exhilarated crews and led them back towards the mother carriers. No sooner had the drone of their engines faded than the second wave of Japanese bombers roared in from the north. By this time, the Americans had manned their remaining guns, and the skies over Pearl Harbor were filled with shell bursts and flaming tracer. The Japanese bombers concentrated on wharves and buildings, many of which were already on fire, and this time they did not get away so lightly. Out of the 170 aircraft involved in the second wave twenty were shot down.

The second wave of Japanese aircraft had left by 1000, leaving behind them a scene of devastation. Four of the mighty US Pacific Fleet's battleships had been sunk by bomb and torpedo, two others were so badly damaged that it was doubtful if they would ever sail again, and a further two suffered slight damage. Three cruisers and three destroyers were crippled, and a 5000-ton minelayer lay on the bottom. Much of the infrastucture of the naval base was in ruins, and the nearby airfields were littered with the wreckage of 164 combat planes. But the cost in life and limb was the greatest, a total of 2,403 servicemen and civilians dead and 1,178 injured. In the space of two hours on that Sunday morning that had begun so peacefully, in return for the loss of twenty-nine Japanese planes and fifty-five men, Pearl Harbor had been reduced to a pile of smoking rubble and sunken ships. Only the submarine base and the fuel storage area remained intact, the latter, ironically, containing almost as much oil as the total of Japan's reserves. As for the United States Pacific Fleet and Far East Air Force, they had ceased to exist as effective fighting forces.

The only good thing to come out of the attack on Pearl Harbor – at least in the eyes of the British – was that it ended two years of American isolationism and brought her into the war. Winston Churchill, writing in his memoirs, said of Pearl Harbor: 'We had won the war. England would live; Britain would live; the Commonwealth of Nations and the Empire would live . . . We should not be wiped out. Our history would not come to an end. We might not even have to die as individuals . . .' Brave words, but a great deal of hard and bitter fighting lay ahead.

It is widely accepted that the bombing of Pearl Harbor signalled the opening of the Second World War in the Far East, but in fact the first shots had been fired – allowing for the time zone difference – some twenty hours before. At around 0500 Singapore time on 7 December, a Catalina flying boat of 205 Squadron RAF, piloted by Warrant Officer Bill Webb, was on patrol over the South China Sea, about 80 miles south of Cape Cambodia, when she sighted a number of unidentified naval ships steering west. The Catalina flew low to investigate, but was pounced upon by ten fighter aircraft, and quickly shot out of the sky. Before she crashed into the sea, killing all her crew, the flying boat's wireless operator succeeded in getting off a report to Singapore.

Singapore, like Pearl Harbor to the Americans, was considered a plum posting by British servicemen. For men coming from a war-ravaged Britain, with its sombre blackout, strict rationing and constant air raids, Singapore offered a warm, pleasant climate, smart shops stocked with luxuries unseen at home, and hotels serving sumptuous food. As an added bonus, the Malay girls were beautiful and, perhaps, available. This was Utopia indeed.

Founded by Stamford Raffles, who bought the island from the Sultan of Johore in 1819, over the years Singapore had developed into the most important port and trading centre in Britain's Eastern Empire. Furthermore, commanding the most convenient route from the Suez Canal to the Far East, its strategic importance was immense. By the outbreak of war in 1939, it was garrisoned by 7000 regular troops, batteries of 15-inch guns protected its seaward approaches, and the naval base had facilities for fuelling, storing and servicing the entire Eastern Fleet. However, the only warship of any size permanently on station at Singapore was the old First World War monitor HMS *Terror*, armed with two 15-inch guns. That the island was wide open to attack from the north seemed to have escaped the military planners.

The British had known for some time that the Japanese planned to invade Malaya with the ultimate aim of capturing Singapore, but such was the air of complacency prevailing in the colony that little preparation had been made to meet the threat. The general opinion in the West was that there was nothing to fear from the Japanese, who were a race of 'comical little men with thick spectacles, bow legs and buck teeth. They suffered from vertigo, and were so near-sighted that only one in five thousand of their rifle shots would ever register'. The War Office in London was confident that the jungle to the north of Singapore was impenetrable, and a request by General Percival, the officer commanding in Malaya and Singapore, for tanks to be sent had been turned down. Whitehall believed that any attack on the island must come from the sea in the south and that Singapore's defences were adequate to cope with this. In reality, the island's seaward-facing guns were only a façade, and on the landward side only a thin fence of barbed wire stood between it and an invading enemy. Around 140 operational aircraft were stationed in Malaya, but these were mainly obsolescent Lockheed Hudson bombers, Vickers Wildebeeste torpedo bombers, and Brewster Buffalo fighters, none of them a match for the Japanese Zero fighters.

Convinced that the Royal Navy could cope with the situation, in December 1941 Churchill despatched two capital ships, the brand new battleship *Prince of Wales*, said to be the finest of her kind in the world, and the First World War vintage battle-cruiser *Repulse*. The 35,000-ton *Prince of Wales* mounted ten 14-inch and sixteen 5.25-inch guns, plus a formidable array of anti-aircraft armament, while the 33,250-ton *Repulse* had six 15-inch and eight 4.5-inch guns, with similar defence against aircraft. Both ships were capable of a speed in excess of 27 knots.

The two big-gun ships, which Churchill envisaged as the first instalment of a new Far Eastern Fleet, were accompanied by the destroyers *Electra*, *Express*, *Tenedos* and HMAS *Vampire*. It was intended that the squadron be joined by the aircraft carrier *Indomitable*, but she had run aground in the West Indies on 3 November and would be out of service for some time. Due to the Royal Navy's heavy commitments in the Atlantic and Med-iterranean, no other carrier was available to take *Indomitable*'s place. This left the capital ships without air cover, but such was the faith of Churchill and his admirals in the power of the big gun that, certainly as far as the Japanese were concerned, the lack of air cover was not considered to be important.

The *Prince of Wales* (Captain John Leach) and *Repulse* (Captain

16

Tennant), along with their destroyers, arrived in Singapore on 2 December, where the squadron came under the overall command of Admiral Sir Tom Phillips. Coincident with their arrival, the Chief of Far Eastern Intelligence reported: 'Aircraft French Indo China approximately North 120 – South 180, including 90 heavy bombers. Assumed minimum troops at South two divisions and mechanised formation. North two possibly three divisions. Majority of 2nd Fleet comprising 12 modern cruisers, 28 destroyers now in Formosa – South China Sea area. In addition, 9 submarines sighted 100 miles north of Camranh Bay on December 2nd course South.' There were, in fact, ten submarines of the 4th Japanese Submarine Squadron operating off the Malay peninsula, and they were strategically spread out to be able to give warning of any attempt by the British Fleet to interfere with the landings on the east coast. Early on the 7th, a Japanese reconnaissance plane had reported two British battleships at anchor at Singapore, and it was these ships that were receiving the closest attention of the submarines.

The Japanese had been in French Indo-China since early 1940, but this was the first indication that they were amassing what could only amount to a large invasion force within easy steaming distance of the Malay Peninsula. The suspicions aroused by the intelligence report were confirmed by the ill-fated Catalina's last message early on the 7th. At 0025 on the 8th (1 hour and 35 minutes before the first bombs fell on Pearl Harbor), any doubts were dispelled by news that thousands of Japanese troops had landed on Malayan soil at Kota Bharu, an anchorage some 450 miles north of Singapore. Later, in the early hours of the 8th, other landings were reported 100 miles further north at Singora and Patami. Japan was at war with the British Empire.

In Singapore, Admiral Phillips decided that he must act at once, to take his ships north and hit the enemy while he was still vulnerable. He made known his intentions to the Admiralty, and requested that Singapore Air Command move fighters up to the northern airfields to provide reconnaissance off Singora from daylight on 10 December, and also to give air cover for his ships in that area. This request was in vain, for the northern airfields had by then already been bombed and made unusable by the Japanese. Furthermore, Singapore Air Command had only a limited number

17

of outdated Brewster Buffalo fighters to call upon, and as air raids were expected at any time, these were required for the defence of Singapore. 'Force Z', as Phillips' squadron was now designated, must fend for itself. This did not unduly trouble Admiral Phillips as, like most Western observers, he had a poor opinion of Japanese air power. Furthermore, his capital ships were well armed against air attack, *Prince of Wales* mounting sixty-four 2-pounder pom-poms, eight 40mm Bofors and twenty-five 20m Oerlikons, and *Repulse* eight 4.5-inch dual purpose, twenty-four 2-pounder pom-poms and sixty-four Oerlikons. Phillips was not aware that the Japanese had modern bombers, torpedo bombers and fighters, flown by highly trained and dedicated crews, based at airfields near Saigon, all of which had the speed and range to strike at his ships when they were in the vicinity of the reported landings. Neither was he aware that the Japanese had been tracking the progress of the Force Z ships since they left Colombo on 28 November, or that the crews of the Mitsubishi G4M1 'Betty' torpedo bombers had been training day and night, ready for the day when they would fly against Force Z. The 'Betty', with an operational range of over 3000 miles and a ceiling of 30,000 feet, had a top speed of 265 mph and carried a torpedo with a 330lb warhead, which could be launched at maximum speed. It was a far cry from the antiquated Swordfish flown by the Fleet Air Arm.

Force Z did not get off to a good start. The *Prince of Wales* was unable to get under way at once as one of her boilers was under repair. Her radar, one of the best afloat in any navy, was also out of action. It transpired that the set had been unserviceable since arrival in Singapore on the 2nd, and nothing appears to have been done about it. Shore technicians were called in as soon the ship was ordered to sea, but in the time available very little could be done. The battleship sailed from Singapore at 1735 on 8 December with only seven of her eight boilers under steam, and without the advantage her sophisticated radar would have given her.

Force Z, *Prince of Wales* and *Repulse*, escorted by the destroyers *Electra*, *Express*, *Tenedos* and *Vampire*, ran into bad weather with frequent rain squalls and low cloud as soon as it cleared the Singapore Strait. This suited Admiral Phillips, who by now had been advised that his ships would almost certainly come under attack from the bombers based in Indo-China when they neared the invasion areas. Bombers required broken cloud and good visibility. Phillips was also convinced that no Japanese torpedo-carrying aircraft had the range to make the long flight across the Gulf of Siam. He pressed on northwards at all possible speed.

Unknown to Admiral Phillips, at 1515 on the afternoon of the 8th, when the two battleships had reached a point 300 miles north of Singapore, they were sighted by the Japanese submarine I-165, under the command of Commander Harada. They were clearly visible through Harada's periscope, and he correctly identified them as the *Prince of Wales* and *Repulse*. The ships were out of torpedo range, so Harada had no opportunity to attack, but as soon as they were out of sight he sent off a signal giving their position, course and speed. This was received by the Japanese Malayan Operations headquarters, and all submarines in the area were ordered to surface and give chase. Vice Admiral Nobutake Kondo's surface force, consisting of the battleships *Kongo* and *Haruna*, along with their cruiser and destroyer squadrons, joined in.

At around 1700 on the 9th, twenty-four hours after Force Z sailed from Singapore, the cover afforded by the squally weather was suddenly lost. The wind dropped, the sun broke through, and the heavy overcast sky gave way to scattered clouds. Conditions were now ideal for enemy aircraft to operate. And the Japanese planes were not long in appearing on the scene.

Lookouts aboard the *Prince of Wales* reported three sightings of unidentified aircraft before the sun went down, and by then it was quite evident to Admiral Phillips that he had lost the advantage of surprise. He was not, however, aware that he had lost this advantage some hours earlier, when Force Z was sighted by a second Japanese submarine at 1345. She radioed the position of the enemy squadron to the 22nd Air Flotilla's base near Saigon, but for some reason her message did not get through until 1600, at which time the Flotilla's 'Bettys' were already being bombed up for a raid on Singapore. Torpedoes were hastily substituted for the bombs, and at 1800 the planes took off and headed south in search of the British ships.

Meanwhile, Force Z continued to move north up the coast, but at a reduced speed of 14 knots. With the vital element of surprise gone, and no hope of air cover, Admiral Phillips was beginning to have doubts as to the wisdom of continuing with the operation.

Then, with the last of daylight fading, the destroyer *Tenedos*, an ageing First World War veteran, signalled that she was running low on fuel, and Phillips had little alternative but to instruct her to return to Singapore. In the Admiral's opinion the loss of a destroyer tipped the scales too far in favour of the Japanese, and as soon as it was fully dark he ordered his remaining ships to reverse course and follow in the wake of *Tenedos*. In doing so, he avoided an attack by the 22nd Flotilla's torpedo bombers, who searched in vain for Force Z, finally returning to base at midnight with their torpedoes unused.

So steeped in the invincibility of His Britannic Majesty's Navy were the men of Force Z, that when Admiral Phillips made known his intention of returning to Singapore, there were loud mutterings below decks. Reg Woods, a gunner in HMS *Repulse*, recounted:

Once news of our intended return to Singapore was announced there was tremendous disappointment on board as we felt cheated out of a rightful confrontation. Later on during the course of the night our spirits were lifted when informed that early in the morning we'd be going to investigate reported troop landings at Kuantan, on the coast of Malaya. As we'd have to pass this area it wouldn't be much out of our way, having the added bonus of a possible show-down with the Japanese Navy, who'd obviously be guarding the beachhead . . .

The report Admiral Phillips had received from Singapore was of Japanese troops landing at Kuantan, about 150 miles south of Kota Bharu. Force Z was then less than 100 miles off the coast in the region of Kuantan, and Phillips decided that, with the element of surprise once more in his favour, intervention was possible. He turned his ships in towards the coast and Kuantan.

Unfortunately for Force Z, luck was not with them. Quite by chance, at 0315 on the 10th another Japanese submarine crossed their path, sighted the British ships, and radioed in their position, course and speed. At 0600, a flight of ten twin-engined GM3 'Nell' bombers, armed with 60kg bombs, took off to conduct a sector search for the British ships. An hour later, a strike force of twenty-seven fully armed 'Nells' and sixty-one 'Betty' torpedo bombers was ordered into the air. Because of reduced visibility, none of the Japanese aircraft discovered Force Z, and flew on past it to the south.

Force Z arrived off Kuantan at first light, but there was no sign of an enemy landing taking place. *Prince of Wales* flew off her Walrus reconnaissance plane, but this could discover no signs of activity on the coast. Still not satisfied, Phillips ordered the destroyer *Express* to investigate. After thoroughly searching the approaches to Kuantan, she returned with a similar negative report: no Japanese naval ships, no landing barges, no invasion force. Admiral Phillips would live to regret those hours wasted off Kuantan.

The Japanese strike force, eighty-eight planes in all, had flown as far south as the Singapore Strait in search of Force Z, and was returning north when, at 1100, they saw the British ships below them, their white wakes streaming astern as they hurried back to Singapore. It was a chance meeting that was to turn into a disaster for Admiral Tom Phillips and Force Z.

The Japanese strike force came in flights of nine aircraft, twin-engined G3M 'Nell' bombers carrying 250kg bombs and flying at 20,000 feet. As they approached, the combined anti-aircraft armoury of the *Prince of Wales* and *Repulse* opened up in unison. Their heavy dual purpose guns, sixteen 5.25-inch and eight 4.5-inch, thundered purposefully, filling the air ahead of the on-coming planes with puffs of black, shrapnel-laden smoke, but this failed to injure or deter the Japanese. Either by design or accident, they concentrated their attack on the thinly-armoured *Repulse*, and although Captain Tennant took violent evasive action, the battle-cruiser was soon lost to sight in a welter of erupting water as the bombs crashed all around her.

Inevitably, the *Repulse* received a direct hit, a 250kg bomb smashing through her vulnerable upper deck to explode in her port hangar near a fan chamber. This was a particularly crowded area of the ship, and many men were killed and injured. To add to the mayhem, a steam pipe burst, filling the space with scalding steam. The *Repulse* was wounded, but she retained her manoeuvring capability, and her guns continued to fire. It was at this point that Captain Tennant sent a radio signal to all British naval ships saying, 'Enemy aircraft bombing my position'. Needless to say, his signal was not answered, as no British warships were within range.

21

Apparently satisfied at having scored a direct hit on the *Repulse*, the high-level bombers flew away, but within fifteen minutes other aircraft were seen approaching low down on the horizon. Lieutenant-Commander Harland, on the bridge of the *Prince of Wales* examined them through his binoculars, and pointed them out to Admiral Phillips, commenting, 'I think they're going to do a torpedo attack.' Phillips, still adhering to the belief that the Japanese had no long-range torpedo bombers, disagreed. He was forced to change his mind as the 'Bettys' dropped to wave-top height and bore down on the battleship relentlessly.

The intentions of the Japanese planes being apparent, the *Prince of Wales* brought her low level guns into action, her quick-firing 40mm Bofors, massed banks of 2-pounder pompoms, aptly nick-named 'Chicago pianos', and 20mm Oerlikons throwing up a curtain of steel which it seemed that no aircraft could fly through. Yet the 'Bettys', their underslung torpedoes now clearly visible, even to the sceptical Tom Phillips, still came on, seemingly oblivious to the shot and shell they were flying through.

The noise of the *Prince of Wales*'s barrage was deafening. One or two of the 'Bettys' faltered and swerved away with smoke trailing behind them, but the others continued to fly straight and level until they were within 2000 yards of their target. Then those aboard the battleship who were not fully occupied manning the guns watched in horror as the torpedoes dropped away from beneath the planes and raced towards the ship. Captain Leach turned to comb the tracks, but he was too late. Suddenly there was a huge explosion, and the ship, which had been travelling at 25 knots, seemed to stop dead as a 330lb Japanese warhead slammed into her port side. Her 16 inch thick side armour was of no avail, the force of the explosion destroying her main steering gear and generator switchboard, which put many of her vital systems out of action, including her 5.25-inch guns. Her speed dropped to 15 knots, and she quickly took on a heavy port list as thousands of tons of sea water poured into her breached hull. Within minutes, unable to manoeuvre, she lay helpless and at the mercy of the enemy.

Having crippled the world's most modern battleship in the space of a few minutes, the Japanese torpedo bombers now turned their attention to the *Repulse*, already hard hit by a bomb burst. At first,

Captain Tennant's brilliant ship handling frustrated their efforts. He threw the 33,000-ton battle-cruiser around like a destroyer, successfully avoiding nineteen separate torpedo attacks, all of which were accompanied by heavy machine-gunning by the low-flying 'Bettys'. But, inevitably, the sheer number of the Japanese planes won the day. The *Repulse* was hit by a total of five torpedoes, and her hull blasted wide open to the sea by the 330lb warheads. She took on a heavy list to port, and within three minutes disappeared beneath the waves, taking 513 of her complement with her.

All attention was now turned to the *Prince of Wales*, then moving to the south-east at about 8 knots under emergency steering gear. Two more torpedoes struck home, reducing her speed further, then she was finished off by a high level bombing attack by a flight of 'Nells'. The *Prince of Wales* capsized and sank at 1320, just two hours after the Japanese attack had begun. Miraculously, only 377 of her crew were lost, but these included both Admiral Tom Phillips and Captain John Leach.

With both British capital ships sunk, the Japanese planes ignored the destroyers, which were picking up survivors, and withdrew. Hardly were they over the horizon than a squadron of Brewster Buffaloes arrived from Singapore, but they were too late to do anything more than offer protection to the destroyers. Later, when questions were asked why air support had not been sent from Singapore earlier, it was said that Admiral Phillips was keeping radio silence, and had not signalled his change of plan on the 9th, so it was assumed he would not require air support until his ships were nearing Singora in the north. The first indication Singapore had that Force Z was in trouble came at noon on the 10th, when Captain Tennant sent out an emergency call for help. By then, nothing could have saved the *Prince of Wales* and *Repulse* from the disaster that overtook them.

When Winston Churchill received the news he was devastated. In his memoirs he wrote:

I was thankful to be alone. In all the war I never received a more direct shock . . . As I turned over and twisted in bed the full horror of the news sank in upon me. There were no British or American capital ships in the Indian Ocean or the Pacific except the American survivors of Pearl Harbor, who were hastening back to California. Over all this vast expanse of waters Japan was supreme, and we everywhere were weak and naked.

The loss of the only two British capital ships in the area left Singapore waters without any real defence against the Japanese seaborne invasion. A few Dutch submarines bravely attempted to intervene and sank several of the enemy's small troopships, but their efforts made very little difference. The Japanese were free to seize local ships and use these to land troops behind the British lines of defence. They also enjoyed almost complete air superiority, able to put in the air large numbers of 'Nell' bombers protected by Zero fighters with a top speed of 332 mph and a range in excess of 1400 miles. The British, on the other hand, due to lack of foresight, had only very limited numbers of near-obsolete Brewster Buffaloes, and even fewer, and more obsolete Vickers Wildebeest bombers, slow, cumbersome biplanes which may have been adequate to control warring Afghan tribesmen in the 1930s, but were completely outclassed by the Japanese.

The defence of the Malay peninsula was in the hands of the 9th and 11th Indian Divisions and two Malay infantry brigades. They probably outnumbered the Japanese, and had the advantage of being familiar with the terrain, but their British officers had a low opinion of the capability of the Japanese, who soon proved themselves able to march light and fast, on foot and on bicycle, manhandling their guns through the dense Malayan jungle. They advanced south at the rate of 10 miles per day, and by the beginning of January 1942 they were at the gates of Kuala Lumpur, and only 200 miles from the Singapore causeway. By the middle of the month they had succeeded in landing five divisions of infantry, and were in control of much of the peninsula. On the 27th, British forces retired to Singapore Island to make their last stand.

Chapter Three

Last Convoy to Singapore

On 1 November 1885 a link between the Atlantic and Pacific Oceans was forged at Eagle's Pass, high in the Canadian Rocky Mountains. With due ceremony, the last spike was hammered home to join east and west in the new Canadian Pacific Railway, which had been under construction for four years. The line ran from Montreal in the east to Vancouver on the west coast, a distance of 2886 miles, reducing a long and hazardous journey that had hitherto taken months to a mere 5½ days. Interconnecting steamship services between Liverpool and Montreal and Vancouver and Pacific ports followed with the formation of the Canadian Pacific Steamship Company, and in 1891 the *Empress of Japan* left Yokohama on 19 August, and arrived in Victoria on the 31st, after a passage of 9 days 19 hours 39 minutes. Passengers and mails were then transferred to the railway, and they reached New York in time to catch the transatlantic mail boat *City of York* sailing on 2 September. The mails were delivered in London on the morning of 9 September, less than twenty-one days after leaving Yokohama. Considering that, until then, the average delivery time for the mails between the Far East and London had been seven weeks via the Cape of Good Hope, the new Canadian Pacific system of rail and sea transport was a resounding success.

The *Empress of Asia*, launched on the Clyde in 1913 on the eve of the First World War, was one of three luxury liners built for Canadian Pacific's Pacific trade. She was a three-funnelled ship of 16,908 tons, with a service speed of 20 knots, and designed to further reduce the time on passage between the Far East and

Europe. However, she was not long in the passenger and mail trade, being commandeered by the Royal Navy on the outbreak of war and converted to an armed merchant cruiser. She resumed passenger carrying in February 1919, and gave distinguished service in the inter-war years. When war came along again in 1939, she was twenty-six years old and showing her age, but she was once again snapped up by the Admiralty, this time being converted for trooping.

On 12 November 1941, with Japan making threatening noises in the East, the *Empress of Asia* sailed from Liverpool for Bombay in a convoy of troopships which included her sister ship *Empress of Japan*, the *Duchess of Bedford* and the *Capetown Castle*. She was under the command of Captain John Bisset-Smith, OBE, and carried a crew of 416. Stopping off at Durban for a few days, the *Empress of Asia* arrived in Bombay on 15 January 1942, where she embarked 2,235 troops for Singapore, where the situation was assuming critical proportions.

In the face of the Japanese onslaught, British forces in Malaya had by then retreated to the southern end of the peninsula, and were attempting to hold a 90-mile front stretching from Batu Pahat in the west to Mersing in the east. Singapore lay only 50 miles behind the front. The attacking Japanese were soon to be reinforced by two fresh divisions, landed from the sea at Singora on the 15th, giving them a total of five divisions in Malaya, including their crack Imperial Guards Division. The British, Indian and Australian defenders, poorly equipped and unused to jungle warfare, were fighting a very gallant rearguard action, but it would never be any more than that. The battle for Singapore was about to begin.

The *Empress of Asia* sailed from Bombay on 23 January in company with three other troopers, Bibby Line's *Devonshire*, the French-flag *Felix Roussel*, also managed by Bibby Line, with the 11th Northumberland Fusiliers on board, and the small Dutch steamer *Plancius*. Four days later, when off the west coast of Sumatra, they joined up with a convoy of eight ships bound for Batavia with more troops, escorted by the 8-inch gun cruiser *Exeter*, two destroyers and three sloops. The Japanese threat to British and Dutch interests in the Far East was at last being taken seriously, albeit too late.

On the night of 3 February, the twelve ships and their escorts passed through the Sunda Strait, which divides Sumatra from its neighbouring island of Java. Once through the narrow strait, the Batavia-bound ships peeled off, while the others carried on for Singapore. The northbound convoy then consisted of five ships, the troopers *Empress of Asia*, *Devonshire* and *Felix Roussel*, and the cargo ships *Plancius* and *City of Canterbury*, escorted by HMS *Exeter* and the three sloops, HMS *Danae*, HMIS *Sutlej* and HMAS *Yarra*. The *Empress of Asia* was bringing up the rear of the convoy and visibly having difficulty in keeping up with the other ships. Captain Smith later said, 'We had been allotted this position on account of our steaming difficulties, the ship almost invariably dropping astern of station when fires were being cleaned. Well-trained Chinese firemen got the best out of the two coal burners from the Pacific Fleet, but by the time World War II broke out there was a real dearth of firemen accustomed to coal, and after our Chinese firemen returned home we had to rely on what the Merchant Seamans' Pool could scrape up.' Smith's diplomatic explanation indicated that all was not well in the *Empress of Asia*'s engine-room.

T. N. Charles, who was serving aboard one of the troopships bound for Batavia, commented more than forty years later: 'I vividly recall seeing the *Empress of Asia* and *Felix Roussel* with her peculiar square funnels and the two other ships turn away to port and head northwards for Singapore . . . I have often wondered what made those in authority send those vessels into Singapore at such a late stage, seeing how much the situation had deteriorated. There is little doubt that a great deal of uncertainty prevailed long before then.'

Charles had good cause to wonder at the futility of reinforcing Singapore, for as *Exeter* led this last convoy into Singapore northwards the battle for the island had already been lost. On 31 January all remaining British forces had retired across the causeway joining Singapore to the mainland, blowing it up after them. In all, 80,000 servicemen and up to one million civilians were crowded into the island awaiting the arrival of the Japanese, who were massing in the thick jungle on the north shore of the Johore Strait. The 70,000 of the British troops who were armed would be forced to defend a front 30 miles long with the help of the few heavy guns which would train north, and their only air cover consisted of one squadron of fighter aircraft with just one usable airfield at their disposal.

The Singapore-bound convoy's first contact with the Japanese came on the morning of 4 February. Captain Bissett-Smith later wrote:

> We were steaming at 12½ knots in single line ahead, led by HMS *Exeter*, the *Empress of Asia* being the last in line, when at 1100 hrs on the 4th February, whilst passing through the Banka Straits a large 'V' formation of Japanese planes flew overhead at high altitude – about 5000ft. One dropped a large number of bombs which all fell together. None of the ships were hit but there were near misses round our ship, the nearest being only 10ft away. The bombs exploded on striking the water, sending up large columns of water to a height of about 20ft which descended on the deck. We received the brunt of this attack, no other bombs falling near the other ships. Two of our lifeboats were pierced by bomb splinters and some splinters were found around the decks . . . All the ships had opened fire, including our escorts . . .

That afternoon, the two faster ships, *Devonshire* and *Plancius*, left the convoy to steam on ahead, hoping to reach Singapore during the night and be under the protection of the guns of the island before dawn came on the 5th, and with it the Japanese bombers. The *Empress of Asia*, the *Felix Roussel* and the *City of Canterbury*, already on their best speed, carried on, their estimated arrival time being mid-morning on the 5th. They would be dangerously exposed on the final run through the Singapore Strait.

At daylight on the 5th, the three ships, led by HMS *Danae*, were 40 miles from Singapore and approaching the Horsburgh light, which marks the eastern end of the Singapore Strait. The weather was fine, with good visibility, a smooth sea and a warm, gentle breeze blowing. For Captain Bissett-Smith, assuming he was able to ignore the sinister presence of the naval ships and the men manning the guns in the bridge wings of the *Empress of Asia*, it might well have been any normal peacetime arrival day in Singapore. It was difficult not to reminisce on the old days: anchor down before noon, and the agent's launch waiting to whisk him ashore for lunch at the Raffles Hotel.

Any pretensions of normality were rudely dispersed a few hours later, when the convoy was nearing Singapore.

We were approaching Sultan Shoal at a reduced speed – about 5 to 6 knots – preparatory to embarking pilots when at 1045 hrs Singapore time on the 5th February a large 'V' formation of about 24 Japanese planes flew over at high altitude and disappeared into the clouds; no bombs were dropped. The planes were of the same type as those which attacked us in the Banka Straits, painted silver with two engines. Fifteen minutes later, at about 1100 hrs, the planes returned singly, or in twos or threes, and attacked the convoy from all directions at both high and low altitudes.

They dived down from about 15,000ft to about 5,000ft, sometimes to 3,000ft but never lower and there was no steep diving. One plane I watched particularly carried out a shallow dive, less than 45 degrees from forward and I followed his bomb down into the water alongside the bridge. It appeared to be a large bomb. The attacks were from forward, aft and athwartships, all the ships in the convoy being attacked. We, as the largest ship with three funnels and well known to the Japanese owing to our peacetime voyages to that country, seemed to bear the brunt of it.

All the ships of the convoy and the escorts opened fire at once on the invaders and the bombs started falling all around us. Terrific concussion shook the ship and standing on the bridge it was difficult to know what were near misses and what were direct hits. Spouts of water were thrown up by the misses, but not very high. At 1105 hrs thick volumes of black smoke came pouring out of the deck on the starboard side in the vicinity of the forward funnel. It was evident that a direct hit had been sustained and that the ship was on fire. Fire parties, under the direction of the Chief Officer, immediately proceeded to the seat of the fire. The attack lasted for about an hour and we sustained at least three direct hits. One bomb smashed its way through the aft end of the lounge and penetrated to the dining saloon on 'B' deck. Looking aft from the bridge, volumes of black smoke covered the whole length of the boat deck and fiddley top.

The *Empress of Asia* had been hit hard, she was on fire below decks in a number of places, and the work of the fire parties was made almost impossible because the deck service water pipes had been shattered by the bombs. Although the fire pumps in the engine-room were working at full pressure, no water was getting through to the fire hydrants, which left the fire parties fighting a losing battle with extinguishers and buckets. At 1125 the Chief Officer reported to the bridge that the fires were out of control. Five minutes later the Chief Engineer informed Captain Bissett-Smith that the engine-room and stokehold were filling with smoke, and that his men would not be able to remain below much longer. Reluctantly, Bissett-Smith gave the order to evacuate the engine spaces. This was a desperate measure, for the ship was then passing through a swept channel in the minefields that lay to the north and south of the strait. Fortunately, she still had considerable way on her, and Bissett-Smith was able to hold her on course until she was clear of the danger area. When he reached Sultan Shoal, where there was room to swing, he decided to anchor. His report illustrates the desperate situation he found himself in:

The lower bridge, chartroom and officers' accommodation were ablaze and it was impossible to remain on the bridge on account of the smoke and heat. Escape by the ladders was impossible so I gave instructions for all bridge personnel and gunners who had collected there to slide down a rope to the fore deck. This was done. I threw the steel box containing confidential documents over the side. The ship, with little way on her, was swinging round towards the position I intended to anchor and finding it impossible to remain on the bridge I followed the others down the rope to the fore deck. Anchors were already let go and the ship gradually swung round to a position about three quarters of a degree east of Sultan Shoal lighthouse and anchored, it then being about noon. We were then some 11 miles to the westward.

30

When Bissett-Smith reached the fore deck, he found the situation was even worse than he had imagined. The entire midships section of his ship, from the fore end of the bridge to the after of her three funnels, was blazing fiercely, the boat deck was enveloped in thick smoke, and the lifeboats were on fire. The two ends of the ship, the fore deck and the after deck, had not been damaged, and into these limited spaces were packed the ship's crew and passengers, 2,651 men with nowhere to go but over the side into the distinctly hostile-looking waters of the Singapore Strait. Panic was not far away.

Fortunately, at that point, a little after noon, the Japanese planes, probably having used up all their bombs, flew away, and a number of small craft began coming alongside the stricken liner. Over 800 men were taken off the forward part of the ship, the rescue boats ferrying them to the Sultan Shoal lighthouse. Those on the after decks, the majority, were still trapped, and with the flame and smoke threatening to engulf them. Urgent action was needed to save them, and this prompted Lieutenant-Commander Wilfred Harrington, in command of the Australian sloop *Yarra*, to risk bringing his ship alongside the stern of the *Empress of Asia*. His bold action saved the day, and by 1300 the *Yarra* had taken off most of the remaining survivors. By the time she pulled away from the burning ship, the little sloop had on board a total of 1,804 survivors, so many that the sheer numbers were threatening to capsize her. Harrington saved her by ordering all those on deck to sit down, so as to lower the ship's centre of gravity.

Those survivors who were left behind had no alternative but to jump overboard. One of them, J. W. Hargreaves wrote many years later: 'Quite a number of us were on the opposite side of the ship to where the *Yarra* was collecting survivors, but we couldn't get to the *Yarra* owing to the fires burning amidships. Therefore when the call to abandon ship came, we on our side had to go overboard into the water. When we went overboard my friend and I went underneath the ship, dropped off the nets and then managed to swim to a life raft. We couldn't feel any ground under our feet, and floated around until nearly dusk, when we were eventually picked up by a motor boat and transferred to the *Yarra* which took us to Singapore.'

Captain Bissett-Smith was the last man to leave the burning troopship, but not before the men stranded on Sultan Shoal were taken off by the Indian sloop *Sutlej* and the Australian corvettes *Bendigo* and *Woolongong*. He later commented: 'During the attack we had no protection from our own fighters. There was not one British plane overhead, but I learned later that this deplorable lack of air support was probably due to the fact that at the same time as the attack on the ships the Japanese were bombing the aerodrome at Singapore and our planes were kept fully occupied in that area. We had not sufficient planes to oppose the vastly superior air strength of the enemy. There was no gunfire from the island itself during the attack but our escorts put up a splendid show. The Oerlikons were very satisfactory, also the Hotchkiss and the naval gunners did fine work, but no planes were shot down. Everyone behaved very well indeed. There was no panic, the troops were splendid and everyone did their job.' Miraculously, when the roll was called, it was found that the *Empress of Asia* had suffered only one serious casualty, namely D. Ellsworthy, a Canadian member of the catering crew, who later died in hospital from his injuries and was buried in Singapore.

The 17,000-ton *Felix Roussel*, which had on board a full complement of troops, mainly of the 11th Northumberland Fusiliers, was also a target for the Japanese bombers. H.J. Godfrey, one of a small group of British personnel placed on board to organise trooping arrangements, later wrote: 'The *Felix Roussel* received two direct hits, possibly three, and a very near miss on the starboard quarter. One bomb exploded in the vicinity of the forward funnel and wiped out some gun crews and the Singapore pilot who was on the bridge received a machine-gun bullet in the shoulder. The decks were continually sprayed by machine-gun fire and we were very glad indeed to get within the protection of the Singapore defences. Sadly, there were 12 fatalities, all Army personnel, but no casualties as far as I can remember among the crew. The dead were buried as the vessel neared Singapore.'

The *Felix Roussel* reached a berth in Keppel Harbour and landed her Northumbrians to swell the garrison of the island. Unfortunately, they landed without their stores and equipment, all of which was still aboard the *Empress of Asia* and about to be devoured by the raging fires. Estimates of the number of troops on Singapore island at the time, including the newly arrived Northumberland Fusiliers, vary from 60,000 to 100,000, of which at least 50,000 were British and Australian. Even taking the lower estimate, the garrison probably outnumbered the attacking Japanese, but there was the smell of impending defeat in the air, and morale was at a very low ebb.

Having discharged her troops, the *Felix Roussel* was not allowed to linger in Keppel Harbour as a target for the Japanese bombers. Next morning, 6 February, she took on board 1,100 passengers, mainly women and children and non-combatant personnel, plus a few survivors from the *Prince of Wales* and *Repulse*. H.J. Godfrey remembers an ugly incident that reflected badly on the ship he had watched burning off Sultan Shoal twenty-four hours earlier:

> Some 30 or 40 *Empress of Asia* crew members also boarded at the last minute, and I regret to say that their behaviour left a lot to be desired and it became necessary for them to be confined to a space at the after end of the accommodation, to which they were escorted at gunpoint. Apparently they had taken advantage of the chaotic conditions in the godowns and had managed to bring on board, in more ways than one, a quantity of hard liquor. These people were handed over in custody on our arrival at Bombay and we were glad to see them go. We few British aboard a French ship were certainly not proud of our fellow countrymen but I must add that I was told afterwards that the *Empress of Asia* crew members who escaped from Java in the *Marella* were very well behaved and those who spent over three years in Changi prison camp were very popular with their fellow prisoners.
>
> We left Singapore in the early hours of February 7 unaccompanied and although enemy aircraft were seen at high altitude over Sunda Straits we were not attacked. The *Empress of Asia*, beached on Sultan Shoal, was still well alight when we passed her. As we were short of both food and water, neither of which had been obtainable at Singapore, we had hoped to make a call at Colombo, but we were directed to Bombay, which we reached about February 22 with only very little food and water remaining.

On the morning of the 8th, large numbers of enemy troops were seen massing on the other side of the Johore Strait, and Japanese guns began shelling the British positions. However, as the strait was a third of a mile wide at its narrowest point, the defenders were confident that their guns would be able to smash any Japanese attempt to cross the strip of water in boats. They had, as all too often happened, underestimated the ingenuity of their enemy, who had brought in armoured landing craft by road. That night, the Japanese crossed under the cover of darkness, and although the defenders inflicted heavy casualties, landings were made at several points. When daylight came on the 9th, the Japanese had penetrated 5 miles inland, and the British forces were falling back. On the 10th, Winston Churchill, made aware of the deteriorating situation, cabled General Wavell: 'The battle must be fought to the bitter end at all costs. The 18th Division has a chance to make its name in history. Commanders and senior officers should die with their troops. The honour of the British Empire and the British Army is at stake. I rely on you to show no weakness in any form.' Brave words.

General Wavell's reply was not encouraging: 'The battle for Singapore is not going well. Japanese, with usual infiltration tactics, are getting on much more rapidly than they should be in west of island . . . Morale of some troops is not good, and none is as high as I should like to see. Conditions of ground are difficult for defence, where wide frontages are to be held in very enclosed country.'

This was the situation that faced Captain Bissett-Smith and his crew when they came ashore in Singapore. Next day, 127 firemen and stewards were lucky enough to leave the island in two ships that were sailing, but the remainder were housed in an Army rest camp outside the city. On the 10th, Bissett-Smith received a request from the Director of Civil Medical Services for help in dealing with the mounting casualties from the bombing, in response to which the entire catering staff of the *Empress of Asia*, 147 men, volunteered. The generosity of these men resulted in their ending up in a Japanese prisoner of war camp.

The fate of the rest of the troopship's crew is best told by three Canadian seamen, J.N. Ewart, Ernie Higgs and Geoff Hoskens, writing in the magazine *Sea Breezes* forty-eight years later:

The Japanese gained a foothold on the island on February 9 and on the 11th a Royal Navy bus arrived at the camp, the driver of which inquired as to the whereabouts of the *Empress of Asia*'s seamen. This 'wee Jock', all decked out in his No.1 whites, soon had a very attentive group of merchant seamen around him, especially when he announced that his orders were to pick us up and take us to the docks. We were broken up into three crews to man three small coasters and subsequently make our escape from Singapore.

We lost no time in piling into the bus. We had no gear, only Army shorts and boots which, of course, we were wearing. After a thrilling ride (due to Jock having consumed much Navy rum) we arrived at about 11 pm at the designated dock where the three little ships were tied up and riding high. A quick inspection was made by all hands and Jimmy Donnelly, the *Empress of Asia*'s 3rd Officer, broke us up into three crews, each with an engineer and several stokers.

The engineers reported that two of the ships were oil fired and one with coal. It was decided that we should wait for day break before proceeding to the various docks for bunkers and food supplies. There was only sufficient fuel aboard each ship to get up steam but proceed we did at first light on 12 February.

Our ship was the *Sing-Keng-Seng*, the coal burner and as we steamed slowly to the coaling dock it was most evident that Singapore was doomed to capitulation. Many oil storage tanks on the inner harbour islands were ablaze, obviously set alight by the defenders in a 'scorched earth' policy.

We had no sooner reached the coal berth than an air raid started. It must have been 10 am as the locals told us that the air raids started each day at that time and continued to 3 pm. Waves of 27 aircraft descended from about 30,000 feet, most of them concentrating on the waterfront and shipping in general. It was about this time that our small crew was joined by two more senior officers from the *Empress of Asia*, Capt Smith and Chief Officer Donald Smith.

In between air raids all hands busied themselves getting coal aboard in wicker baskets, two men to a basket, and helping themselves to canned food from a nearby warehouse. Army personnel were pushing new Ford lorries, Bren gun carriers and the like over the séa wall into the harbour. This new equipment had undoubtedly only arrived a week before in the ships of our convoy and if the *Empress of Asia* had arrived no doubt our cargo would have gone the same way.

All the time our little ship was fueling and storing a member of the Military Police kept close guard on the gangway to make sure that only *Empress of Asia* personnel got aboard. However, some RN and RAN personnel, survivors from the *Repulse* and *Prince of Wales* asked if we had any objection to their joining us and when we agreed they simply told the MP that they were *Empress of Asia* crew and came aboard. None of us had any documents, anyway, and no one really cared.

One of these chaps was a Jim Fields and although he had been a member of the *Prince of Wales*'s 'A' turret gun's crew, he served as cook in our little vessel.

In the opposite direction, some of us were seriously considering approaching some RN MTBs which were provisioning nearby. Obviously they were preparing to escape as well and to us they appeared to have a much better chance of making their destination than we did. However, we decided to stay with the *Sing-Keng-Seng*, which was just as well, as none of the MTBs made it to Java.

Our bunkering and provisioning operation took us until just after noon on February 12 when the RN authorities ordered us to anchor in the harbour and await a signal to go alongside later in the day and embark some nurses and other civilians. However, several hours later we received another message by Aldis 'Do not come alongside. Get us out as best you can'.

We weighed anchor immediately and as we cleared the harbour we steered away from an Empire cargo ship of approximately 10,000 tons which was getting quite a beating from Japanese dive bombers. She had taken some direct hits and was on fire and her speed had dropped considerably because with our top speed of 7 knots we were able to overtake her quite handily.

Our first evening at sea was uneventful but on the following day, just before noon, a pontoon-equipped aircraft headed straight for us at about deck level. Prior to the intrusion of this visitor our officers had wisely advised us to drape white towels around our waists to disguise any evidence of khaki or anything symbolic of military personnel.

As the aircraft got nearer the Japanese 'rising sun' on its wings and fuselage were quite clear but after circling around it flew away and another sigh of relief was emitted by us all. We must have been too small to bother with, plus the fact that we were an uncrowded vessel and not displaying any armament.

We plodded along and either on that evening or the next we ran into quite a storm with torrential rain and wind on our starboard beam, and with our coal bunkers as our only ballast we soon took on quite a list. Stored on deck were about a dozen 45-gallon drums full of oil and we immediately shifted these from the lee side to the weather side. This helped to square her up and lessened our fears of capsizing.

Someone found a bar of soap and with the warm tropical rain descending in torrents all hands stripped off and had their first fresh water shower for many a week.

On the following day Capt Len Johnson of the *Am Pang*, which was keeping us company, signalled that they were low on fuel and asked if we had charts for Sumatra as he wished to seek a port where he could refuel. We had such charts and readily gave them to him, although I cannot remember how the transfer was made. These same charts subsequently took the ill-fated *Am Pang* to Palembang.

There was little variation in our menu aboard the *Sing-Keng-Seng*, rice, canned peas and more of the same, but this was the least of our worries as it became quite apparent that our bunkers were insufficient to see us into Batavia. However, our fireboxes could handle material up to 2ft in length and an assessment of the wood supply was made and a search instigated for a saw. One was found and all hands went to work breaking up bunks and chairs and cutting them to size. Dunnage from the ship's hold was also brought up, cut to size and passed down to the engine-room.

The weather was now more favourable but the change from coal to wood proved inadequate to maintain steam and our speed was reduced to 5 knots and dropping. Fortune was still with us, and on the following day with very little wood remaining a ship was seen off our starboard bow. When she came nearer she was seen to be a man-of-war but our concern, of course, was her nationality – friend or foe?

She proved to be a Dutch destroyer, and she wasn't long in coming alongside and making arrangements to take us in tow. Some time before noon on the following day, February 17, we nosed alongside a wharf at Tandjong Priok. The Dutch authorities housed us in the Netherlands Bank in Batavia.

When she slipped out of Singapore on the afternoon of the 12th, the *Sing-Keng-Seng* left behind a city under heavy siege and in a state of rapidly worsening chaos. The Japanese had control of the reservoirs on the mainland that supplied the island, the fresh water supply was drying up, many of the depots containing reserves of food and ammunition for the troops were in enemy hands, and most of the local labour had deserted. And now, a programme of organised demolition was in progress: all guns and ammunition not in use were being destroyed, petrol supplies set on fire, and secret documents burned. In the dock area the floating dry dock had been sunk, and work was in hand to immobilise all equipment. There could be no surer signs of impending collapse.

General Wavell telegraphed General Percival on 15 February:

So long as you are in position to inflict losses and damage to enemy and your troops are physically capable of doing so you must fight on. Time gained and damage to the enemy are of vital importance at this crisis. When you are fully satisfied that this is no longer possible I give you discretion to cease resistance. Before doing so all arms, equipment, and transport of value to the enemy must of course be rendered useless. Also just before final cessation of fighting opportunity should be given to any determined bodies of men or individuals to try and effect escape by any means possible. They must be armed. Inform me of your intentions. Whatever happens I thank you and all your troops for your gallant efforts of last few days.

Hostilities ceased at 8.30 pm on that day, Sunday, 15 January 1942, thus bringing to an end a disastrous campaign that reflected no credit on Britain's military commanders. For the men involved

38

in the fighting, the defeat was no less humiliating. When the fighting stopped, 8,000 of their number had been killed or wounded and 130,000 made prisoner, 10,000 of whom later died in captivity.

Singapore and its aftermath was due largely to a complete underestimation by the British of the capability of Japan's forces. Ronald Searle, the famous cartoonist and illustrator, volunteered for the Royal Engineers in 1942, aged 19, and was immediately drafted to Singapore to assist in its defence. Sixty-three years later, interviewed on radio recently, he summed up the fiasco succinctly:

> For all of us the Japanese were Fu Manchu. No one knew anything about them at all. Our commanders simply said to us 'No problem, you know. They're slit-eyed, they can't shoot straight, they're just a lot of yellow dwarfs.' Searle and his comrades were soon disillusioned: 'All we did basically was to run backwards.'

About the cruelty the Japanese showed to them when they were captured, Searle is just as explicit: 'You were in fact dirt, available to your captor to do anything he wished.'

Chapter Four

Dunkirk Again

On Friday, 13 February 1942, 'Black Friday' as it was inevitably dubbed, the authorities in Singapore decided to save what they could out of the crumbling shambles of the island, and arranged a mass evacuation of key personnel, senior officers not involved in the fighting, technicians, nurses, any specialist whose services would be of more use elsewhere. This involved nearly 3,000 people. The bigger ships had already left Singapore, and eighty small ships, including yachts and harbour launches were commandeered to make the hazardous 500-mile voyage to Batavia, which was then still in Allied hands. Among this motley armada was HMS *Li Wo*.

The 707-ton *Li Wo*, built at the Hongkong & Whampoa dockyard in Hong Kong in 1938, was a flat-bottomed coal burner designed for passenger service on the upper Yangtse. Owned by the Indo China Steam Navigation Company, she was the smallest, and almost certainly the ugliest, ship in their fleet, with tiers of box-like cabins perched on her main deck and extending the whole length of the ship. But with a draught of only 8 feet and twin rudders, giving her an ability to manoeuvre that belied her awkward appearance, she was ideally suited for negotiating the tortuous upper reaches of the Yangtse. This she had done with considerable profit to her owners until the Japanese decided to expand their boundaries.

In December 1941, the humble *Li Wo*, one of the few ships to escape from Hong Kong when the colony fell, was requisitioned by the Admiralty, given a coat of grey paint overall, an old 4-inch gun, twin Lewis machine-guns and a depth charge thrower, and became the armed auxiliary HMS *Li Wo*. Her master, Captain Tam Wilkinson, who had no naval training, became Lieutenant (Temporary) Thomas Wilkinson, RNR.

When Chief Petty Officer Charles Rogers was ordered to join HMS *Li Wo* in Singapore on 13 February, he had no idea of the bizarre operation he was about to be involved in. Rogers was a 'big ship' man with seventeen years' service in the Royal Navy, much of it in battleships, and a survivor of the battle-cruiser *Repulse*. Since losing their ships to the Japanese bombers, Rogers and a number of other survivors from *Prince of Wales* and *Repulse* had been manning naval cutters, each with six heavily armed Gurkhas on board, patrolling the coast of the Malayan peninsula to prevent Japanese troops infiltrating behind the British lines.

As instructed, CPO Rogers reported to the Orange Hotel in Singapore on the afternoon of 13 February, where he found that he was to take charge of a party of eighty-three men made up of *Prince Of Wales* and *Repulse* survivors, men from various Army and RAF units, and one civilian, and to join HMS *Li Wo* without delay. As the hotel was under mortar fire, the men wasted no time in loading the lorries allocated to them with provisions, and drove through the smoking ruins of Singapore to Keppel Harbour, where the *Li Wo* was anchored a mile off shore.

On boarding the armed auxiliary, CPO Rogers discovered that his party was to replace the *Li Wo*'s Malay crew, which had been put ashore. Rogers was appointed Chief Boatswain's Mate of the ship, and instructed by the First Lieutenant, Sub-Lieutenant Stanton, to detail off guns' crews, lookouts and engine-room hands. As the ex-*Prince of Wales* and *Repulse* men were experienced with guns, they were the natural choice for the 4-inch gun's crew, while the Army and RAF personnel were allocated throughout the ship.

At around midnight, Lieutenant Wilkinson found that his signals to the shore were not being answered, and decided it was time to leave. However, having weighed anchor, he found that most of the channel buoys were missing or unlit, and rather than risk running aground, he re-anchored. At daylight on the 14th, in company with another auxiliary, the 1670-ton *Vyner Brooke*, an ex-Straits Steamship Company's ship, the *Li Wo* cleared Singapore Roads and set course for the Banka Strait, the destination of both ships being Batavia. The *Vyner Brooke*, commanded by Captain R.E. Borton, which had on board 330 evacuees, including 65 Australian Army nurses and a number of survivors from the *Prince of Wales*, led the way, and being the faster ship, was soon out of sight.

The *Li Wo* and *Vyner Brooke* were only two of a fleet of some forty small craft that left Singapore in the flight south. A Dutch pilot flying overhead likened the spectacle to a regatta. But it was a regatta which very few survived. Most of the ships involved lacked any form of navigational equipment, and were manned by men without even basic seamanship training. Many came to grief on the reefs and islands strewn across their path before they had sailed many miles. Those who managed to stay afloat had even greater dangers to face.

Early that afternoon, Japanese bombers found the *Li Wo* and attacked, but she was unharmed, and the planes flew away. Presumably they considered her too small to warrant any more attention. When dusk began to close in, she was off the Lingga Islands, 100 miles south of Singapore, and having come thus far, Tam Wilkinson decided to find a quiet bay and anchor the ship for the night. She was under way again before dawn next day, but the Japanese bombers, by now constantly flying overhead, soon spotted her. They attacked, but made the mistake of flying low and were beaten off by fierce machine-gun fire, the *Li Wo*'s Lewis guns being manned by an RAF flight-sergeant who was a formidable gunner.

Wilkinson was aware that his ship would be at her most vulnerable when she entered the Banka Strait, now 90 miles to the south, and decided to press on at all speed, hoping to pass through the narrowest stretch of the 80-mile long strait during the hours of darkness.

The *Li Wo* was destined not to reach the Banka Strait. At around 5 o'clock that afternoon, when near the northern entrance to the strait, a number of ships were sighted on the starboard bow, all heading south on a parallel course. The *Li Wo*, by the sheerest bad luck, had sailed blindly into the midst of a Japanese troop convoy on its way to invade Sumatra. The convoy was escorted by an aircraft carrier, two cruisers and several destroyers.

Lieutenant Wilkinson suspected the strangers might be Japanese and called for anyone in the crew who might be able to confirm

42

this. Leading Seaman Thomas Parsons, ex-*Prince of Wales*, who had spent two years on the China Station and was familiar with Japanese warships, came to the bridge. Wilkinson handed him the telescope, and it only took a few moments for Parsons to identify a Japanese light cruiser and two destroyers.

It is feasible that if the *Li Wo* had now put her stern to the Japanese ships and made a run for it, she could possibly have escaped into the oncoming darkness. But Lieutenant Tam Wilkinson, perhaps sickened by what he had seen happening in Singapore, had other plans. He addressed his crew, saying: 'A Japanese convoy is ahead, I am going to attack it, we will take as many of those Jap bastards as possible with us.'

These were brave words indeed from an ex-merchant seaman in command of a Yangtse River steamer masquerading as a gunboat, but not one of his equally makeshift crew would have had it differently. Battle ensigns were hoisted, one at the gaff and one at the masthead in true Navy style, and the *Li Wo*, black smoke steaming from her funnel, headed purposefully for the enemy ships.

Only Leading Seaman Tom Parsons, who was gunlayer on the 4-inch, had any doubts. He had checked the 4-inch ammunition and found that the magazine contained just sixteen shells, three of which were practice shells and could be discounted, while only six of the remainder were semi-armour piercing and capable of doing any real damage. In later years Parsons wrote:

Do you think I can ever forget that moment? The hopelessness of knowing that I had only six shells that could do any damage and realising that two shells would probably be wasted before we found the range and target. The *Li Wo*'s Gunnery Officer joined us, I cannot remember his name but he was ginger-headed and was I believe a New Zealander. I had only a hurried conference with him and I said to him, 'Look, sir, I have only six shells that can do any damage, four that can do harm if we fire at the superstructure as anti-personnel shells, then our last hope is to set the AA shells at Fuse 2 and hope for the best.' I also pointed out that unless we were lucky with our first shot, as all we had was gunlayer's control and gunlayer's firing, with no rangefinder and no inclinometer to help, we might waste two shells at least before

43

we were on target – should we use the practice shells as our ranging shots? He paused for a moment, then replied, 'It might be a good idea, but then again it might not as, if we can get in close enough and we find our target, it is a wasted effort.' I then received the order to load with SAP.

The *Li Wo* closed on the Japanese ships at 15 knots, her battle ensigns streaming in the wind and giving plain warning of her intentions, and yet, possibly because she was a most unwarlike looking man of war, the enemy did not open fire. Leading Seaman Tom Parsons' six-man guns' crew, all survivors from the *Prince of Wales* and *Repulse*, crouched behind the shield of their 4-inch gun and waited.

Lieutenant Wilkinson had picked out a transport of around 5000 tons as his target, and when the range was down to 4000 yards he gave the order to open fire. Tom Parsons retained vivid memories of what happened next: 'The first shell was over target. I ordered "Fixed sight, rapid salvos". I know that at least three of our remaining five SAP shells were bang on target, as fire broke out on her immediately. Soon she was blazing furiously. In less than two minutes our ammunition was expended.'

With the Japanese transport on fire, and having run out of 4-inch ammunition, Lieutenant Wilkinson would have been fully justified in withdrawing at this point and attempting to make a getaway, but his blood was thoroughly up. Using his twin rudders to full effect, Wilkinson cleared the forecastle head, slewed the little gunboat around and headed for the next ship in line, a transport of about 2000 tons.

The *Li Wo* hit the other ship squarely amidships, burying her sharp bows deep in the transport's hull. The two ships drifted, locked together, with the *Li Wo*'s twin Lewis guns engaged in a deadly duel at point blank range with a 40mm cannon on the Japanese ship. The accuracy of the RAF flight-sergeant handling the *Li Wo*'s guns won the day, killing the transport's guns' crew and setting the ship on fire. The Japanese began to abandon ship.

Ringing for full speed astern, Lieutenant Wilkinson now backed away from the Japanese transport, and the *Li Wo* began to limp away, her bows buckled, but still watertight. She did not go unmolested. A Japanese cruiser had appeared on the scene and headed in at full speed, her guns blazing. Tom Parsons takes up the story again:

It was a fearful experience as it took the Japs five to ten minutes to find our range, their gunnery was lousy and the noise of their shells whistling overhead always expecting the next one to land inboard, knowing that we had to just sit there and take it, with the helplessness of not being able to do anything about it. When they eventually found the range, it was all over.

The *Li Wo* listed to starboard and sank stern first. When we survivors were swimming in the water, the Jap transports closed in. I myself was on one of two rafts, which for safety we had tied together. The transports came towards us and picked up their own survivors, we were then under the impression, when they came slowly towards us, that they were going to pick us up as well. But we were in for a shock. They came right at us and deliberately rammed us but we realised just before what their intentions were, and hastily dived into the sea. With my own eyes, and there are times when the memory of it is most vivid, I saw that transport go among a group of survivors and manoeuvre amongst them with churning screws, killing at least a dozen.

Chief Petty Officer Charlie Rogers had similar memories:

The last sight I had of the *Li Wo* as she started on her last voyage to the bottom of the ocean was something I shall never forget – her ensigns were still flying and the Captain was standing on the bridge, and although listing to port, she was still under way. Then she suddenly disappeared.

The few remaining men who had escaped were at the mercy of the sea – there was no land in sight. Eventually in the distance a lifeboat was sighted bobbing up and down on the swell. Leading Seaman Thompson and myself struck out towards it, but just as we were approaching it we noticed a ship from the convoy coming towards us. We swam away as fast as possible and on glancing back saw the ship ram the lifeboat. Around this area were about 30 men struggling for

45

their lives, little realising that the worst part was yet to come – the Japs were not content to leave us to our fate, but circled around and opened up a murderous attack with machine-guns, hand grenades, coal and wood. It was just plain cold blooded murder. Amidst the hell men could be heard crying out for mercy, but still the Japs continued their 'sport'. I lay back with my arms outstretched and luckily no more shots came in my direction.

When the Japanese had gone on their way, of the *Li Wo*'s total complement of eighty-six only nine men appeared to be alive, and three of these were injured. As darkness fell, they helped each other to board the drifting lifeboat, which they found was submerged to the gunwales. There were no oars in the boat, no food or fresh water, and no first aid kit. The senior survivor was Sub-Lieutenant Stanton, who had a bullet wound in the head, but was still able to take charge. Before dawn came on the 15th, the only other officer in the boat died of his wounds. Later that day, just before dark, they came across an abandoned naval whaler, which was found to be damaged and partially waterlogged, but still had its oars and sails. They transferred to the whaler, rigged the mast and sails, and set course for the land. After dark, shouts were heard, and two rafts drifted close, on which were four more survivors, one of which was Leading Seaman Tom Parsons. The rafts were taken in tow, and using oars and sail they reached Banka Island just after sunrise on the 16th. Unfortunately, the Japanese were there before them, and after a few days roaming the island, all ten men were taken prisoner, and remained in captivity until the end of the war.

While the *Li Wo* had been valiantly attacking the Japanese invasion convoy on the afternoon of the 14th, the *Vyner Brooke* was some miles ahead, having already entered the Banka Strait. Her decks crowded with men, women and children and short of food and water, the elderly ship was piling on all steam in a frantic dash to reach Java before the Japanese caught up with her. Captain Borton, who for many years had been trading peacefully between Singapore and Sarawak, and had in the dying days of the colony had his ship requisitioned by the Admiralty, armed with a 4-inch gun and classified as an 'armed trader', was still coming to terms with his new-found situation, but at least he was no stranger to these waters. Although darkness was still some hours away, he was confident they would make good their escape. And it seemed that his confidence might indeed be justified, when, out of the blue, came a flight of six twin-engined bombers.

The alarm was sounded on the ship's whistle, and all passengers ushered below decks for protection. As the bombers dived, Borton threw the little ship into a series of erratic zig-zags and the first stick of bombs fell wide, the muted explosions rattling the wheelhouse windows, but throwing up only harmless fountains of water. But when the planes came back again they found their mark. One bomb dropped straight down the *Vyner Brooke*'s funnel to explode with devastating results in her engine-room, another demolished the bridge, and a third blasted the fore deck. The crippled ship drifted slowly to a halt, black smoke pouring from her bowels and flames licking at her accommodation.

Predictably, many of the passengers panicked, young children fighting with the elderly to escape from below decks. The Australian nurses restored a measure of order, while the crew fought to clear away the lifeboats. Despite the heavy list, three boats were lowered with a full complement in each, and two of these cleared the ship's side. The third became entangled with its own gear and was dragged down with the ship when she sank. From the time the Japanese bombers first attacked until the *Vyner Brooke* disappeared beneath the waves, just fifteen minutes had elapsed.

The sunken ship left behind her two crowded lifeboats, a few small rafts, and a sea of wreckage to which over a hundred bewildered and frightened survivors were clinging, many of them injured or with severe burns. Then the planes came back again, this time spraying the wreckage with machine-gun fire. More bodies joined those already floating face down in the water. And through this pathetic flotsam ploughed a fleet of Japanese invasion launches crowded with heavily armed troops. The Japanese ignored the plaintive cries for help of those still alive in the water. They had more pressing work in hand. The sinking of the *Vyner Brooke* had coincided with the Japanese invasion of Banka Island.

Over the next eighteen hours, groups of exhausted survivors came ashore on the beaches of Banka Island. The largest group assembled on Radji beach, where by morning some sixty men, women and children, and twenty-two Australian nurses were huddled together. They had no food or water, and no shelter from the burning sun, which shone down out of a cloudless sky. In desperation, a party of nurses set out to find help. They eventually found a village, but the locals, fearing a Japanese reprisal, refused to help them. The women finally found a fresh water spring, which satisfied the thirst of the survivors on the beach, but they were now nearly forty-eight hours without food, and hunger was adding to their misery.

That night, a lifeboat containing about twenty British soldiers, many of them injured, landed on the beach, swelling the group to over a hundred. Next morning, it was decided that the women and children should find the Japanese and throw themselves on their mercy. That left only the men and the nurses, who refused to leave the wounded, and one civilian woman, who opted to stay with her husband.

When the Japanese soldiers arrived some hours later, those remaining on the beach , unarmed and unable to offer any resistance, surrendered willingly, expecting to be marched into captivity. At this early stage of the war no one believed the Japanese were capable of the brutality the prisoners were about to suffer. Half the men were ordered to their feet and herded at bayonet point until they were out of sight behind a headland. Shots were heard, then after a while the Japanese returned to collect the remaining men and march them away. Left alone on the beach, the women tried hard not to believe what they knew must be happening behind the headland. Minutes later, when the Japanese returned and sat on the sand in front of them cleaning their rifles and wiping the blood off their bayonets, the frightened women were left in no doubt as to the barbarity of their captors. Sister Vivian Bullwinkel, one of the Australian nurses, survived to tell the story:

We just looked at each other. We didn't have any emotion about it. I think by this time we'd had shock added to everything else. The Japanese came and stood in front of us and indicated we should go into the sea. And we walked into the sea with our backs to them. We knew what was going to happen to us, but all I can remember thinking was, 'I am sorry Mother will never know what has happened to me but it will be nice to see Dad again'. We didn't talk among ourselves. It was quite silent. We were drained of emotion. There were no tears. Perhaps I was thinking, 'How can anything as terrible as this be happening in such a beautiful place?' I am not sure I heard the shooting . . . yes, I think I did hear a rat-tat-tat and I suppose it was a machine-gun. I got hit. The force of the bullet, together with the waves, knocked me off my feet. I just lay there, swallowing a tremendous amount of salt water until I was violently ill. And after a while it sort of penetrated that I wasn't dying right there and then. I thought I'd better stay low until I couldn't stay low any longer. The waves brought me right up into the shallow water. Finally, when I did sit up and look around, there was nothing. The Japanese had gone and none of the other girls were to be seen . . .'

Vivian Bullwinkel was the only survivor of the twenty-two nurses and one civilian woman who had fallen into Japanese hands on Radji beach. With a bullet in her hip, she survived in the jungles of Banka Island for another thirteen days before giving herself up to the Japanese. She spent the remainder of the war in a prison camp.

One of the last little ships to sail out of Singapore before the surrender was the 585-ton gunboat HMS *Grasshopper*. Built to patrol the tortuous Yangtse River, with triple rudders, a draught of 7 feet and a maximum speed of 12 knots, this highly manoeuvrable little craft was armed with two 4-inch guns, a 3.7-inch howitzer, four 2-pounders, and eight machine guns. In command was Commander J.S. Hoffman RN (Retired), an elderly officer recalled to service, who made no bones of the fact that his eyesight was not of the best.

Grasshopper left Singapore in the early hours of 14 February in company with a sister ship HMS *Dragonfly*. She had on board fifty passengers, comprising civilian men and women, Army officers, Royal Marines and a small party of Japanese prisoners of war. By dawn both ships were 50 miles south of Singapore, and running clear of Bintan Island, having emerged from the Riouw Strait. Ahead of them lay a 170-mile-long passage to the Banka Strait, most of which they would have to cover in daylight and exposed to marauding Japanese aircraft. It was a daunting prospect.

Soon after sunrise, the gunboats were joined by a Fairmile

launch, loaded to her gunwales with men of the Gordon Highlanders and also making a dash for safety. Japanese planes were now passing overhead, fortunately without seeing the three British ships – or perhaps they had more worthwhile targets in mind. Then, at 0900, a lone seaplane found them and carried out two dive bombing attacks on each of the gunboats. *Dragonfly* escaped without damage, and *Grasshopper* sustained only slight damage from a near miss, but this was enough to persuade all three ships to make for the nearest land, with the object of laying up until darkness came. But they had left it too late. At 1130 they were only 2 miles off a group of islands to the north of Singkep when two formations of Japanese bombers with fighter escort, some eighty planes in all, flew over at about 4000 feet, heading in the direction of Singapore. Then, having passed overhead, the Japanese suddenly broke formation and dived on the little flotilla, attacking in flights of nine at heights between 2000 and 4000 feet. *Dragonfly* was sunk by the first wave, the Fairmile was machine-gunned and beached herself. Then the planes turned on *Grasshopper*.

The Japanese planes came at the gunboat from all directions at five minute intervals. Her machine-gunners fought back, and Commander Hoffman, unable to see the planes clearly because of his poor eyesight, but directed by Lieutenant Ian Forbes, a *Prince of Wales* survivor seconded to the *Grasshopper*, successfully dodged the sticks of bombs that rained down. The two men working together saved the *Grasshopper* from between fifteen and twenty determined attacks, always altering course in the right direction at the last minute. But there seemed no end to the enemy planes; they just kept on coming.

When the *Grasshopper* was only half a mile from the nearest island, and seemed to be within reach of shelter, the Hoffman/ Forbes combination made their first mistake, altering course just that fraction of a minute too late. A Japanese bomb exploded in her after messdeck, wrecking the after part of the ship and starting a fire. Lieutenant Forbes rushed aft and found the flames already licking at the after magazine. He was unable to flood the magazine, as the flooding valve had been smashed by the explosion.

Forbes reported the situation aft to Commander Hoffman, who, realizing that the magazine could go up at any moment and take the rest of the ship with it, immediately ran *Grasshopper* ashore on the nearest beach. Two more attacks were fought off while the gunboat was beached, but by then the fire was spreading rapidly, and Hoffmann gave the order to abandon ship and swim for the shore.

Eventually, there were over a hundred survivors from the two gunboats gathered on the island, many of them wounded. The island was uninhabited, so Hoffman ordered Lieutenant Forbes to get help. Accompanied by two Army officers, Forbes swam to the next island, and from there they embarked on a series of boat and land journeys, finally reaching the Dutch-occupied town of Djambi on the mainland of Sumatra on 18 February. From there he despatched a ship to pick up the survivors he had left behind far to the north.

While Ian Forbes and his party were approaching Djambi, the *Sing-Keng-Seng*, manned by survivors from the *Empress of Asia*, completed her escape passage, finally tying up alongside a wharf in Tandjong Priok, the port for Batavia on the north coast of Java. J.N Ewart continues with her story:

The Dutch authorities housed us in the Netherlands Bank in Batavia until February 20, when we were told to get back to Tandjong Priok as quickly as we could and muster alongside the Burns Philp liner *Marella*.

The original intention had been that we should take over from the ship's Lascar crew, who were refusing to sail. However, in the event they decided that they would rather sail than endure more daily bombings and the prospect of being taken prisoner by the Japanese. As a result, with the exception of two or three who were asked to perform quartermaster duties, our party went aboard as DBS (Distressed British Seamen). Also on board were civilians of many nationalities, including women and children, survivors from a Norwegian ship and Australian and New Zealand Air Force ground crews whose airfields in Malaya had had to be evacuated.

We sailed on February 21 and soon joined a convoy of eleven ships escorted by a British destroyer HMAS *Yarra* and HMS *Exeter*. The latter two stayed with us just long enough to see us through the Sunda Strait and then left us for more urgent duty in the east . . . Rumour had us going to Fremantle and six days later, after an uneventful trip we entered this port in Western Australia.

Amongst the ten men who survived the sinking of the Li Wo was Leading Seaman Tom Parsons, ex-*Prince of Wales*. At the end of February, Parsons, Lieutenant-Colonel Dalley and Lieutenant Eno of Military Intelligence and Counter Espionage in Malaya, and Australian Sergeant Ken Wharton, escaped from a prisoner of war camp on Banka Island. The four men persuaded some local fishermen to sell them a boat, and sailed to Java, where they were betrayed by Javanese villagers and, once again, fell into Japanese hands. Many years later, Tom Parsons recalled these traumatic events:

Within an hour they came and what happened next was unbelievable. Thirty to forty Japs, heavily armed and two of them carrying a heavy machine gun appeared and surrounded us. When the Commanding Officer realised that he had turned out in force to capture a mere four unarmed European servicemen he literally went berserk. He beat the informer to the ground and kicked and jumped on him, he was so angry. He was like a very excited chimpanzee, with his short bandy legs, jumping up and down. It was the first inkling we had of the Jap mentality and reasoning. What seems to have happened was this. Whilst the informer had told the Japs that four Europeans had landed in a boat and were in his village, owing to the language interpretation the Japs understood it to be four boatloads of Europeans that had landed. Hence the backup of thirty to forty Jap soldiers. The Jap officer's thinking and reasoning was that they had lost face – and to them it was unbearable!

The Japs tied our hands behind our backs and marched us to the road where we boarded one of the two lorries that had brought the Japs to the village. They then drove us to what we believed had been a Police Administrative building. We were then lined up outside with our backs to a wall and eight Japanese soldiers were no more than five yards in front of us while the rest of the Japs moved off. Soon a crowd of jeering Malay and Javanese natives gathered and I could not believe the hatred they had for us. Some other Japs soon cleared them away and the officer who captured us came back and alerted the Jap soldiers facing us to be ready to fire. Just then a senior Jap officer who spoke good passable English came on the scene and dismissed the firing squad. The officer who captured us then began to protest most strongly and once again we witnessed another insight into Jap mentality. The English speaking officer shouted angrily at the officer who had captured us and suddenly he was bowing and grovelling to his superior. We all more or less summed up the incident thus: the Jap officer who captured us felt he had lost face by turning out with between thirty and forty heavily armed troops to take four unarmed enemy prisoners and felt that executing us would remove the stigma. After that episode we were marched away for interrogation one by one separately. We all stuck to the same story that was previously agreed upon, as we all knew and were well aware, that anyone who escaped and was recaptured was executed by decapitation.

Our agreed story was this: all four of us left Singapore on a small steamer, most were civilians and the few military men on board were there to run the ship as crew members and to look after the safety of the civilians. We were intercepted by the Jap Navy and sunk but managed to reach the shore in a boat, and hence we headed south until we met the Malay Chinaman who the Japs had released when we were taken prisoner. To further questions we replied: no, we did not know that Bangka Island, Sumatra or Java had been captured by the Japs. After the interrogation we were tied by our thumbs to a beam and it was very painful.

The following day we were once again interrogated separately, booted and thumped and knocked about. I was forced to kneel and a Jap officer who was interrogating me unsheathed his Samurai sword and placed it at the back of my neck flatwise. Opposite me and facing me was a Jap soldier with rifle and fixed bayonet, grinning and really enjoying the situation. I was told to get up and the officer sheathed his sword and told me if I told the truth he would let me go. 'Did you escape?' he asked me and I told him no, this was the first time I had been taken prisoner. I was then allowed to join the others. The following day I had a very high fever. I had contracted malaria and was put on a mattress, on my own for several days separated from the others. How long that fever actually lasted I don't know as I lost all count of time.

Tom Parsons did recover from his fever, and was moved from camp to camp, eventually ending up back at Singapore, and spent a while in the notorious Changi Jail. He was repatriated to Britain in October 1945.

Chapter Five

The Other Pearl Harbor

After the fall of Singapore on 15 February, the now invincible Japanese forces moved quickly south and east through the islands of the East Indies. Bali fell on the 18th, and Timor was awaiting invasion at any time. Japanese troops were rapidly drawing close to the Australian mainland, while the same fast carrier group that had launched the attack on Pearl Harbor cruised menacingly in the Timor Sea.

Belatedly, it now came home to the Australians that their homeland was under serious threat of attack, if not invasion, with their northern port of Darwin first in the line of fire. Yet the Australian authorities still took no steps to improve the defences of the port, which had become an important base for the supply of troops and war materials to Java and Sumatra, both now awaiting a Japanese attack.

The full strength of the Royal Australian Air Force in the Darwin area consisted of seventeen Hudson light bombers and fourteen Wirraway fighter patrol planes. Both types were antiques in terms of modern air warfare, and certainly no match for Japanese fighters and bombers of the day, especially the Mitsubishi A6M Zero, which had a top speed of 332mph, and was armed with two 20mm cannon. Visiting the RAAF Base, having arrived on 15 February, were ten P40 Kittyhawks, one B17 and one B24 bomber of the US Army Air Force, all in transit to Java. Three PBY Catalinas flying boats of the US Navy were in the harbour.

Faced with the threat to Timor, the Allied Command took steps to strengthen the Australian garrison on the island. A convoy consisting of the Burns Philp ship *Tulagi*, and the US transports *Mauna Loa*, *Meigs* and *Portmar*, between them carrying nearly 1,700 Australian and American troops, left Darwin on the 15th bound for Koepang, on the south-west coast of Timor. The convoy was well defended, being escorted by the US light cruiser *Houston*, the old four-funnelled destroyer USS *Peary*, and the Australian sloops *Swan* and *Warrego*. However, the transports had no air cover, and when, on the morning of the 16th, two four-engined Japanese seaplanes appeared, the escorting ships kept them at a distance with anti-aircraft fire, but could do nothing to stop them reporting the position and strength of the convoy.

The dive bombers, four squadrons flying in tight formation, arrived some five hours later. *Houston* ordered the convoy to scatter, and all ships began zig-zagging and opened fire on the bombers with every gun that could be brought to bear. But seemingly oblivious to the curtain of fire put up, the Japanese came relentlessly on, splitting up into formations of nine planes each as they singled out the troop transports for their attack.

The *Mauna Loa*, the largest ship in the convoy at 11,358 tons displacement, and carrying 500 troops, was the first to come under attack. She was making violent alterations of course to throw the bombers off their aim, but at her maximum speed of 10 knots she could not escape. A near miss close to her No. 2 hold caused her to take on water and killed one crew member and one soldier. The other transports all had some damage, but thanks largely to the fierce barrage put up by the escorts, none received a direct hit.

However, once having been detected by the Japanese, the convoy was ordered to return to Darwin, where it arrived on the 18th. *Houston* sailed immediately for Java, but the other ships remained in port, the *Tulagi* still having 560 men of the US Army 148 Field Artillery Regiment on board.

On 19 February 1942, Darwin awoke to another busy day. Including those from the returned invasion convoy, there were now forty-six ships in the port, berthed alongside, or anchored in the harbour, loading or discharging supplies, under repair, refuelling, or in the case of the Australian hospital ship *Manunda* on standby to receive casualties from the fighting further north. With so much shipping concentrated in the harbour, there were many in Darwin who feared they would soon become a target for Japanese bombers. They were not to be kept in suspense for long.

At 0815 one of the US Navy's Catalinas, PBY VP22, took off from the harbour, the roar of its powerful Wasp engines drowning the clatter of cargo winches coming from the wharves. Piloted by Lieutenant Tom Moorer, the 'Cat' was on a routine patrol keeping watch for any threatening Japanese activity. At 0920 the flying boat was 140 miles north of Darwin, when Moorer sighted an un-identified merchant ship below. He descended to 600 feet to investigate, and was immediately pounced upon by eight Japanese Zeros. Moorer took violent avoiding action, but his plane was raked by cannon fire. The port engine caught fire, and one of the fuel tanks exploded. With his plane now well on fire, Moorer quickly lost height, and made an emergency landing on the sea. He and all his crew were able to evacuate the plane before it blew up. Fortunately for them, the merchant ship they had been about to investigate was the *Florence D.*, a supply ship on charter to the US Navy, which was then bound south for Darwin with a cargo of ammunition. By this time the Zeros had gone away, leaving the ship free to pick up Lieutenant Moorer and his crew of seven.

The Catalina's attackers were from a Japanese force consisting of the aircraft carriers *Akagi*, *Kaga*, *Hiryu* and *Soryu* which, accompanied by cruisers and destroyers, had sailed from Palau on 15 February and, quite unknown to Darwin, were then 250 miles to the north-west of the port. At 0845 these carriers had launched an attack force of eighty-one 'Kate' high level bombers, seventy-one 'Val' dive-bombers and thirty-six Zeros. Led by Commander Mitsuo Fuchida, who had commanded the raid on Pearl Harbor, their target was the port of Darwin.

Having downed Lieutenant Moorer's Catalina, the eight Zeros continued south towards the land, passing over Bathurst Island, 50 miles north of Darwin, at about 0930. Father John McGraph, who ran the Catholic mission station on Bathurst, saw the planes passing overhead, correctly identified them as Japanese, and radioed a warning to the RAAF base at Darwin. It must then have been obvious to those on the base that an attack on the port was under way, but for some reason they failed to notify either the town or the ships in the harbour. The *Florence D.*, meanwhile, had been attacked near Bathurst Island by Japanese bombers, which sank her. Fortunately, her cargo did not explode, and only three of her crew of thirty-seven lost their lives. With them died one of PBY VP22's crew, who had been plucked from the water only a few hours before. The survivors were picked up by the Australian minesweeper *Warrnambool* and the Bathurst Island Mission boat *St. Francis*. The *Warrnambool* was bombed by a Japanese seaplane while she was involved in the rescue, but suffered no damage.

The *Florence D.*'s attackers also came across the 3261 ton Philippine-flag *Don Isidro*, also carrying supplies for the US Army, and bound for Darwin. She received a direct hit and was run ashore on the north coast of Bathurst. Eleven of her sixty-seven crew died on the beach while awaiting rescue, which did not come until the 22nd, when the *Warrnambool* came in to pick them up. Two others died after the minesweeper returned to Darwin on the 23rd.

Earlier that morning, the USAAF Kittyhawks had taken off from Darwin on the final leg of their flight to Java, where they were to help strengthen the defences of the island. Led by Major Floyd Pell, and accompanied by the B17 bomber, which was acting as navigator, at 0930 the Kittyhawks were only a few miles on their way when bad weather over Java forced them to return to Darwin. They were back over the town at 0938, by which time Major Pell had been notified of a possible Japanese air attack. He allowed five of his flight to land, keeping the other five in the air to provide cover. His caution achieved nothing, for at that moment the same Zeros that had shot down Moorer's Catalina appeared overhead. The five Kittyhawks still in the air met the Zeros head-on but they were outgunned, and four out of the five were shot down. The other Kittyhawks tried to take off again, but, caught at a disadvantage, were shot down before they could gain height.

There were now no Australian fighters in the air, and if there had been, the antiquated Wirraways must have suffered the same fate as Pell's Kittyhawks. When Mitsuo Fuchida led his bombers in, the skies over Darwin were clear. Flying in tight formation at between 8–10,000ft, and ignoring the anti-aircraft fire, the 'Kates' attacked first, their target the closely packed ships in the harbour below. Commander Fuchida reported: 'The airfield on the outskirts of the town, although fairly large, had no more than two or three small hangars, and in all there were only twenty-odd planes of various types scattered about the field. No planes were in the air. A few attempted to take off as we came over but were quickly shot down, and the rest were destroyed where they stood. Anti-aircraft fire was intense but largely ineffectual, and we quickly accomplished our objectives.'

Stoker 2nd Class Charlie Unmack, serving in the 480 ton minesweeper HMAS *Gunbar*, was an early eye-witness:

On the morning of Thursday, 19 February 1942, my ship was heading out of port and those of us who were not on duty were sitting on deck. We had not cleared the harbour when we noticed a formation of planes approaching over East Head. It would have been close to 10.00 am when we first saw them. The planes were glinting in the morning sun, and we remarked on the good formation they were keeping.

At first we thought these planes were ours, and then we noticed some silver-looking objects dropping from them. It was not long before we knew what they were as they exploded in smoke and dust on the town and waterfront. More Japanese planes came in from another direction. These were dive bombers, and they attacked the ships in the harbour. We saw a couple of planes crash into the sea. I thought they were ours.

Then it was our turn for some attention. They began strafing us from almost mast height. As the only armament we had against aircraft was a Lewis machine-gun, and this had been disabled by a Japanese bullet hitting the magazine pan, the skipper was firing at them with his .45 revolver. This strafing went on for approximately half an hour before my first taste of action ended. Our casualties were nine wounded out of a crew of thirty-six, and one of these died on the hospital ship *Manunda* on the following day. The skipper had both knees shattered by Japanese bullets.

We transferred our wounded to the *Manunda*, and then our motor boat began rescuing survivors in the water.

The scenes in the harbour during the raid were horrific, with ships on fire, oil and debris everywhere, ships sinking and ships run aground . . .

It was unfortunate that the first ship to be hit was the 5952-ton Burns Philp motor ship *Neptuna*, which had been requisitioned by the Admiralty to carry military stores. Under the command of Captain W. Michie, she had arrived in Darwin on 12 February after loading a cargo at Sydney and Brisbane, which included 200 depth charges and a very large quantity of anti-aircraft shells. She was a very vulnerable target.

When the Japanese bombers arrived over Darwin, HMAS *Swan* was berthed alongside the *Neptuna* replenishing her magazines with anti-aircraft shells from the merchant ship's hold, having exhausted her supply in defending the Timor-bound convoy. The transfer of this ammunition was being carried out by sailors from the sloop. On the shore side of the *Neptuna*, dockers were discharging general cargo from the ship onto the wharf. This seemed like a perfectly sensible arrangement, the *Swan* being short of shells, but Australian dockers are sticklers for 'union rules', even in wartime. When they realized that someone else was doing what they rightfully regarded as their work, they threatened to walk off the ship, so bringing the whole cargo operation to a stand-still. The dispute had become very heated, with the Petty Officer in charge of the naval party threatening to throw the union delegate into the dock, when someone noticed the aircraft overhead. Seconds later the bombs began to fall, and the argument was settled decisively and finally. The *Swan* cast off and backed away to give herself room to fire her guns, the 'wharfies' ran for the hills, and the *Neptuna*'s crew went to their emergency stations. They were not a moment too soon. A bomb landed on the wharf close to the *Neptuna*'s bow, the blast from which damaged her hull, and she began to take on water.

Other bombs followed the first, causing devastation to nearby installations, including an oil storage tank, from which oil gushed into the dock, turning the water around the *Neptuna* black. Then the ship received two directs hits one after the other, which wrecked much of her superstructure and started a number of fires. Captain Michie, his chief and second officers were killed, leaving Third Officer Brendan Deburca to take command. The ship, which was now listing heavily, was obviously finished, so Deburca wasted no time in organizing the rigging of a temporary gangway to the shore – the original gangway had been destroyed by the first bomb – and evacuated all surviving crew to the wharf.

Once ashore, Deburca called the roll, and established that in addition to Captain Michie and the deck officers, fifty-two men were missing: three engineers, a cadet, the three radio officers, and forty-five Chinese ratings. There was no going back to look for them, for the *Neptuna* was now blazing furiously, and with hundreds of tons of ammunition still on board, she was liable to blow up at any minute. She did in fact explode in a sheet of flame soon after the survivors were taken off the wrecked wharf by small boats, and put on board the depot ship HMAS *Platypus*. One of the survivors died on board the *Platypus*, bringing the number lost with the *Neptuna* to fifty-six.

Another target singled out by the Japanese bombers was the *British Motorist*, a 6891-ton motor tanker owned by the British Tanker Company and commanded by Captain Bates. She carried a crew of sixty-five, and was armed with a 4.7-inch and a 12-pounder, both mounted aft, and four .303 Lewis machine-guns. The *British Motorist* had arrived in Darwin on 11 February carrying 9,500 tons of diesel oil from Colombo for the Admiralty. She completed discharging on the 17th and then moved out to an anchorage in the bay, where she was to carry out engine repairs. Her log book reports that on the morning of the 19th the weather was extremely good, with light variable airs, a calm sea, and very good visibility. At about 0930, the Third Officer, who was on anchor watch on the bridge, saw a V formation of nine aircraft approaching, which he recognized as being Japanese. He immediately sounded the alarm, and the tanker's crew went to their action stations. Second Officer Pierre Payne wrote a detailed report of what happened next:

> On my way to the after gun station I saw a salvo of bombs explode on the jetty. About 5 minutes later, when standing by the 12 pdr., I sighted a second wave of nine planes coming in from a south-easterly direction also in V formation. I saw nine bombs, which were released from a height of about 10,000 feet, fall about 15 feet from the starboard side of the vessel. The explosions were terrific and caused the vessel to roll and pitch violently and it was found that the starboard side and bottom had been blown in and the deck buckled up in an arch amidships, and, on looking over the side the water could be seen pouring out of the ballast tanks as she listed . . . Owing

to the height of the planes, we did not open fire during the attack, as they were out of range of our guns.

Some Japanese planes then carried out dive bombing attacks, the planes coming in from a general south-westerly direction, and we were attacked once or twice but were not hit, the nearest bombs falling about 50 yards away. Meanwhile the other ships in the harbour, the jetty and the town were attacked, resulting in a great deal of damage being done.

Our 12 pdr. H.A. gun was in action throughout the attack, and we concentrated our fire on the planes attacking us. Our firing was effective, definitely disturbing the aim of the attacking planes, which gave us a lull of about 15 minutes.

I told the gun's crew to stand by for further developments, meanwhile the ship was gradually sinking. After a quarter of an hour, at about 1030, we sighted another wave of planes coming in from the south-east. These planes dropped a salvo of bombs, one of which hit the fore deck, the other eight being dropped into the sea near the starboard bow. These near misses caused the ship to pitch and roll; the direct hit made a terrific explosion, the bridge ladders being blown away and the fore side of the saloon accommodation and bridge being severely damaged. A great deal of debris was thrown up into the air, and I could see fire had broken out amidships.

At about 1045 dive bombing was resumed, during which a direct hit was scored on the port wing of the bridge, destroying all the midship accommodation, and completely destroying the port lifeboat. I was still in the main gun pit aft, firing my gun. The Chief Officer was attempting to put out the fire with the help of other members of the crew, using pyrene fire extinguishers and a small hand pump. The water service lines were completely destroyed, and the ship was increasing her list to port.

The Captain had visited the gun position previous to this latest bombing but had decided to go amidships to direct the machine-gun fire from the bridge guns and when the bomb exploded both he and the Second Wireless Operator were very severely injured.

There was one more bombing attack at about 1100 which

was ineffective owing to the accurate fire from our gun which prevented the planes from taking up a good position . . .

When the Japanese bombers had gone away, and there was no sign of any more coming in, Second Officer Payne left his gun and went forward to ascertain the state of the ship. This was not good. Much of her superstructure had been destroyed, she was on fire in several places, listing heavily to port, and seemed to be on the point of capsizing. There was obviously not much more to be done for her. Captain Bates was lying severely injured, and the Chief Officer could not be found, so Payne took command and ordered the ship to be abandoned.

Payne supervised the launching of three lifeboats, and while this was being done, a number of small naval craft came alongside the tanker, taking off the injured men and transferring them to the hospital ship *Manunda*. The nearest landing point for the lifeboats was the jetty which juts out into the harbour, but the two ships on each side of the jetty, had been hit and were burning. Oil had spilled from their ruptured tanks into the water, and this too was on fire. Payne decided to take his lifeboats to the nearest beach, which proved to be a wise precaution. As they were passing within 100 yards of the jetty, one of the ships, the *Zealandia*, blew up, throwing burning debris in all directions.

When the *British Motorist*'s boats reached the shore, the survivors reported to the company's agent in the town, but such was the state of confusion reigning in Darwin that he could do nothing for them, except to take a list of their names. No food or shelter was available, so Payne led his men back to the beach, where for the next two days they camped out alongside their boats, living off the emergency provisions they carried. At last, on the 22nd, they were accommodated at an old hospital building near the beach, and were fed by the Army. The last they saw of their ship was her lying capsized, with her port side, most of which had been ripped open by the bomb blasts, about 3 feet above the water. The *British Motorist* would never sail again.

The Burns Philp ship *Tulagi*, participant in the ill-fated Timor convoy, was also anchored in the harbour, and still had 560 US Army men on board. When she came under attack from the air, her master, Captain Thompson, slipped his anchor and ran the ship aground in a muddy creek with the object of landing his troops before the Japanese planes came in again. Using lifeboats and rafts, all troops and crew were put ashore, and the ship temporarily abandoned.

Next afternoon, Captain Thompson reboarded the *Tulagi*, but only five members of his crew, one engineer, three wireless operators and the Purser, volunteered to come with him. With the assistance of a naval working party and some of the *Neptuna*'s officers, the *Tulagi* was floated off the mud and re-anchored in the harbour. Nine days later, after repairs had been carried out, she left Darwin for Sydney, crewed by volunteers from the *Neptuna*, the *British Motorist*, and a naval party consisting of a Chief Petty Officer and six ratings.

HMAS *Swan*, having pulled clear from the *Neptuna* before she blew up, did not escape the attentions of the enemy planes. Despite the extremely accurate anti-aircraft fire she put up, she was attacked on seven separate occasions. Several near misses caused considerable damage to the sloop, three of her crew were killed and nineteen injured.

USS *Peary*, the largest naval ship berthed in Darwin at the time of the raid, for all her great age, carried a formidable anti-aircraft armament of six 3-inch dual-purpose guns, and these she put to good use when the Japanese planes came over. But at 1045 she became the main target of the 'Kate' dive-bombers, and was hit by five bombs in quick succession. The first bomb exploded right aft, over her steering gear, the second, an incendiary, hit the galley deckhouse, the third failed to explode, the fourth dropped on the fore deck, causing her forward magazine to blow up, and the fifth, also an incendiary, landed in the after engine-room, completely wrecking it.

The American destroyer was hard hit, on fire, and sinking, but she was not about to give up without a fight. Her six 3-inch guns hurled their shells skywards as fast as their crews could load and fire, while the two machine-guns mounted aft raked any of her attackers that dared to come within their range. All guns continued to fire until the Japanese planes had gone away, by which time the *Peary*'s after deck was under water. She finally sank stern first at 1300. Eighty-one of her total complement of 136 died, and thirteen were injured.

Darwin's first air raid was over by 1040, when the Japanese planes, their mission accomplished, returned to their carriers. In a momentous forty minutes, they had sunk ten Allied ships, including the *Florence D.* and the *Don Isidro,* and damaged many others. A total of 187 people were killed in those ships, while another 107 were left injured, some seriously. In addition, twenty-two of the dock workers engaged in discharging the *Neptuna* lost their lives when they were trapped on the jetty by burning oil.

While the bombs were falling on Darwin's harbour, the hospital ship HMAHS *Manunda* found her services to be very much in demand. The 8853-ton ex-Adelaide Steamship Company's passenger liner, under the command of Captain James Garden, had arrived in Darwin on 14 January, and over the intervening weeks her medical staff, led by Lieutenant-Colonel John Beith, had been in constant training to cope with the casualties that the war, which was moving ever nearer, might bring.

When the Japanese bombers arrived over Darwin on the morning of 19 February, the *Manunda*, although she must have been easily recognized as a hospital ship by her white painted hull and prominent red crosses, soon became a prime target. A near miss sprayed her decks with lethal fragments of shrapnel, causing widespread damage and a number of casualties. A second bomb narrowly missed her bridge and exploded on B and C decks, totally destroying the medical and nursing quarters and starting a number of fires, which could not be controlled as the fire mains were cut.

Eleven members of the *Manunda*'s crew were killed, including Third Officer Alan Scott Smith, eighteen were seriously wounded, and forty others slightly wounded. Three of her medical staff, including Nursing Sister Margaret De Mestre and Captain B.H. Hocking, a dentist, lost their lives. In spite of the terrible carnage wrought by the Japanese bombs, the *Manunda* continued to function as a hospital ship, using her boats to pick up hundreds of casualties from the wrecked ships in the harbour and from the water. When she sailed for Fremantle in the early hours of the 20th, she had on board 266 wounded, many of whom were stretcher cases.

While the Japanese dive bombers concentrated on the ships in the harbour, the high-level 'Vals' had been systematically bombing the town of Darwin. The devastation they caused was widespread. One of the first buildings to be hit was the Post Office, where the Postmaster, his family and all the staff on duty were killed. The Police Barracks, the Police Station, Government House, the Cable Office, and the local hospital, along with a number of private houses were all either hit or damaged by blast. And no sooner had the people of Darwin recovered from the shock of this raid than they found themselves under attack again. A few minutes before noon, the air was once more filled with the sound of high-flying aircraft. This second wave of Japanese planes consisted of fifty-four twin-engined land-based bombers flying from Kendari, in the island of Sulawasi and from Ambon. They had no fighter escort, not did they need one, for all Darwin's air defence force had already been crushed. Ignoring the sporadic anti-aircraft fire, they proceeded to pattern-bomb the RAAF airfield, destroying eight aircraft still on the ground and most of the buildings, and causing serious damage to the hospital.

In the two raids on Darwin that day, a total of 243 Japanese planes dropped 628 bombs, nearly three times the number dropped on Pearl Harbor. No exact figure is on record of the number of civilians killed in the town of Darwin during the raid. Army Intelligence sources at the time put the figure at 1,100, while the Mayor of Darwin estimated that 900 had been killed. The Australian Government, on the other hand, anxious to avoid any panic, claimed that casualties amounted to only seventeen killed and thirty-five injured. Their reassurances fell on deaf ears. The population of Darwin was convinced that a Japanese invasion was only hours away and streamed out of the town, heading south in what became known later as 'The Adelaide River Stakes'.*At least half of the civilian population left, the panic spreading to the Australian servicemen based in Darwin, who deserted their posts in great numbers. Three days after the attack, 278 soldiers and airmen were still missing.

*Also "The Darwin Handicap!"

Chapter Six

The Battle of the Java Sea

Soon after the outbreak of war in 1939, Winston Churchill, then First Lord of the Admiralty, wrote: 'Singapore is as far from Japan as Southampton is from New York. The operation of moving a Japanese army, with all its troopships and maintaining it during a siege, which would last at least four or five months, would be liable to be interrupted, if at any time Britain chose to send a superior fleet to the scene.' In fact, the siege of Singapore lasted exactly seven days, ending on 15 February 1942, and going down in history as one of the most ignominious defeats ever suffered by British arms.

The loss of Singapore left open the way to the fabled Spice Islands of the Netherlands East Indies, wherein lay the oil so coveted by the Japanese, who wasted no time in moving towards this goal. Already, beginning on 9 February, convoys of troop transports had been sailing from Camranh Bay, in French Indo-China, their destination Sumatra and then Java. Covering these convoys was the Japanese 7th Cruiser Squadron, under the command of Vice-Admiral Ozawa, flying his flag in the cruiser *Chokai*, with the aircraft carrier *Ryujo* and a division of destroyers.

On the 13th the first Japanese troop convoy entered the Banka Strait, and Admiral Ozawa then positioned his squadron to guard the northern approaches to the strait against any Allied attack. The state of the British and Dutch navies in these waters being what it was, this was not a likely eventuality. The only ships to come up against Ozawa's guns were those of the pathetic armada of little ships escaping from the shambles of Singapore. Crowded and defenceless, some forty of these ships were sunk in the space of two days.

The assault on Sumatra began on the morning of the 14th, when 460 Japanese paratroopers were dropped on Palembang at the southern end of the island. Twenty-four hours later, the main invasion force landed from the ships. A spirited resistance was put up by British and Dutch troops, but they were outnumbered and outgunned. By the time night fell, much of Southern Sumatra was in Japanese hands.

There was worse to come. On 18 February, an invasion force comprising fifty-six troop transports left Camranh Bay and sailed south for Java. A day later, another forty-one transports set out from Jolo in the Sulu Sea, also heading for Java. The two convoys came together 50 miles or so to the north of Bawean Island, where they were joined by a powerful escort force under Rear-Admiral Takeo Takagi, consisting of the two 8-inch gun cruisers *Haguro* and *Nachi*, the light cruisers *Naka* and *Jintsu*, and fourteen destroyers.

When news of the approaching invasion forces reached Admiral Conrad Helfrich, in overall command of Allied naval forces in the area, he ordered the Eastern Striking Force, led by Rear-Admiral Karel Doorman in the light cruiser *De Ruyter*, to proceed to sea and attack the enemy. Doorman's force consisted of the two Netherlands Navy light cruisers *De Ruyter* and *Java*, the British heavy cruiser *Exeter*, the American heavy cruiser *Houston*, the Australian light cruiser *Perth*, and nine destroyers, three British, five American and one Dutch. The ships were assembled in Sourabaya, on the north coast of Java, and although outwardly an impressive force, they had not really exercised together as a squadron, *Houston*'s forward turret was out of action, and they had no air cover. Moreover ship-to-ship communication was abysmally slow, as Admiral Doorman's orders were given in Dutch, and had to be first translated into English by an interpreter stationed on each British and American ship. None of this was a recipe for success. Time was short, and at a meeting of Commanding Officers hurriedly called in Sourabaya Doorman's briefing was short and to the point, giving only the order of sailing, the method of attack, and night recognition signals. The Admiral had no comprehensive battle plan.

The Eastern Striking Force left Sourabaya at 1906 on 26 February, and having cleared the minefields at the entrance to the port, formed up in their pre-arranged cruising order. The British destroyers, *Electra, Encounter, Jupiter*, with the Dutch destroyer *Kortenaer*, screened ahead, the cruisers, led by Doorman's flagship *De Ruyter*, followed in line astern, while the American destroyers, *Alden, John D. Edwards, John D. Ford* and *Paul Jones* brought up the rear as a separate unit. The latter were all 1920 vintage four-stackers, long outdated, and with only 3-inch guns, but they each carried twelve torpedo tubes loaded with 21-inch 'Long Lance' torpedoes. Doorman's battle plan was for the cruisers, supported by the British and Dutch destroyers, to engage the enemy escort force, while the US destroyers dashed in to sink the troop transports with their torpedoes.

Not having any definite information regarding the enemy's position, Doorman first led his ships to the east parallel to the coast of Madura Island, but at 0100 on the 27th, with nothing seen, he reversed course to the west. The remainder of the night passed quietly, but shortly after dawn a Japanese reconnaisance plane appeared and began to circle out of range of the Allied guns. The bombers appeared in the forenoon, but their attacks, mostly by single aircraft, were half-hearted. A number of bombs were dropped, but they all went wide, and no damage resulted.

At about 1030, when 60 miles west of Sourabaya, having sighted no enemy ships, and fearing that he might be on a wild goose chase, Admiral Doorman decided to abandon the search and return to port to await more definite information. Some four hours later, when the Allied ships were about to enter the swept channel into Sourabaya, word was received that a Japanese force of two cruisers and six destroyers had been sighted 90 miles to the north and heading south at high speed. Doorman immediately led his ships through a 180° turn, and set off to the north at 20 knots. The only order he gave to the others was 'Follow me'. The weather at the time was fine, with light airs and excellent visibility.

At approximately 1610 masts were sighted on the horizon to the north, soon to be followed by funnels. By the time the approaching ships were hull-up they had been identified as two Sendai class cruisers, each leading a flotilla of six destroyers. This was in fact the vanguard of Admiral Takagi's force, the 5.5-inch cruisers *Naka* and *Jintsu* with their attendant destroyers. Confident that he had the superior force, Doorman increased to 27 knots and steered to engage.

The Japanese were first to open fire, their shells falling around the starboard wing destroyer HMS *Electra*. She was not hit. Minutes later, *Exeter* came within range, and Captain Gordon ordered his 8-inch guns into action. The range was extreme, 27,000 yards, but after twelve salvoes from her A and B turrets *Exeter* was straddling the leading Japanese ship, forcing her to run away under cover of a smoke screen. Fire was then shifted to the second cruiser, and soon she was seen disappearing under cover of smoke, some of which Gordon was convinced his shells had caused.

While *Exeter* was engaged with the two four-funnel cruisers more masts were seen on the horizon behind them. These proved to belong to the heavy cruisers *Nachi* and *Haguro*. They were formidable ships, 15,000 tons and each mounting ten 8-inch guns, and although launched as far back as 1929, they had been completely modernised in 1941. Suddenly, the odds had swung in favour of the Japanese.

It now fell to the big guns of *Exeter* and *Houston* to take on the recent threat, the new arrivals being beyond the range of the light cruisers *De Ruyter*, *Java* and *Perth*. With one turret out of action, *Houston*'s fire was erratic, but *Exeter* got away fifteen salvoes, eventually forcing one of the enemy cruisers to make smoke and retire. Unfortunately, *Exeter*'s determined attack attracted the fire of all the other enemy ships, and before long she was being straddled. She staggered under a direct hit on the waterline aft, and a few minutes later another shell exploded in her boiler-room, putting six of her eight boilers out of action and killing fourteen men.

With her speed dropping away to 11 knots, and her main armament rendered temporarily inactive by a power failure, *Exeter* was forced to break off the action and turn away, covered by smoke made by the destroyers *Encounter* and *Jupiter*. In view of the damage to the British cruiser, Admiral Doorman ordered to her to return to Sourabaya. As Captain Gordon hauled his ship out of the line, the enemy destroyers, led by the light cruiser *Jintsu*, raced in for a torpedo attack on the Allied squadron. They fired no fewer than sixty-eight torpedoes, but only one found its mark, slamming into the Dutch destroyer *Kortenaer*'s engine-room. Her main magazine blew up and she broke in two.

The loss of the *Kortenaer* and the withdrawal of the *Exeter* left Admiral Doorman at a considerable disadvantage. Nevertheless, he continued to take the fight to the enemy. Having re-formed his cruiser line, he ordered the British destroyers to attack. By this time *Electra* (Commander C.W. May), *Encounter* (Lieutenant Commander E.V. St. J. Morgan) and *Jupiter* (Lieutenant Commander N.V.J.T. Thew) had become widely separated, and were hampered by the smoke screen laid down for *Exeter*. However, without hesitation each launched an independent attack on the Japanese light cruisers and the fourteen destroyers accompanying them. *Encounter* fought a close-range duel with the 5-inch guns of the destroyer *Minegumo* without either ship inflicting damage on the other. *Electra* was more successful when she faced up to *Minegumo*'s sister destroyer *Asagumo*. She scored a direct hit on *Asagumo*'s engine-room, and the Japanese ship was seen to stop. Commander May then took on the light cruiser *Jintsu*, inflicting slight damage on her, but in return the *Electra* came under fire from the guns of both *Asagumo* and *Jintsu*, and was hit time and time again. Under the hail of Japanese shells, the British destroyer's guns were soon silent, and she was heavily on fire. She sank as the sun was going down, with the loss of ninety of her crew. Commander May went down with his ship.

With smoke being made by both sides, the battlefield had come to resemble Dante's Inferno, with tongues of flame lighting up the murk as the opposing sides fired blind at each other, the Japanese having the advantage of their spotter planes overhead. Their destroyers made another attack with torpedoes, prompting Admiral Doorman to order the American destroyers to retaliate. The four-stackers attacked enthusiastically, firing first their starboard tubes, and then reversing course to fire their port tubes. Unfortunately, the range was nearly 8 miles when they fired, with the result that all their torpedoes were wasted.

Admiral Doorman was now attempting to work his way around behind the Japanese force in order to get at the troop transports they were shielding, but by now the sun had gone down, and with darkness closing in it was even more difficult to distinguish ship from ship. At 1930, by the light of the full moon, there was a brief

71

scuffle when the *Jintsu* and three destroyers were sighted 5 miles to port. Fire was exchanged for a few minutes, but when the Japanese cruiser was seen to fire a spread of torpedoes, the Allied ships broke off and turned away.

The four American destroyers, who had used up all their torpedoes, now signalled the flagship, reporting that they were all running low on fuel, and Doorman had no other option but to order them back to Sourabaya. HMS *Encounter* was astern picking up survivors from the *Kortenaer*, and that left only *De Ruyter*, *Houston*, *Java*, *Perth* and the other British destroyer *Jupiter*, but Doorman was still determined to come to grips with the Japanese troop convoy. Forming his depleted squadron into line astern, he led the way to the south, and then to the westward, keeping 4 miles off the coast. Japanese spotter planes followed them, dropping flares which revealed every movement of the Allied ships.

At 2125, with no Japanese ships visible, *Jupiter* suddenly blew up and sank. At first it was thought she had been torpedoed by a submarine, but nothing was picked up by the Asdics. As the squadron was then only 3 miles north of a minefield that had been laid by the Dutch that morning, it was assumed that *Jupiter* must have hit a drifting mine. Some of her crew reached the shore, while others, including Commander Thew, were picked up by a Japanese ship.

The depleted Allied squadron continued to the west at full speed under the light of the full moon, but the elusive Japanese troop convoy was nowhere in sight. Then, just after 2300, the two heavy cruisers *Haguro* and *Nachi* suddenly appeared on the port beam 8 miles off. The enemy ships altered course towards the Allied squadron, coming round onto a parallel course when within 7 miles. Doorman's ships opened fire at 2310, the Japanese ten minutes later. The night was filled with the thunder of guns, but no hits were scored on either side. Then the enemy cruisers launched a torpedo attack, *Nachi* firing eight, and *Haguro* a spread of four. Within minutes, both *De Ruyter* and *Java* were hit, the Japanese torpedoes striking home with devastating effect. *De Ruyter*, now on fire, turned to starboard, and the other ships followed her round, but then both the *Java* and the flagship blew up and sank. Admiral Karel Doorman was last seen on the bridge of his ship. His final order to the remaining ships, *Houston* and *Perth*, was to ignore survivors and retire to Batavia.

Captain Waller of HMAS *Perth*, being the senior surviving officer, now found himself in charge of this ill-fated expedition. With only the two cruisers left under his command, and with *Houston* short of ammunition, Waller realized it was futile to carry on with the odds so heavily in favour of the Japanese. He did consider ignoring Doorman's last order and attempting to pick up survivors from *De Ruyter* and *Java*, but that would have meant putting *Perth* and *Houston* in even greater danger of being sunk. He decided to make for Batavia without delay. His decision was later criticized, to which criticism Waller replied, 'I now had under my orders one undamaged 6-inch cruiser, and one 8-inch cruiser with very little ammunition and no guns aft. I had no destroyers. The force was subjected throughout the day and night operations to the most superbly organized air reconnaisance. I was opposed by six cruisers, one of them possibly sunk, and twelve destroyers.'

The Battle of the Java Sea was a gallant attempt by the Eastern Striking Force to delay the invasion of Java, but it had ended in disaster for the Allied ships. The two Dutch light cruisers *De Ruyter* and *Java* were lost, as were the destroyers *Kortenaer*, *Electra* and *Jupiter*, taking with them over 1,000 men in all. And all this for nothing. Just one Japanese destroyer was damaged, and no contact was made with the troop transports. Captain Waller, commanding HMAS *Perth*, criticized Admiral Doorman for not closing the range to allow the 6-inch gun cruisers to play a greater part, but Captain Gordon of the *Exeter* summed up the difficulties involved in a report written after the war:

This action demonstrated in a very marked manner the difficulty of working with a heterogeneous squadron, composed of ships of different nationalities, all of whose methods, but in particular those of signalling and fire distribution, differ from our own and with whom there had been no opportunity of even the briefest discussion on such matters.

It was clear that the Dutch cruisers were outranged for most of the daylight action and their splashes only made spotting more difficult for the remainder.

The enemy made use of a number of spotting aircraft.

During the action an attack was made on the enemy cruisers by land-based bombers from Sourabaya, and several bomb splashes were observed. The enemy appeared to be unaffected by this attack. About the time that the Allied squadron reversed course and when the enemy torpedo attack had developed, the four American destroyers previously stationed astern fired torpedoes. It was not clear what was their target but the majority of these torpedoes were seen to be running on the surface in the direction of the Japanese destroyers.

HMS *Exeter*, accompanied by the Dutch destroyer *Evertsen*, limped back to Sourabaya, arriving there late on the 27th. Next day, with the assistance of the Dutch authorities, *Exeter*'s fourteen men killed in action were buried with full naval honours.

Two of the battered remnants of Admiral Doorman's Eastern Striking Force, USS *Houston* and HMAS *Perth*, reached Tandjong Priok early in the afternoon of the 28th to find the port reeling under an almost constant attack by Japanese bombers, and expecting invasion at any moment. Five and a half hours later, they sailed again with orders to make for Tjilatjap 400 miles away on the south coast of Java, where they were to evacuate American troops before making good their escape to Fremantle or Colombo. *Perth* was low on fuel, having been allowed only 300 tons from the dwindling supplies in Tandjong Priok, so the two ships had agreed to proceed at an economical speed, timing their arrival in Tjilatjap for early on 2 March. The *Evertsen* was to accompany them, but in the confusion reigning she had not received orders to raise steam. *Perth* and *Houston* sailed without her, clearing the port at 2100.

With *Perth* as the senior ship leading and *Houston* five cables astern, the Allied cruisers set course for the Sunda Strait, hugging the coast at 22 knots. Before sailing, Captain Waller had received an air reconnaissance report to the effect that shortly before dark there were no enemy ships to be seen in the Sunda Strait. He was also warned to keep a lookout for Allied corvettes which were said to be patrolling the strait. All of this indicated a trouble-free passage. However, soon after sailing, another reconnaissance report came in of an enemy convoy sighted at 1600 about 50 miles north-east of Tandjong Priok on an easterly course. This consisted of ten transports escorted by two cruisers and three destroyers. It was obviously an invasion force, but with such a small escort as to be unlikely to bother *Perth* and *Houston*.

It was a fine night, the sea calm, the wind light, and with a full moon shining down out of a cloudless sky, visibility was excellent. With *Perth* leading and *Houston* following close in her wake, the cruisers made good time, the light on Babi Island being abeam to starboard at 2245. Another forty minutes would see them rounding St. Nicholas Point and entering the Sunda Strait.

At 2306 the Allied ships were crossing Bantam Bay when a vessel was sighted 5 miles ahead by *Perth*'s lookouts, which Waller took to be one of the Allied corvettes said to be patrolling the Sunda Strait. She was challenged by lamp, but her reply was unintelligible. The challenge was repeated, and she turned away making smoke, at which point she was recognized as a Japanese destroyer. With only nine miles to go to St. Nicholas Point, *Perth* and *Houston* steamed straight into the midst of the Japanese Western Invasion Force, which was escorted by six cruisers, twelve destroyers, an aircraft carrier and a minelayer. Fate had dealt them a very heavy blow.

Perth was first to open fire, her target the destroyer first sighted. This was the signal for the night to erupt into a mad chaos of star shell, soaring flares and sweeping searchlights. The Allied cruisers found themselves surrounded by Japanese warships, their guns traversing to seek out the enemy that threatened their charges, the transports then heading into the bay to land their troops.

Lieutenant-Commander Harper later described the action:

I cannot attempt to estimate what force was opposing us. During the action a large number of destroyers engaged us from all directions; at least one and probably more cruisers were engaging us from the northward and one officer on the bridge reported sighting a large number of vessels in close formation, probably transports. At about 2340 one set of torpedo tubes was fired from the bridge at a target – I do not know what. The other set was fired before the ship was abandoned, but I do not know if they were fired at a target or not. Due to a large number of enemy destroyers opposing us it was impossible to engage all targets at once, and so some were

75

eventually able to close enough to illuminate us with their searchlights from a range of about 3000 yards.

Captain Tameichi Hara, commanding the Japanese destroyer *Amatsukaze* recorded his impressions:

Nine minutes past midnight on March 1, destroyer *Fubuki* spotted two unidentified ships. They were located some 10,000 metres east of Babi Island, near Banten Bay, roughly 500 nautical miles from the scene of the Java Sea battle. Commander Yasuo Yamashita, *Fubuki*'s skipper, had no idea what these ships were. *Fubuki* swung around and followed some 8,000 metres behind the two mysterious ships. The ships were *Houston* and *Perth*, and the mystery is how they ever made the 24-hour voyage without being observed during the day by Japanese scout planes.

After the long hours of fighting in the running battle of the Java Sea, these ships were low in ammunition. They had made a 500-mile voyage at some 20 knots and were also running low on fuel. They were in no shape to strike back at a vastly superior Japanese force. The two ships, headed for fuel and ammunition supplies, must have been astounded to sight a 56-ship Japanese convoy in Banten Bay, ready for landing. They bravely started to shell these transports at 37 minutes past midnight.

Japanese destroyer *Harukaze* dashed forward to lay smoke screens. Destroyer *Fubuki* fired 9 torpedoes. Rear Admiral Akisaburo Hara's 12 escorting warships scrambled in confusion and chaos. *Fubuki* had notified them of 'two mysterious ships entering the bay', but they were still not fully prepared for a battle. There were just too many opposing the Allied ships. Some of the skippers told me later they were busy the whole time evading friendly shells and torpedoes.

Perth and *Houston* put up a magnificent fight, but the odds against them were too great. *Perth*, short of ammunition, was reduced to firing star shells when she was hit, firstly by one torpedo in the engine-room, and then by a second one a few minutes later which exploded under her 'A' turret. Torpedoes were now coming at her

76

from all sides, and within the next ten minutes two more found their mark. Captain Waller gave the order to abandon ship, and as her men were scrambling over the side, the gallant Australian cruiser rolled over and sank. Hector Waller was last seen on the bridge of his ship, leaning over the forward rail and calmly surveying the chaos of his decks. Two hundred and three of his crew died with him.

USS *Houston* fought on alone for a while before she too succumbed to the overwhelming firepower of the enemy. Lieutenant Commander Arthur L. Maher, her Gunnery Officer, describes her end:

> The disposition of the enemy vessels was such as to completely encircle the *Houston* on all offshore bearings. Light patrol and torpedo boats operated with the transports in Bantam Bay. Enemy planes were overhead. Enemy ships, believed to be cruisers or carriers, were firing at the *Houston* from about 1,200 yards to seawards. Having established hitting range, they were pouring fire into the ship and causing considerable damage. Destroyers were operating in formations of three to four ships and making repeated attacks on the bows and quarters of the *Houston* using both guns and torpedoes. The proximity of the ship to shoal water and the strong currents running were additional hazards to manoeuvring . . . All communications systems which were still operative were hopelessly overloaded with reports of damage received or approaching torpedoes or new enemy attacks begun, or changes in targets engaged.

The *Houston* was hit by four torpedoes in all. Captain Rooks was killed by a bursting shell at 0030, and as the battered cruiser gradually slowed to a halt Japanese destroyers closed in on her and swept her decks with machine-gun fire. She went down a few minutes later with her ensign still flying proudly. Of her complement of 872 only 368 survived.

In this swift-moving battle between eighty-five and ninety torpedoes were believed to have been fired at the Allied cruisers. Three Japanese transports were badly damaged, and the troop command ship with the Army Commander on board was sunk. It has never been established who really inflicted this damage on the convoy, but is is strongly suspected that in the confusion that reigned Japanese shells and torpedoes were responsible.

HMS *Exeter* also received the order to quit Java as soon as possible, and at 1900 on the 28th she sailed from Sourabaya accompanied by the destroyers HMS *Encounter* and USS *Pope*. Captain Gordon's routeing instructions were to proceed '20 miles to the eastward from Sourabaya northern entrance, thence northward to pass eastward of Bawean Island, thence northwestward and westward and through Sunda Strait to Colombo'. This would take them well to the north of Japanese forces known to be off the coast in the region of Bantam Bay. At the time of sailing very little in the way of repairs to *Exeter*'s boilers had been completed, and she still had only two of her eight boilers serviceable. Gordon estimated this would give the cruiser a maximum speed of between 15 and 16 knots, which was hardly satisfactory, but the alternative was to remain in port to complete repairs, and with Japanese troops rapidly advancing on Sourabaya this was not possible.

Having cleared the Sourabaya minefields, with the two destroyers screening her, *Exeter* set course to the east. The night was fine and clear, with a light east-north-easterly wind and a slight sea, and all went well. At midnight, Gordon altered course to the north to pass 25 miles to the east of Bawean Island, by which time steam had been raised on two more of *Exeter*'s boilers, and she was making a speed of 23 knots.

At 0400 on 1 March, the adrenaline ran high in the Allied ships when three vessels which appeared to be two merchantmen escorted by a cruiser or destroyer were sighted to the west in the light of the setting moon, and on a reciprocal course. If they were Japanese – and they most probably were – *Exeter* and her escorts were more than a match for them, but Gordon's orders were to avoid confrontation. He turned stern on to the strangers to avoid being sighted, and then worked around to the northward, resuming course half an hour later when the other ships were out of sight. Daylight came, and the horizon was clear of enemy ships or aircraft. So far, so good.

When the sun came up visibility was extreme, and at 0750 *Exeter*'s crow's nest lookout reported the mast tops of two ships almost right ahead. These were soon identified as the topmasts of warships, cruisers or larger, steering to the north-north-east. Gordon immediately reversed course and ran away from the threat. *Exeter*'s radar screen showed no sign of any spotter plane being flown off by the unidentified warships, and once again she appeared to have escaped detection.

Unfortunately for the Allied ships, their dash for safety had led them straight into the arms of the force protecting the Japanese landings in Bantam Bay. They were confronted by the four heavy cruisers *Ashigara*, *Haguro*, *Myoko* and *Nachi*, each mounting ten 8-inch guns, and accompanied by at least five destroyers.

On sighting the enemy, Gordon altered course to the east and called for more speed. *Exeter* was making 23 knots at the time, but working with a sense of urgency that matched the emergency, her engineers managed to raise steam in a fifth boiler, and speed was increased to 25 knots. But there was no escape for *Exeter* and her destroyers. The Japanese launched their spotter planes, and although *Encounter* and *Pope* laid down a smoke screen, every move of the Allied ships was watched from the air and reported back.

Closing the range to 18,000 yards, the enemy cruisers took up position, two on *Exeter*'s starboard beam, and two on her port quarter. Caught in a trap, Gordon considered reversing course, but decided this would gain nothing. He had little alternative but to try to force his way through, engaging the enemy ships on both sides and hoping, at the very least, to cripple one or two of them.

The guns roared, and *Exeter*, returning shell for shell, was continually straddled by the Japanese as she tried to snake her way through. The inevitable happened at 1120, when an 8-inch shell exploded in the British cruiser's boiler-room. Fire broke out, and within minutes was raging so fiercely that the boiler spaces had to be evacuated, and it was necessary to flood the 4-inch magazine, which was only a bulkhead away from the boiler room. *Exeter* gradually lost way through the water and came to a halt, and as she did so all electrical power failed, leaving her unable to traverse her turrets. Stopped and unable to defend herself, the cruiser was at the mercy of the Japanese shells, which were showering down on her. Captain Gordon decided that he had no alternative but to scuttle his command and abandon her.

Although she was still under fire, the *Exeter* was abandoned in an orderly manner. When the survivors pulled away from her, she had a heavy port list which was increasing by the minute. Her agony was ended at 1145, when a torpedo slammed into her starboard side. She righted herself, then rolled to starboard and sank.

While *Exeter* had been lying helpless under the enemy's guns, *Encounter* and *Pope* were fighting a desperate action against the Japanese destroyers, which heavily outnumbered them. *Encounter* was eventually sunk by shellfire, while USS *Pope*, having fired all her torpedoes and 140 salvoes with her 4.7s managed to make her escape, only to be sunk by enemy dive bombers an hour later.

Around 800 survivors from *Exeter* and *Encounter*, including Captain Gordon and Lieutenant Commander Morgan, who commanded *Encounter*, were picked up by Japanese destroyers during the next 24 hours.

The loss of HMS *Exeter* signalled the end of Allied sea power in the Java Sea. Of the ships of Admiral Karel Doorman's Eastern Striking Force, only the four American destroyers *Alden*, *John D. Edwards*, *John D. Ford* and *Paul Jones* survived. All had expended their torpedoes, were running short of fuel and dropped out of the one-sided fight, returning to Sourabaya on the evening of the 27th. Having topped up their tanks, they sailed again at 1700 on the 28th with orders to attempt a breakthrough to Australia.

Steaming in single line at 28 knots with the *John D. Edwards* in the lead, the four ships hugged the north coast of Java, arriving off the Bali Strait, which separates the eastern end of Java from the island of Bali, at 0200 on 1 March. It was a clear, moonlit night, and they were only a few minutes into the strait when an unidentified ship which looked suspiciously like a Japanese destroyer, was sighted ahead.

It was too late to turn back, and the Americans could do no more than press on at full speed, hoping that the enemy ship's lookouts were not alert. This was not to be. The stranger altered onto a parallel course, and she was soon joined by three other destroyers. The American squadron had fallen in with the Japanese guard on the Bali Strait. They were the crack *Hatsuharu*-class destroyers *Hatsishimo*, *Hatsuharu*, *Nenohi* and *Wakaba*, each armed with five 5-inch guns and six 21-inch torpedo tubes.

A lamp flashed out a challenge from one of the Japanese destroyers, and when the Americans failed to answer, the enemy ships opened fire from a range of about 6000 yards. A fierce gun battle ensued, with the Japanese shells falling uncomfortably close all around the American destroyers. In a display of superb seamanship the 4-stackers manoeuvred so close in to the coast that the Japanese were unable to follow them. When they had successfully opened the range, the Americans made smoke, and then ceased fire, calculating that the Japanese destroyers were most unlikely to be radar-equipped, and would be unable to target them. The ruse worked. For another fifteen minutes the Japanese continued to fire blindly into the smoke, then gave up the chase. *Alden, John D. Edwards, John D. Ford* and *Paul Jones*, all unscathed, reached Fremantle on 4 March.

While Japanese and Allied cruisers and destroyers fought it out in the Java Sea, there were a number of US Navy submarines on patrol in the immediate area, yet they took no part in the battle. Incredible though it may seem in hindsight, no one had seen fit to warn the submarines that the action was taking place, nor was Admiral Doorman informed of their presence.

It is just possible that the American submariners would have been able to tip the balance in favour of Doorman's ships, and so change the course of history. As it transpired, the only contributions the submarines made, and that was in the aftermath of the battle, was when S-38 plucked fifty-eight HMS *Electra* survivors from the water, and when S-37 found one of the *De Ruyter*'s lifeboats with sixty survivors on board and gave them food and water and directions to reach land.

Chapter Seven

An Island in Peril

On the first day of March 1942, after the catastrophic routing of
the Allied naval forces with which it had been hoped to forestall
any Japanese landings on Java, the island was in a perilous state.
The situation in the Far East was such that it had been decided in
London that any reinforcements available for this area of conflict
must go to the defence of Burma and India in the north and
Australia in the south. Java must stand alone.

The Supreme Commander of the Allied forces on Java, General
Archibald Wavell, had at his disposal three Australian battalions,
a light tank squadron of the 3rd Hussars, and a makeshift
defence force composed of clerks, RAF ground crew, and a
number of US Army artillerymen without their guns, around
8,000 men in all. This was supported by 25,000 Dutch troops,
mainly natives, whose loyalty to the Dutch command was in
question. Air cover was provided by five RAF squadrons,
in which only around forty aircraft were serviceable, ten Dutch
squadrons whose aircraft were mostly unserviceable, and a
handful of American planes. The Japanese, on the other hand,
were in the process of landing up to 100,000 troops trained in
the art of jungle fighting, backed up by their powerful and
already victorious naval force and hundreds of modern fighters
and bombers. General Wavell had already appraised Churchill of
the dire situation, saying: 'I am afraid that the defence of
A.B.D.A (America, British, Dutch, Australian) area has broken
down, and the defence of Java cannot now last long. It always
hinged on the air battle . . . Anything put into Java now can do

little to prolong the struggle; it is more a question of what you will choose to save . . .'

In a last desperate attempt to bolster General Wavell's forces the American seaplane tender USS *Langley* was pressed into service. The 11,500-ton *Langley* was a ship with a long and chequered history. Launched in 1912, when the last of the great windjammers were still plying their trade on the wide oceans, she started life as the *Jupiter*, a lowly fleet collier for the US Navy. In October 1914 she moved from the Pacific to the Atlantic, being the first vessel to transit the Panama Canal from west to east. This was followed by three uneventful years servicing naval ships on the east coast of America and in the Gulf of Mexico, hard, dirty work that was finally relieved by America's entrance into the war in 1917. Two voyages to France with cargo followed, and then a spell coaling ships bringing troops back to the United States after the war. In March 1920 she was taken into the Navy Yard at Norfolk, Virginia, and after extensive conversion work she re-emerged as America's first aircraft carrier, USS *Langley*. There followed a long spell with the Pacific Battle Fleet, and in 1936 she returned to Mare Island for conversion to a seaplane tender, resuming her duties with the Pacific Fleet in 1939.

On 22 February 1942, USS *Langley* sailed from Fremantle in a convoy bound for Colombo, escorted by the cruiser USS *Phoenix*. The *Langley* was carrying thirty-two Lockheed P-40 fighters and thirty-three USAF pilots, the planes lashed down on her flight deck wing tip to wing tip. In the same convoy was the American freighter *Sea Witch* with another twenty-seven P-40s in crates on board. The original intention had been for these aircraft to be landed in Ceylon or India, but while the convoy was at sea Admiral Helfrich, recently installed as Chief of the Allied Naval Command, ordered *Phoenix* to detach *Langley* and *Sea Witch* and divert them to Java. Helfrich planned to land the aircraft from the two ships at Tanjong Priok or Sourabaya, where they could be easily transported to an airfield nearby, but the subsequent invasion of northern Java and the likelihood that these ports would soon fall resulted in the ships being routed to Tjilatjap in the south. This was not an ideal option. Tjilatjap, once the main port for Java's sugar exports, had long fallen into disuse, and its facilities were minimal. The aircraft would have to be discharged into barges, and ramps built to land them on the shore, from where they would be manhandled through the town to a hurriedly constructed runway. All this involved a great many people, including a large part of the local native population, with the inevitable result that the impending arrival of *Langley* and *Sea Witch* off Tjilatjap was no secret. Word was not long in reaching Vice Admiral Nobutake Kondo, whose 2nd Fleet, consisting of three battleships and six aircraft carriers, escorted by cruisers and destroyers, unknown to Admiral Helfrich, was already operating in the waters south of Java.

Langley, commanded by Captain Robert P. McConnell, left the convoy some hours ahead of *Sea Witch*, and on the afternoon of the 26th was met by a Dutch mine layer and two Catalinas of the Royal Dutch Air Force. Unfortunately, the escorting mine layer was hard pressed to make even 14 knots, and the *Langley* soon found herself having to slow down to allow her to catch up. Eventually, McConnell had to make the decision to carry on alone at full speed, leaving his escort behind. He informed Tjilatjap of his decision, and next morning the American destroyers *Whipple* and *Edsall* arrived to escort him in. These 1920s vintage four-funnel flush-deck types still had the speed, but they were armed with only six 3-inch dual purpose guns and two machine-guns. Their ability to ward off attacking aircraft, which was the main threat then facing them, was very limited.

It had been originally planned for the *Langley* to hold back to wait for the *Sea Witch* to join her, and then the two ships with their escorting destroyers would approach Tjilatjap under the cover of darkness that night. But by now the Battle of the Java Sea had been fought and lost, and Japanese troops were landing on the north coast of Java. General Wavell's greatest need was for fighter planes to ward off the never-ending stream of Japanese bombers pounding his forward positions. *Langley*'s aircraft were ready to go into action as soon as they were landed, and they were needed without delay.

At sunrise on 27 February the *Langley* was 150 miles south of Tjilatjap and zig-zagging north at 15 knots under a clear blue sky dotted with a few scattered clouds resembling balls of cotton wool. The wind was light north-easterly, the sea flat calm. *Edsall* and *Whipple* cruised on either side of the carrier, their sonars pinging as they searched for danger below the surface. All three ships were at first readiness, guns manned and lookouts alert.

The early morning passed without incident. Then, at 0900, an unidentified aircraft appeared overhead, flying high. The plane began to circle, and Captain McConnell knew that what he had been dreading most had become reality. The enemy had found the *Langley*, and the bombers were bound to arrive soon. As the *Langley* was carrying thirty-two of America's most modern fighters, along with their pilots, there should have been no fears for her safety, but there was no room on her crowded flight deck for these planes to take off. McConnell sent an urgent signal to Admiral Glassford requesting fighter cover, but as there were fewer than twenty Allied fighter aircraft still flying in Java, his request was in vain. The defence of the carrier was in the hands of her AA gunners and those of her accompanying destroyers.

USS *Edsall* was first to sight the bombers, at 1140 reporting nine twin-engined aircraft approaching at 15,000 feet. The attackers were not from Admiral Kondo's carriers, but from Kendari on the island of Celebes, and were part of the 11th Japanese Airfleet.

The bombers made straight for the *Langley*, and as they dived to attack, and the guns opened up, McConnell took violent evasive action. When the first stick of 500lb bombs, a cluster of tiny black dots, were seen dropping away from the underside of the leading plane, he called for full right helm, and the *Langley* veered sharply to starboard. The enemy bombs fell 100 feet to port of the carrier, spraying her decks with splinters and shrapnel, but she suffered no casualties or serious damage. Other bombs followed, but apart from a violent shaking up, and thanks to Captain McConnell's brilliant handling of his ship, the carrier escaped unscathed.

The Japanese planes circled and came back again, but flew over without dropping bombs, perhaps studying McConnell's tactics. On their third run the bombers made no mistake, and the *Langley* steamed straight into a rain of bombs. McConnell put his ship into a frenzy of twists and turns, but he was unable to avoid disaster. The enemy bombs showered down on *Langley*, scoring five direct hits and three near misses. One bomb exploded right forward, two crashed through the flight deck near the elevator, a fourth hit the base of the port funnel, and another penetrated the flight deck aft.

As the Japanese bombers flew away, a flight of six fighters swooped down and machine-gunned the crippled ship.

The *Langley* was sorely hit. The aircraft on her flight deck were on fire, other serious fires raged below deck, she was holed below the waterline forward, and she had developed a heavy port list. Some of the burning planes were pushed overboard, but blast had smashed the fire main, and the fire hoses lay limp and useless. Fortunately, for all the devastation, the *Langley*'s engines were still running, and her steering gear working. McConnell manoeuvred her so that the wind ceased to fan the flames, and it was then possible to tackle the fires, but it was too late. Water was pouring into the engine-room, and the list was increasing.

McConnell was not yet prepared to abandon ship, but as a precaution he gave the order to make the boats ready, which unfortunately started a panic. Some men had been blown overboard in the bombing, others had been forced to jump when trapped by the flames; now, at the mention of abandoning ship, others followed them over the side. Reluctantly, at 1332, McConnell gave the order for the remaining crew to go.

When Captain McConnell signalled his intention to abandon ship the Japanese planes had already flown away, and *Whipple* and *Edsall* were able to close in and pick up survivors. Miraculously, out of the *Langley*'s total complement of 495, only five men had been killed and five were missing. When the rescue operation was complete, Edsall having picked up 177 survivors and Whipple 308, the destroyers sank the *Langley* with gunfire and torpedoes. With her went Java's last hope of mounting a credible air defence. When they were certain that no more survivors were left in the water, *Edsall* and *Whipple* steamed to the west at full speed, anxious to put as much distance between themselves and the Japanese bombers as possible.

Sea Witch, heading north in the wake of the *Langley*, was blessed with better luck. Having avoided the attention of the Japanese bombers, she slipped into Tjilatjap on the morning of the 28th, but she also was unable to influence the outcome of the battle for Java. Admiral Doorman's fleet had been defeated, Japanese troops were about to land, and even if there had been time to assemble her twenty-seven crated P-40s, no technicians were available for the job, and there were no pilots to fly them. The aircraft were destroyed to avoid their falling into the enemy's hands. *Sea Witch* then left port and escaped to the south.

News of the bombing of the *Langley* spread quickly amongst other ships in the area, one of which was the US Navy fleet tanker *Pecos*. The 14,500-ton *Pecos*, commanded by Commander Elmer P. Abernethy and escorted by the destroyer USS *Parrott*, had left Tjilatjap on the morning of the 27th with orders to proceed to Colombo. When the news of the *Langley*'s sinking came through, the two ships immediately altered course to pass well clear of the area. Shortly afterwards, a signal was received ordering *Pecos* to proceed to Christmas Island to pick up the *Langley*'s survivors from *Edsall* and *Whipple*, the destroyers being urgently needed elsewhere. At about this time *Parrott* was also called away for other duties.

The *Pecos* arrived off Christmas Island on the morning of the 28th, and rendezvoused with *Edsall* and *Whipple* in Flying Fish Cove, at the north-east end of the island. The transfer of survivors was under way when three Japanese twin-engined bombers appeared from the direction of Sumatra. As the bombs began to fall, all three ships left the anchorage, and taking advantage of the cover of a rain squall, made for the open sea. The remainder of the *Langley*'s survivors were ferried across to the Pecos early next morning, 1 March, after which the tanker, now with a total of 727 men on board, set course for Fremantle unescorted.

Only an hour or two after *Pecos* left the destroyers, a single-engined Japanese spotter plane appeared overhead and began to circle out of range of the tanker's guns. It was surmised that the aircraft was radioing the tanker's position back to her base, and that an attack by bombers, probably carrier-based, would soon follow. This was, in fact, more than a probability, for not far over the horizon was the huge Japanese Second Fleet, recently arrived in the waters south of Java. Under the command of Vice Admiral Nobutake Kondo, the Second Fleet consisted of the battleships *Haruna*, *Hiei* and *Kirishima*, the battle-cruiser *Kongo*, the aircraft carriers *Akagi*, *Hiryu*, *Kaga*, *Shokaku*, *Soryu* and *Zuikaku*, and the cruisers *Atago*, *Chikuma*, *Maya*, *Takao* and *Tone*, with five flotillas of destroyers and twelve fleet tankers.

Enemy carrier-based bombers arrived one hour and forty-five minutes later, the first wave consisting of six planes. *Pecos*'s gunners, manning her 3-inch, four twin 40mm and four twin 20mm AA guns, opened up with HE and tracer, but the Japanese planes came in one by one, each dropping one bomb. The first three bombs were wide, but the fourth was a direct hit, which destroyed the 3-inch gun and killed most of its crew. The planes made a second run, one of their bombs scoring a hit amidships which left the *Pecos* with a substantial port list.

The second wave of bombers roared in hard on the heels of the first. This time the six aircraft attacked simultaneously, their bombs hitting home with deadly accuracy. Fires were started on deck, part of the foremast came down, bringing with it the wireless aerials, the centreline bulkhead was breached, and two boilers were knocked out. Now listing 15 degrees, on fire above and below decks, and limping along on reduced speed, the *Pecos* was dangerously vulnerable. No order had yet been given to abandon ship, but due to a misunderstanding, two lifeboats and a number of rafts were put over the side, and several men jumped overboard before order was restored. And a third wave of Japanese planes was on the way in. Among these was Naval Aviation Pilot 1st Class Shinsaka Yamakawa, at the controls of a 'Nell' twin-engined dive bomber from the carrier *Kaga*. He recorded his impression of the attack:

Soon after take-off, we sighted the *Pecos*. The altitude of our formations was 5000m. Although there were patches of clouds, it was very fine weather for bombardiers. We broke the formations off to make assaulting run. The enemy flak fired heavily, but we were not bothered by any of it. At first the commander's plane dived, and a second one and third one followed. My plane should dive as a last one, because we were a guest of the unit. We were going to look on their bombing, since I thought they would sink her so easily that we wouldn't need to wait for our turn. As I saw, the first plane and the second one were diving deeper and deeper. The enemy ship was heading straight forward. All the planes except for us had gone to steep-dive. Pom-pom guns of the enemy ship were firing up vigorously. After a while, the first plane dropped a bomb and pulled itself up. *Pecos* steered to starboard drawing a long white wake. When the wake drew white arc, a large water column sprouted in front of her port side. Then the second plane bombed. She was still steering to starboard, and it looked desperate the way she turned herself. The second one missed too, the bomb made a splash before her port side bow. Her wake turned to 45 degrees and the third one bombed. She was steering with a heavy careen, and its bomb deflected too. 'Gee!' If either her steering had been slower or the plane had assumed her turn enough, we would have got her; but she was doing her job very good. Her captain must have been able enough to dodge our bombs. When the fourth plane and the fifth one dropped bombs, she was still steering hard on starboard, and had already turned more than 90 degrees. Both bombs exploded about 10m away from her port side bow, to our regret, and merely made big water columns. Praiseworthy job she was doing. On our side, the sixth plane and the seventh one were successively on dive-bombing run toward her. Usually bombs were to be released at 450m of height. We had never missed the aim like this. I was still looking on their bombing, wondering why. I observed her wake and the points where the bombs had fallen, thinking they would hit her this time anyway, but the ripple caused by the bombs paralleled the wake, bombs from the sixth, seventh and eighth plane completely missed her . . .

Due to the masterly handling of the *Pecos* by Commander Abernethy, the third wave of Japanese planes scored no direct hits, but their bombs exploded near enough to cause more serious damage. By 1530, after fighting off her attackers for more than three hours, the tanker at last succumbed to her wounds, and began to go down by the head. Those of her crew who were still on board went over the side with anything capable of floating. As they struck out away from the sinking ship other Japanese planes attempted to strafe them, but were driven off by one brave gunner who stayed with the *Pecos*, continuing to fire his machine-gun until the ship took her last dive.

Fortunately for the survivors, the *Pecos*'s wireless operator was able to send out an SOS before the ship sank. This was picked up by USS *Whipple*, which immediately reversed course and raced back to the scene of the sinking. Of the 727 men on board the

Pecos, the *Whipple* found only 220 alive, 149 from the *Langley* and 71 from the *Pecos*. She landed them at Tjilatjap the next day.

The other destroyer involved with the *Langley*, USS *Edsall*, failed to reach Tjilatjap. Late on the afternoon of 1 March she was unfortunate enough to meet up with the Japanese 3rd Battleship Division and the 8th Cruiser Division, which included the battleships *Hiei* and *Kirishima*, accompanied by two cruisers. The odds were heavily stacked against the ageing American ship armed only with six 3-inch guns, but she fought like a tiger at bay. During the action that lasted for over an hour, the Japanese battleships expended 297 14-inch and 132 6-inch shells, while the cruisers fired 844 8-inch and 62 5-inch. This huge concentration of firepower could have only one conclusion. *Edsall*, battered beyond recognition and on fire fore and aft, went down with her battle ensigns still flying. The Japanese picked up eight survivors, all of whom subsequently died in captivity.

By 1 March, large Japanese forces having landed at two points on the northern coast, the situation in Java was rapidly becoming untenable for the Allies. Rear Admiral Glassford, commanding US naval forces on the island, in consultation with Admiral Helfrich, ordered all remaining American warships to sail for Australia. This did not involve a great number of ships, namely the destroyers *Parrott* and *Pillsbury*, the gunboats *Asheville*, *Isabel*, *Lanakai* and *Tulsa*, and the minesweepers *Lark* and *Whippoorwill*. These survivors had already retreated to Tjilatjap, the only port still open to Allied ships, and in view of the powerful Japanese forces now known to be operating in the waters south of Java, the survival of any Allied ships attempting to break through to Australia was in doubt.

The *Asheville*, commanded by Lieutenant Jacob W. Britt, with her fine lines, tall funnel and raked masts looking more like a potentate's private yacht than a man of war, was first to run into the Japanese net. On the morning of 3 March, the minesweeper *Whippoorwill*, commanded by Lieutenant Commander C.R. Ferriter, picked up a radio message from the *Asheville* saying she was 'being attacked' 300 miles south of Tjilatjap. Ferriter immediately altered course to go to her assistance. A later message from *Asheville* said her attacker was a surface ship. Although the gunboat did not specify the size of the enemy, Ferriter decided that it would be suicidal for the little *Whippoorwill*, armed only with one 3-inch gun, to intervene. He resumed his dash for Australia.

Nothing further was heard from the *Asheville*, and her story did not come to light until the war was over. Japanese records show that the gunboat had run into the guns of Admiral Kondo's 2nd Fleet, her attackers being the destroyers *Arashi*, *Hayashio* and *Nowaki*. Completely outgunned by the trio – each of which mounted six 5-inch guns – the *Asheville* was soon reduced to a burning wreck, but she went down fighting, leaving only a few survivors behind. The Japanese destroyers picked up just one man from the water, Fireman 1st Class Fred L. Brown, leaving the rest to their fate. Brown himself died in a prisoner of war camp a few months before the war ended.

The *Pillsbury*, another of the US Navy's First World War four-stackers involved in this hopeless war against the overwhelming might of the Imperial Japanese Navy in these waters, also met her end at the hands of Admiral Kondo's 2nd Fleet. She left no survivors, but interrogation of Japanese naval officers after the war revealed that the American destroyer was involved in a night action with three enemy cruisers and two destroyers, a fight which could have only one conclusion.

The gunboat *Lanakai* – if she could be called such – had a very narrow escape on her way south, possibly because the Japanese thought she was not worth bothering with. The *Lanakai* was a most unlikely warship, a schooner-rigged, diesel-powered yacht of 150 tons, built in 1914, taken over by the US Navy in December 1941 and armed with a 3-pounder gun. Under the command of Lieutenant Kemp Tolley, with a Filipino crew, she had performed a useful role in spying on the Japanese Fleet in Camranh Bay, and took part in the evacuation of Manila before ending up in Tjilatjap. While heading south for Australia under full sail, on 1 March she sighted a large Japanese naval force – probably Admiral Kondo's 2nd Fleet – but her innocent appearance again undoubtedly saved her. The Japanese ignored her, and she reached Fremantle on 18 March. She was transferred to the Royal Australian Navy, and served as a harbour defence vessel until the end of the war.

With the departure of the last surface ship, all that remained of the US Navy in the waters off Java was a handful of submarines of Submarine Division 14. These were ordered to inflict as much damage as possible on the Japanese invasion force before they too left for Australia. Two of these submarines patrolled south of Java looking for Admiral Kondo's carriers, while the others patrolled north of the island between the Lombok Strait in the east and the Sunda Strait in the west. There was no shortage of targets in the north, for Japanese cruisers and destroyers seemed to be everywhere, particularly off Sourabaya. But although the American boats carried out a number of attacks, their torpedoes failed to hit home. Their only success was against the seaplane carrier *Kamogawa Maru*, sunk by USS *Salmon* in the Lombok Strait.

One of the submarines patrolling in the shallow waters off Sourabaya was USS *Perch*, under the command of Lieutenant Commander David A. Hurt. On the night of 1 March, *Perch* was on the surface some 20 miles north of Sourabaya. It was a cloudy night with no moon and limited visibility, and two Japanese destroyers were less than a mile off when the submarine's lookouts sighted them. Hurt immediately dived, but *Perch* hit the bottom at 140 feet and became stuck in the mud, where she lay helpless as the Japanese depth charges rained down. Fortunately, the destroyers did not persist in their attack, moving away after dropping three patterns of charges.

Perch lay on the bottom for the rest of the night, Hurt bringing her to the surface again in the early hours of the 2nd to assess the damage. This proved to be serious. Two of *Perch*'s four engines were out of commission, water was seeping into the hull from numerous leaks, both her periscopes were damaged, and the deck gun was a mess of tangled metal. There could be no question of diving again, and she lay stopped on the surface while emergency repairs were carried out.

At 2030 on 1 March, the Japanese 6-inch gun cruiser *Jintsu*, accompanied by four destroyers, left Sourabaya with orders to hunt down American submarines believed to be in the area. Once clear of the swept channel, they formed up into line abreast with 2,500 metres between each ship, and zig-zagging at 18 knots, began to trawl back and forth, their sonars searching the shallow waters for the enemy. The Japanese ships were not equipped with radar, and were relying on lookouts using powerful binoculars to spot anything on the surface.

For six hours the vigilance of the squadron's lookouts went

unrewarded, then, at 0340 on 2 March, the destroyer *Amatsukaze* reported a submarine on the surface at 6000 metres. Without waiting for orders from *Jintsu*, Captain Hara increased speed to 26 knots and raced in to attack. A second destroyer, the *Hatsukaze*, followed his lead. At 2700 metres Hara hauled *Amatsukaze* hard round to port to bring her six 127 mm guns to bear, and switched on his searchlight. The brilliant beam of the big light swept from side to side, and then settled on the long, low shape of USS *Perch*, still on the surface, her crew working feverishly to effect repairs, and probably caught unawares due to their preoccupation. The destroyer's guns barked in unison. Captain Hara reported:

> I saw seven crewmen running around helplessly on the deck. A moment later, two yellow explosions burst among them, followed five seconds later by a second salvo! One of these six shells hit the target. Then the third salvo, and again one direct hit. The submarine blazed fiercely.
>
> *Hatsukaze*'s first salvo was over. The second salvo barely missed, and there was no third salvo. The submarine sank so fast that it had disappeared among the waves before we arrived on the spot. We dropped six depth charges to cinch the job. We cut down our speed to 12 knots and combed the area together with *Hatsukaze*. Our sonars did not pick up any targets, but the area smelled strongly of heavy oil. We abandoned the search at 0359 and left the scene.

Once again, the Japanese assumption that *Perch* was finished proved to be wrong. In spite of the risk involved, Dave Hurt had taken her down to the bottom as soon as the Japanese destroyers were sighted. *Amatsukaze* and *Hatsukaze* followed her down with five patterns of depth charges, the first of which was wide, but the second, third, fourth and fifth spreads of the deadly canisters exploded close all around her. The American submarine was hard hit, but by no means finished. She lay on the bottom throughout the rest of the day, while her plucky crew fought to save her.

Hurt brought his battered command to the surface after sunset on the 2nd, determined to escape to fight another day. Only one of *Perch*'s engines was still functioning, and with half its holding-down bolts sheared it vibrated wildly, but with careful nursing it produced 5 knots. Survival was now the top priority, and Hurt headed east, hoping to escape to Australia through the Flores and Banda Seas, a route he judged the Japanese might not be watching.

At dawn on 3 March, Hurt sent his men to diving stations and took *Perch* down to see how she would handle underwater. As the boat began to sink, the true extent of her damage was revealed. She went down with a rush, and it quickly became obvious that she was plunging straight to the bottom. All ballast tanks were blown, and while this checked *Perch*'s headlong descent, she ended up half-submerged with her bow out of the water.

Frantic efforts were made to right the trim of the crippled submarine, and Hurt succeeded in bringing her to the surface again, but only her conning tower was above water. As *Perch* drifted half-submerged, and with no means of defending herself, three Japanese destroyers appeared, and came charging in with their guns blazing. The situation was now hopeless, and in order to save his crew Hurt gave the order to abandon ship and scuttle. *Perch* went down, and all sixty-two men were picked up by one of the Japanese destroyers and taken to Makassar. They spent the rest of the war in a Japanese prison camp, where nine of their number died.

The remaining American submarines, realizing the battle for Java was over, abandoned their patrol and made their way to Australia. And so ended the US Navy's role in the defence of the Dutch East Indies.

Chapter Eight

The Rout Begins

Rotterdam Lloyd's 7395-ton *Langkoeas* left Sourabaya, bound for Haifa on 1 January 1942 while the Japanese were still fighting their way down the Malaysian peninsula towards the gates of Singapore. The Java Sea was at that time far removed from the war, its only menace the many uncharted reefs that lurked below its surface. It therefore came as a very unpleasant surprise to Captain Jan Kreumer when, on the evening of the 2nd, a torpedo exploded deep in the *Langkoeas*'s engine-room. I-158, the first Japanese submarine to arrive in the Java Sea, had claimed her first victim.

Twelve men died in the devastated engine-room of the *Langkoeas* that night; the remaining eighty-two men of her Dutch, Chinese and Javanese crew left the sinking ship in four lifeboats, one of which was damaged in launching. When the boats were clear of the ship, Captain Kreumer, who was in the motor lifeboat, began rounding up the others, with the intention of taking them in tow. But as Kreumer was thus engaged, Lieutenant-Commander Kitamura brought his submarine to the surface, closed in on the boats, and set about disposing of the survivors with his machine-guns. In the midst of wanton slaughter, one man escaped by throwing himself overboard from his bullet-riddled lifeboat. He was Fourth Engineer Jan de Mul, who attempted to swim away from the scene of the massacre, but before he had gone more than a few yards the Japanese submarine moved in closer. Desperate to save himself from being run down, de Mul grabbed the submarine's forward hydrophone, and found himself being dragged along for some distance, before being hauled aboard by one of Kitamura's crew. He later described what happened to him:

> Under the threat of a revolver I was being pushed towards the conning tower. In the meantime I felt a severe pain in my left leg (some blood dripped off it), so that I could hardly walk. Having come to the tower I saw a Chinese sailor and a Javanese steward of the *Langkoeas* standing there, who like I had got hold of the sub and had been pulled up by the Japs – as I recognized them now in the dark by their uniform and the little flat khaki cap.
>
> With pushes and hits we were brought to the commander, who interrogated me under all sorts of threats. When, however, he realized that I was not the master of the *Langkoeas* and could not give any information useful to him, he murmured something like, 'You go home', and suddenly I was being seized. There followed a punch and a kick in my right side and I was pushed overboard to land with a thud in the sea. The Chinese and the Javanese were thrown in after me, and the submarine motored away, leaving us to our fate.

Although they were not aware of it, Fourth Engineer Jan de Mul, the Chinese sailor, Lam Dai and the Javanese steward Lajar were the only three left alive out of the *Langkoeas*'s crew of ninety-four. And now they were alone and at the mercy of the sea, for while they had been on board the submarine their ship had sunk. Fortunately, all three still wore their lifejackets, but at some time during the remainder of the night they drifted apart. When daylight came on 3 March, Jan de Mul found himself alone in an empty sea.

The young Dutch engineer had no conception of how far he was from the land, or in which direction it might lie. His kapok-filled lifejacket was rapidly becoming saturated and losing its buoyancy, and he was bleeding from the wound in his leg. The thought that the sharks must sooner or later scent his blood was never far from his mind, and in desperation he took off the sodden lifejacket and began to swim. Without a sense of direction, this was a largely futile gesture, but to him anything was better than drifting, waiting for the sharks to come for him.

Several hours later, as darkness was beginning to descend again, a tired and thoroughly dispirited Jan de Mul had finally reached the point where he could see no sense in continuing the fight for survival, and was prepared to let himself slip quietly below the waves. Then, in this moment of his lowest ebb, he was thrown against a large piece of wreckage, and he reached out eagerly for support. He then discovered that his luck was even greater than he had dared to dream in all the long, tortured hours of semi-delirium. The wreckage turned out to be a wooden life-raft from the *Langkoeas*, badly damaged by Japanese machine-gun fire, but still floating. Summoning up the last of his dwindling reserves of strength, the engineer hauled himself aboard the raft, and sank into the blessed oblivion of sleep.

It was light when de Mul awoke from his exhausted slumber. He looked around, and to his great surprise found the Chinese seaman Lam Dai floating nearby supported by his cork lifejacket, which had not lost its buoyancy. With de Mul's help, Lam Dai boarded the raft. Some time later, the two survivors were joined by the Javanese steward Lajar. Another two hours went by, during which, without shelter, the three men suffered agonies under the blazing sun. Then, out of the empty wastes of sea around them, the *Langkoeas*'s work-boat drifted into their path. They boarded it filled with new hope.

The work-boat was little more than a dinghy, ideal for painting ship, but hardly suitable for the open ocean. It did, however, contain two oars, a mast and a small sail. Now, at last, the survivors could put an end to their aimless drifting. Unfortunately, there was no food or water in the boat, and Jan de Mul and his two companions were to suffer increasing thirst and hunger for two more days and nights. Sailing before the wind, they came in sight of land on 5 March, land which proved to be Bawean Island, some 90 miles north of Sourabaya. Local fishermen found them lying exhausted on a beach in the south of the island, and took them to the nearest village. It was some days before the outside world heard the story of the only three men to survive the sinking of the *Langkoeas* by Kitamura's I-158. The sheer barbarity of the massacre of the other crew members sent a wave of fear and disgust surging around the Dutch East Indies. Was this the way the Japanese intended to wage war against merchant seamen? It was not long before an answer to this question was forthcoming.

As February 1942 drew to a close it was becoming increasingly clear that the days of Allied control of Java were numbered. Having summarily disposed of Admiral Doorman's ships, the Japanese had successfully landed in excess of 100,000 troops in the north of the island, and were rapidly overcoming the poorly organized and ill equipped British and Australian forces. Preparations were going ahead to clear all shipping from the main ports, Tandjong Priok and Sourabaya in the north, and Tjilatjap in the south, all of which were heavily congested with merchantmen who had streamed south from Singapore in search of sanctuary or, at least, breathing space. Now they were being forced to run again. One of the first ships to leave Tandjong Priok was the Dutch-flag tanker *Augustina*.

The 3110-ton *Augustina*, owned by the Netherlands Indies Steam Tanker Company, and commanded by Captain Moerman, left Tandjong Priok in ballast on the morning of 27 February. She was clear of the minefields outside the port before Captain Moerman informed his crew that his orders were to take the ship to Australia. What he omitted to tell them was that the *Augustina*'s chances of reaching her destination were very slim indeed, and in the event of being stopped by the Japanese he was under orders to scuttle the ship.

Before sailing, Moerman had been warned that his shortest route, through the Sunda Strait, was already blocked by Japanese warships, so he set course to the east, hoping to slip through the Lombok Strait, the passage between Bali and Lombok Island, while the enemy was busy in the west. Unfortunately, neither Moerman nor the authorities in Tandjong Priok were aware of the true strength of the Japanese forces threatening Java.

The voyage went well for the first two days, with the *Augustina* bowling along at a good speed in calm seas and under blue untroubled skies. Of the enemy there was no sign. Then, on Sunday, 1 March, the tanker's run of good fortune came to an end. Lunch was over, and Captain Moerman, more relaxed than he had been for many a day, was pacing his deck enjoying the warm sunshine. Suddenly, the drone of aircraft engines stopped him in his stride. He raced to the bridge, where Second Officer Kuyper pointed out a number of low-flying aircraft approaching from the north. Moerman snatched up a pair of binoculars and focused on the planes. They were twin-engined bombers and seaplanes, undoubt-edly Japanese. The *Augustina* was caught out in the open, with not even a passing rain squall to offer a hiding place.

The tanker was unarmed, and Moerman could only zig-zag and wait for the bombs and torpedoes to rain down on his ship. To his complete surprise, the anticipated attack did not come. The enemy planes roared past, completely ignoring the *Augustina*, and continued to the south. Shortly afterwards, explosions were heard in the direction of the Lombok Strait. Some other unfortunate ship was receiving the attention of the Japanese bombers.

Moerman had no other option open but to continue on course, and this the *Augustina* did for another half an hour. Then the drone of engines was heard again, and the Japanese planes reappeared, flying north. Moerman and his crew steeled themselves for the attack that must now surely come. But again the bombers seemed either not to have seen the Dutch tanker or to be prepared to ignore it. The heavy twin-engined planes carried on to the north, and a collective sigh of relief was breathed on board the *Augustina*. Then, the tanker's luck changed. There was a warning cry from one of the lookouts, who had seen some of the Japanese seaplanes peel off, and soon they were diving on the unarmed ship.

Captain Moerman had prepared for this eventuality by having a makeshift air raid shelter constructed amidships using sandbags. He now sent all men who were on the bridge or on deck to this shelter, and took the wheel himself.

As the seaplanes approached, Moerman threw his ship around in a crazy zig-zag to spoil their aim, but, much to his surprise and relief, the anticipated attack did not come. The Japanese planes dived and roared over the *Augustina*, but they dropped no bombs or torpedoes, neither did they machine-gun the ship. Moerman surmised that they must have used up all their ammunition on that other unseen target to the south. After a few threatening passes, the enemy flew away.

The afternoon passed uneventfully, and at around 1500 the tall peak of the island of Bali was abeam to starboard, and beyond it the Lombok Strait. Darkness would soon draw its comforting cloak around the fleeing tanker, and Captain Moerman might have been forgiven for believing that the way to Australia was clear. But his hopes were dashed when smoke appeared on the horizon in the north-east, and soon the menacing outlines of a Japanese destroyer could be discerned. She was the *Mutuki*-class destroyer *Harukaze*, fresh from the furious Battle of the Java Sea, where a lucky hit had damaged her rudder, and her commander was in no mood to observe the niceties of war. There could be no escape for the *Augustina* as the *Harukaze* bore down on her at full speed, and with obvious intent. As she neared, she fired two shots across the tanker's bow.

Having nothing to defend his ship with, and unable to run away from the enemy, Moerman surrendered to the inevitable. He rang his engines to stop and passed the word to clear away the lifeboats. At the same time, he ordered Chief Engineer Osseman to open all the sea valves and tank stop valves in the engine-room, allowing the sea to flood into the hull. The *Augustina* would not fall into Japanese hands.

At 1500, two lifeboats, containing all forty-two men of the *Augustina*'s crew, ten Dutch officers and thirty-two Chinese ratings, pulled away from their sinking ship. They had not gone far before the *Harukaze* closed with them and ordered the boats to come alongside. Reluctantly they complied, and when the two boats were made fast to the destroyer's rails, Moerman and Osseman were ordered aboard. There they suffered the humiliation of being sprayed with disinfectant before being taken to *Harukaze*'s bridge, where the destroyer's commander interrogated them, and then ordered them to return to the *Augustina* to try to save her. The two men, surrounded by Japanese sailors armed with rifles and fixed bayonets, were obliged to comply. They were bundled aboard a cutter and ferried back to their ship.

An uneasy fear of the unknown settled over the two lifeboats, where the remainder of *Augustina*'s crew lay back on their oars, wondering if they would ever see their captain and chief engineer again.

They did not have long to wait. Within an hour the Japanese cutter returned to the destroyer from the *Augustina*. Moerman and Osseman were still alive, but they had failed to save the *Augustina*, being unable to reach the engine-room valves, which were under water when they reboarded the doomed ship.

The two senior officers were unceremoniously bundled into one of the waiting lifeboats, and it was then that the *Augustina*'s men began to have serious doubts about their fate. The Japanese sailors stripped both their boats of provisions, fresh water, and small gear, all the things they would need if they were to survive. Then the destroyer took the boats in tow and, in full sight of the already fearful survivors, a machine-gun was set up in the stern of the *Harukaze*. This was clearly a warning to the men that any attempt to escape would be swiftly dealt with.

At about 1800, as the sun was sinking below the horizon in the west and darkness approaching, the *Harukaze* stopped, and the Japanese cast off the crowded lifeboats and signalled them to row clear of the ship. While the oars were being shipped, the boats drifted up on the destroyer, one on each quarter. When they were within fifty yards of her stern, the machine-gun suddenly opened up, spraying the boats and the sea around with a fusillade of bullets.

The survivors, who by this time had naively assumed that they were free to go, were taken completely by surprise. Several men who were standing up were shot down before they could take cover behind the gunwales, others hurled themselves over the side, seeking safety in the sea. One of these was Third Engineer Meyer, who escaped the hail of bullets and became an eyewitness to the carnage that followed.

Treading water, Meyer saw one of the boats drift alongside the destroyer, its occupants still bemused by the ferocity of the attack. As the boat bumped against the hull of the *Harukaze*, a Japanese sailor armed with a sub-machine-gun quite deliberately shot everyone in the boat, and then turned his gun on those in the water.

Meyer, who was a strong swimmer, saved his life by diving deep, and staying down while bullets splattered the water around him. He remained submerged until his lungs were on the point of bursting, and when he finally came to the surface he found that he was still close to the boat, but on the other side, and hidden from the destroyer. By this time darkness was coming in, and after stripping off his sodden clothing, the engineer struck out strongly, desperate to put as much distance as possible between himself and the murdering Japanese.

Meyer had no idea how long or far he swam, but sometime later he saw a dark shape looming up ahead of him. Cautiously, he swam closer, and soon he realized he was swimming towards his own ship. The *Augustina* had a very heavy list, and was low in the water, but she was still afloat. To Meyer it seemed that his prayers had been answered, and he swam to the low side of the ship, hoping and intending to board her, but as he approached he heard voices – Japanese voices. He stopped and trod water, listened for a while. His ears had not deceived him; the shrill voices confirmed that his ship was in the hands of the enemy. He slowly circled the Augustina, and on the high side he saw that a destroyer lay alongside, most probably the one responsible for his predicament.

Unwilling to approach closer, Meyer trod water while he tried desperately to form a plan of action. As he did so, the destroyer cast off from the *Augustina* and steamed away. Very cautiously, lest the Japanese had left men aboard the drifting tanker, Meyer circled the ship again, watching and listening. He could detect no sign of life. The *Augustina* was by now listing at least 35 degrees, and looked to be about to capsize at any moment, which, Meyer concluded, was why the Japanese had abandoned her.

The risks involved in boarding the ship were very great, but by this time Meyer was so cold and tired that he was prepared to take any risk. Climbing aboard on the low side, where the rails were only inches above the water, was not difficult, but the deck of the listing tanker sloped upwards like the side of a steep mountain, and in his weakened state progress was painfully slow. Crawling on all fours, he eventually reached the officers' accommodation, and groping around in the complete darkness he found a dressing gown in one of the cabins with which to cover his nakedness. Then he began to search for food, making his way to the *Augustina*'s mess-room. The ship was now creaking and groaning ominously, and he feared she might turn turtle at any moment. When he came across a parcel that seemed to contain food and a bucket containing water, he wasted no more time. Snatching up his booty, he scrambled out onto the open deck.

Meyer now needed some means of keeping himself afloat, and he made his way to the boat deck. The lifeboats were gone, of course, drifting somewhere in the surrounding darkness, full of bullet holes and waterlogged. But there was one boat left. The tanker's small work boat was still hanging from its davits, and having stowed his precious provisions aboard, Meyer lost no time in getting the boat into the water. Once clear of the ship, he lay down in the bottom boards and fell sound asleep.

102

The sun was high in the sky when Meyer awoke from his deep sleep. His throat was dry, and he reached for the water he had brought with him from the *Augustina* during the night. Unfortunately, he discovered that in his haste to get away from the dangerously poised ship he had brought with him a bucket containing soapy washing-up water covered in dirty scum. Even in his parched state, the water was totally undrinkable. His shock was compounded when he opened the parcel of 'food'. It contained someone's dirty clothes.

In desperation, Meyer stood up in the boat and looked around him. Much to his surprise, the *Augustina* was still afloat, lying some 4 miles away. He decided he must return to her in search of food and water, or die. Then came yet another disappointment. The boat contained only a single oar, and the stern was so badly damaged that sculling was an impossibility.

Cursing in frustration, Meyer sat with his head in his hands, not knowing what to do next. Meanwhile, his boat drifted further and further away from the *Augustina*. By sunrise the next day, 3 March, the engineer could see only the masts and funnel of his ship showing above the horizon. With her had gone all his hopes for survival.

That afternoon, as Meyer, who was growing weaker by the hour, drifted in and out of consciousness, he heard the sound of engines and looked up to see a low-flying aircraft heading directly for his boat. He had just sufficient grip on reality to throw himself over the side before the plane roared overhead, and the Japanese pilot opened up with his machine-guns. The boat survived, the plane did not return for a second attack, and Meyer was able to reboard.

The day wore on, the sun beat down, and the lone survivor began to hallucinate. The land was all around him, near enough to touch, and there were cool streams and coconut trees, and yet nothing was real. Tortured by hunger and thirst, Meyer finally found oblivion in sleep when the sun went down, only to be rudely awoken by a bright light shining in his eyes a few hours later. He sat up. Now he could hear the engine of a motor launch, and a few minutes later, voices jabbering in unintelligible Japanese.

Still terrified by the memory of the slaughter of his shipmates in the *Augustina*'s boats, Meyer threw himself over the side, hoping to find refuge in the sea again. This time he could not hide. The beam of a searchlight picked him out, and he found himself being hauled over the gunwales of a Japanese destroyer's cutter.

Contrary to his expectations, Meyer was not badly treated aboard the enemy ship. He was transferred to another destroyer, where he joined the survivors of the crew of the American destroyer *Pope*, sunk while escorting the cruisers *Exeter* and *Houston* two days earlier. The prisoners were landed in Makassar on 7 March, where Meyer was kept in the local jail for seven months. In October 1942 he was sent to a prisoner of war camp in Japan, and remained there until liberated by the Americans in September 1945.

Third Engineer Meyer's statement of events which took place in the approaches to the Lombok Strait on the afternoon of 1 March 1942 was corroborated by two of the *Augustina*'s Chinese ratings, who also survived the massacre and landed on a part of the north coast of Java still occupied by the Allies. No trace was ever found of the remaining thirty-nine men of the Dutch tanker's crew, including Captain Moerman, and it must be assumed that they were brutally murdered by the Japanese for no other reason than that they took the honourable course of trying to avoid delivering their ship into the enemy's hands. As the war progressed, the treatment of captured Allied merchant seamen by the Imperial Japanese Navy became ever more bestial.

The tanker *British Judge* had sailed from Tandjong Priok a few hours after the *Augustina*, under orders to sail to Sourabaya, and there take on a full cargo of oil, presumably to prevent it falling into Japanese hands. The 6735-ton *British Judge*, operating under orders of the Admiralty and commanded by Captain T. Gaffney, was two hours out of port when Gaffney received an urgent radio signal ordering him to return to Tandjong Priok and await further orders. In these confused early days of the war in the Far East, order and counter-order were to be expected as the natural run of things, but to Gaffney this was ominous. Before leaving Tandjong Priok he had been warned that the Japanese were bombing Sourabaya, and he now concluded that the port must be already untenable. His conclusion was correct.

Returning to Tandjong Priok, the *British Judge* lay off the port until late the same night, when the order came for her to put to sea again. Things had gone from bad to worse; the Battle of the Java Sea had been fought and lost, and it was time for the remaining

Allied ships, merchant and naval, to make good their escape. At around midnight, the tanker joined up with a motley collection of ships to form a small convoy, the sole purpose of which was to break out through the Sunda Strait into the Indian Ocean. From there each ship would go her own separate way, the *British Judge* to sail north to Colombo.

Swiftly, and with the minimum of signalling to betray its presence, the convoy formed up within sight of Tandjong Priok, and when complete consisted of, in addition to the *British Judge*, the 3470-ton depot ship HMS *Anking* and the fleet oilers *Francol*, 4800 tons, and *War Sidar*, 11,000 tons. Escorting these four ships were the sloop HMAS *Yarra*, the corvette HMAS *Wollongong*, and the motor minesweeper MMS 51. It was not an impressive line-up, with nothing bigger than a 4-inch gun between them, and limited by the slowest member to a maximum speed of 6 knots.

With HMS *Anking*, whose commanding officer had been designated Senior Officer Escort, in the lead, the convoy sailed at midnight and headed west, hugging the coast. Disaster struck swiftly. Two hours out of Tandjong Priok, the *War Sidar* ran aground on a shoal, and was left behind struggling to free herself. The *Francol* also touched bottom on the patch, but was able to steam clear without any serious damage.

By 0630 on the 28th the convoy had reached St. Nicholas Point, at the northern end of the Sunda Strait, where an additional escort, the Royal Indian Navy sloop *Jumna* joined. Course was then altered to the south-west for the 75-mile-long run through the strait. At the convoy's speed of 6 knots there lay ahead of the ships a 12-hour passage, during which they would be dangerously exposed to the enemy's sea and air patrols.

Aboard the *British Judge*, a 10-knot ship reduced to crawling along at a little more than half-speed, the tension mounted as the sun rose higher in a cloudless sky. The tanker was armed with a 4-inch and 12-pounder guns mounted aft, and two Hotchkiss .303 machine-guns on the bridge. All these were constantly manned, the heavy guns by teams of crew members supervised by two DEMS gunners, and the machine-guns by two officers, Second Officer Coke and Third Officer Whattler.

The first attack from the air came just an hour later, when the convoy was passing abeam of Thwart Way Island, one of the

105

number of small islands that litter the Sunda Strait. It was an uncharacteristically poor effort, the Japanese planes making a few half-hearted passes at the ship, and dropping a handful of bombs, all of which went wide. It was all over in ten minutes. But that was only the opening move. The bombers were back again after half an hour, this time in greater numbers and pressing home their attacks with customary determination. Throughout the rest of the day they returned again and again, seven or eight times in all, coming in high in line ahead from the north, and diving down to about 300 feet before dropping their bombs. However, they were not unopposed. Between them, the ships put up a fierce barrage of cannon and machine-gun fire, and in all the attacks not one Japanese bomb found its target. The defence of the *British Judge*, as described by Captain Gaffney, was typical of the ships: 'The 2nd Officer, Mr M.A. Coke, and 3rd Officer, R.F. Whattler, manned the Hotchkiss guns throughout these attacks, and although they did not succeed in bringing down any of the enemy aircraft, they scored many hits with tracer bullets. The enemy machine-gunned us during every attack, but not a single man was hit, although the bullets were flying about from all angles, often ricocheting off the water.'

The enemy planes made their last pass at 1600, after which the convoy, shaken but unscathed, continued on its way without further molestation. At 1800, with the short equatorial twilight drawing its cloak, the ships ran clear of the Sunda Strait. At this point, the *British Judge* received orders from the SOE to leave the convoy at 2000 and make for Colombo independently. The rest of the convoy was to go south to Fremantle.

As the ships left the shelter of the land, the weather took a turn for the worse, rain squalls sweeping in with the wind gusting up to Force 5. The accompanying decrease in visibility was welcomed in the convoy, for the next few hours were crucial. The more distance they put between themselves and the coast of Java without being discovered by the enemy, then the greater were their chances of escaping. However, it is a fact of life that one ship's hiding place is often another's ambush – and for the *British Judge* this turned out to be the case.

Since his ruthless disposal of the *Langkoeas* and most of her crew eight weeks earlier, Lieutenant Commander Kitamura had moved I-158 into the Indian Ocean, sinking two more Dutch steamers, the

Pijnacker Hordijk and the *Boero*, only this time exercising rather more humanity. When the *British Judge* cleared the Sunda Strait, Kitamura was lying in wait 10 miles south of Prince's Island.

At 1945, shortly before *British Judge* was due to leave the convoy and go north, Kitamura's torpedo streaked towards the tanker, and she was staggered by a huge explosion which blew a hole in her port side below the waterline, in way of her No.3 cargo tank. She quickly settled by the head, at the same time taking on a heavy list to port.

Experience in this war had shown that a large tanker sailing in ballast was notoriously difficult to sink. Her longitudinally strengthened hull is divided into as many as twenty separate water-tight compartments, at least fifty percent of which needed to be flooded before the ship sank. In the case of the *British Judge*, an inspection of the damage found her No's 2,3,4 and 5 cargo tanks on the port side were flooded, but she appeared to be in no imme-diate danger of sinking. This was in spite of the fact that Kitamura's torpedo had blown a hole in her side some 50 feet in length, and extending from her keel to several feet above the waterline. There was also considerable damage on deck. Two heavy steel tank lids had been blown away, and several others were buckled. No. 2 lifeboat had disappeared, and the port side of the bridge was in a shambles. Mercifully, however, she had suffered no casualties, and her engine-room was intact.

Captain Gaffney had stopped his ship to assess the damage, and having decided she would stay afloat, he trimmed her onto an even keel by running water into one of the after tanks. During the fifty minutes or so that the *British Judge* lay stopped, HMAS *Wollongong* stood by her, and when Gaffney was ready to get under way again, the Australian corvette offered to escort him into Tjilatjap, 250 miles to the east. Tjilatjap was still under Allied control, and had a floating dry dock where temporary repairs could be effected. Gaffney agreed.

Twenty-four hours later, on 1 March, when the two ships were within 50 miles of Tjilatjap, *Wollongong* signalled that she had been ordered to leave the *British Judge* to her own devices and proceed at all speed to Australia. In view of this, Gaffney was advised to take his damaged ship to Colombo, giving the coast of Sumatra a wide berth. The *British Judge* reversed her course, and

107

passing 200 miles south of Christmas Island, she avoided the attentions of the enemy, eventually reaching Colombo on 16 March. She was not destined to play any significant part in the war at sea for some considerable time.

While in Colombo making temporary repairs, the British tanker's gunners were called upon several times to defend their ship when Japanese planes raided the port. She was further damaged by the bombers, and the weeks under repair dragged on into months. When she did finally sail, Captain Gaffney planned to make for Durban, 3700 miles to the south, but the tanker ran into heavy weather on the way, lost the temporary patches on her hull, and started to take in water. Gaffney put into Mombasa, where work began to patch the breached hull again, but repair facilities in the port were minimal and already stretched to their limit. Nine months elapsed before the *British Judge* was able to put to sea again. She was dry-docked at Cape Town, but once more the extent of her bottom damage proved too much for the local facilities. Patched up again, she set out across the Atlantic for America. When she reached the repair yard in Mobile, in the Gulf of Mexico, where it was at last possible to make a permanent repair, she had completed a voyage of 20,000 miles with a hole in her bottom 'the size of a medium-sized house'. The story of her survival was a glowing tribute to the determination of Captain Gaffney and his crew.

Chapter Nine

Java Abandoned

Long before Japanese carrier-borne aircraft delivered their devastating blow against the US Pacific Fleet at Pearl Harbor, the Dutch authorities in Java were busy laying plans to meet an invasion from the north which they knew was inevitable. The island possessed only three deep-water ports, Tandjong Priok, the port for the capital Batavia, Sourabaya on the northern coast, and Tjilatjap in the south. The northern ports would almost certainly be the first to be closed in the event of an invasion, leaving only Tjilatjap through which to bring in supplies and reinforcements, and, if their worst fears were realized, as an evacuation port.

Tjilatjap, situated on the Indian Ocean coast of Java, 150 miles south-east of Batavia, had steadily declined in importance after the collapse of the sugar market in 1929 until it was little more than a backwater playing host to the occasional coastal vessel. When war broke out in Europe ten years later, and the threat from Japan already loomed on the horizon, matters had not improved. The buoyed approach channel was not lit, so ships were able to enter and leave only in daylight, and there were only five somewhat ramshackle wharves, one of which was for tankers, no cranes, no tugs, no lighters and no bunkering facilities. Fresh water was available, but this had to be sterilized before use. However, being at the mouth of the River Donan, Tjilatjap possessed a large natural harbour capable of sheltering a great number of ships, although the holding ground for anchors was poor. The demands of war gave the port a new lease of life. The entrance channel was dredged, and thirteen sets of mooring buoys were laid in the harbour providing safe berths for ocean-going ships. Bunkering pipes were laid, fresh water facilities were improved, an 8000-ton floating dry dock was brought in, and extra housing built for the large number of officials and labourers drafted in to run the harbour. From a run-down, hardly used outport, Tjilatjap became a bustling centre for the import of essential war supplies into Java. Following the fall of Singapore, the flow of incoming traffic into the port was dramatically swelled by ships carrying refugees, with the roads packed with anchored ships awaiting berths. When the Japanese landed on the north coast of the island, Tjilatjap assumed even greater importance. All berths were full, and ships were triple-banked on the buoys, discharging troops and war supplies. It seemed that nobody in the world outside had yet realized that Java's days were numbered. Captain W.A. Peters, of the Royal Dutch Mail Line's 8187-ton *Tawali*, recorded the situation in the port in his diary: 'We were anchored in the port of Tjilatjap as of February 7th 1942, together with another 65 ships, all of us waiting for our turn to discharge our cargoes. In spite of the extensive efforts in order to increase port facilities, it appeared not easy to get a berth. There was a shortage of lighters, insufficient storage facilities and poor railway transportation. Only three berths for ships were available, which was hopelessly insufficient. Bottle-necks in all directions . . .'

It was not until news of the cataclysmic defeat of Admiral Doorman's fleet came through late on 26th February that Java woke up to the threat facing the island. Early next day, the order came from the Allied headquarters at Bandoeng for all merchant ships not required for special duties to leave Tjilatjap without delay. The text of the message received by the Commanding Officer Maritime Resources in Tjilatjap, Lieutenant Colonel Schokking, was as follows: 'All merchant ships, seaworthy and with sufficient radius of action to reach Australia or Colombo to leave the port immediately and await radio orders in position 200 miles south of Tjilatjap.'

At the time, the harbour was crammed with ships, mainly Dutch-flag merchantmen, while the town overflowed with human flotsam, refugees from the rout of Singapore, including many women and children, and swarms of Dutch, British, Australian and American servicemen, all confused and looking for leadership. Although Schokking had been told by Bandoeng that the immediate priority was to get the ships to sea where they would be less vulnerable to air attack, and that later some of them could be brought in to evacuate the troops and civilians, he was reluctant to allow any ship to leave empty.

During the course of that night, twenty-four ships left Tjilatjap. They ranged from Rotterdam Lloyd's 10,000-ton *Kota Gede* with nearly 2,000 British and Australian Air Force personnel on board, to the tiny 982-ton *Tomohon* of the Royal Packet Navigation Company carrying forty crew and passengers. Because of a threatened air raid – which subsequently failed to materialise – the exodus from Tjilatjap was hurried and somewhat chaotic.

The first ship to leave was the *Tawali*, after three weeks in the port, during which Captain Peters had fought a constant battle with the authorities to land his cargo of military stores, which included a large consignment of explosives. With this potential to blow Tjilatjap off the map in her holds, she had lain at anchor in the crowded harbour for day after day, with the situation in Java worsening by the hour. Finally, Peters was able to persuade the authorities of the great danger this lethal cargo presented to the port, and he was allowed to put the explosives ashore, along with a quantity of small arms. As to the rest of the *Tawali*'s cargo, it was still on board when she was ordered out of the port on the 27th. Amid scenes of great panic and confusion, she sailed an hour before midnight, and feeling her way out through the entrance channel which was poorly lit, she promptly ran aground on a sandbank and stuck fast.

Following the *Tawali* out was the 8917-ton *City of Manchester*, commanded by Captain Harry Johnson. She narrowly missed colliding with the stranded Dutch ship in the darkness, before reaching the open sea. Owned by Ellerman Lines of Liverpool, and built by Cammell Laird's Birkenhead yard in 1935, the *City of Manchester* was a twin-screw general and refrigerated cargo liner. Until the advent of Japan's aggression in the Pacific, she had ploughed a regular furrow between Australia and British ports carrying wool, meat and dairy produce. Now, caught up in the tide of war, she was at the beck and call of the Ministry of War Transport, and like so many of her contemporaries, engaged in carrying troops and their equipment.

In January 1942, the *City of Manchester* sailed from Melbourne with a contingent of Australian troops, which she landed in Singapore. Within weeks, she was called in to lift troops, possibly the same ones, off the beaches of the east coast of Malaya when they were cut off by the relentless advance of the Japanese down the peninsula. She landed these troops in Tandjong Priok, and with a cargo of 6,400 tons of military stores still on board, was sent south to Tjilatjap to join the other merchantmen assembled there. On the evening of the 27th, she was ordered out again. Captain Johnson later reported:

> On February 27th at 1800 local time, whilst at Tjilatjap, a Dutch naval officer came on board and told me I must proceed to sea that night. Owing to being short of fuel, I had reduced steam while in harbour in order to save oil, and I told him that it would take some time for me to raise steam, and it would probably be daylight before I could get away. At 2000 a British naval officer came to see me and said that it was very urgent and important that I should get away from the port that night. I sent for the Chief Engineer and told him that we had orders to sail that night and that he must rush the raising of steam, and at about 2030 I received an official notice in writing from the Dutch Naval Authorities to proceed to sea immediately.

Captain Johnson does not say whether he was fully informed of the extent of the Japanese threat to Tjilatjap, but he must have been told enough to convince him of the need to get his ship out of the port, and before midnight the *City of Manchester* had cast off her moorings. After narrowly avoiding a collision with the grounded *Tawali*, she cleared the buoyed channel at 0150 on the 28th, and set course to the south at full speed.

It was a fine night, very dark, but with good visibility, light variable winds and a smooth sea. The *City of Manchester* settled down on a zig-zag course, eventually working up to 14½ knots, with Captain Johnson becoming more confident as the miles slipped by that he had every chance of covering the 1,500 miles to Fremantle without meeting the enemy. Should the worst happen, however, his seventeen DEMS gunners, manning their 4-inch, 12-pounder, four Hotchkiss and eight Lewis machine-guns, would be able to give a good account of themselves.

Johnson's confidence was about to be badly shaken, for Lieutenant Commander Kitamura in I-158 was already manoeuvring
to bring the *City of Manchester* into his sights. At precisely sixteen
minutes past four on the morning of 28 February, when the British
ship was about 35 miles to the south of Tjilatjap, she was shaken
by a violent explosion as Kitamura's torpedo struck her on the starboard side in way of her No. 4 hold.

The explosion registered on the bridge of the *City of Manchester*
as no more than a dull thud, but the column of water seen soaring
high into the sky from the after deck left Captain Johnson and his
officers in little doubt as to what had happened. Their fears were
confirmed when, a few minutes later, the silence on the bridge was
shattered by the pealing of the engine-room telegraph bell. The
engine-room had rung the engines to 'Stop'. This was followed by
the appearance of the Chief Engineer on the bridge to report that
the starboard engine was out of commission, the torpedo having
smashed its propeller shaft, which ran through No. 4 hold. He was
quick to add, however, that the port engine was still serviceable and
the engine-room intact, all watertight doors having been closed as
soon as the torpedo struck. Reassured, Johnson rang for full speed
ahead on the port engine, and put the helm hard over. With luck,
he would be back in Tjilatjap in just over two hours.

Johnson's hopes of slipping away into the night were dashed
fifteen minutes later, when Kitamura fired a second torpedo,
which went home forward of the *City of Manchester*'s bridge.
This time the noise of the explosion was deafening, and the devastation it wreaked so obvious that Johnson immediately stopped
the ship and ordered the boats cleared away and made ready for
lowering.

The *City of Manchester* carried a crew of 136, the majority of
whom were Lascar ratings, and just one passenger, an RAF officer
who was wounded. If the ship was to be abandoned without confusion, then time was needed. No such luxury was forthcoming, for
even before all the way was off the ship Kitamura brought I-158 to
the surface and opened fire with her 4.7-inch deck gun, the first
shell starting a fire in the British ship's refrigerated chambers, while
other shells started fires on deck. Johnson's gunners searched in
vain for a target to hit back at, but the flash of I-158's gun was
barely visible to them.

113

The fires spread rapidly, and accepting that the situation was beyond his control, Johnson gave the order to abandon ship. The *City of Manchester* carried six lifeboats and four wooden life-rafts, all of which were quickly put into the water, with the exception of one raft that jammed in its launching chute. Although Kitamura's shells were crashing all around them, there was no panic in the crew, and it seemed that all 137 men would get away safely. Then, as the last boat was being manned, a shell burst on the ship's side about 8 feet above it. One man was killed and twelve wounded, eight of them seriously, by shell splinters, and the boat was badly damaged. Captain Johnson, the last man to leave the burning ship, was about to board this boat, but with many of its crew lying wounded it drifted away from the ship's side, leaving him stranded on board. He shouted to the other boats, but they were now too far away to hear him. Johnson was left with no alternative but to swim for his life.

Kitamura finished off the *City of Manchester* at his leisure, and before quitting the scene of his conquest, he came alongside one of the drifting lifeboats with the intention of taking a prisoner. An amusing insight into this incident appeared in the magazine *Sea Breezes* many years after the war:

In 1950 I sailed with a survivor of the *City of Manchester*. As I recall, his name was Broadbent and he had been 2nd Mate on her. After the torpedo struck he got his lifeboat clear (he did not mention any others). When the sub surfaced he gave instructions that all the officers should remove their epaulettes. The Chief Steward refused to do so.

When the sub had finished off the ship with gunfire, it came alongside the lifeboat. A Jap officer pointed a gun at the Chief Steward, telling him that as an officer he must come aboard the sub. The Chief Steward denied being an officer, and pointed out the 2nd Mate. 'He's the officer,' he said. 'I'm only in the catering department.'

And so Broadbent became a prisoner of war somewhere in the Dutch East Indies. He had one burning ambition, and that was to catch up with the Chief Steward of the *City of Manchester*.

1. Aerial view of
   Tjilatjap and harbour
   taken in 1940.
   Photo: N. Dorlas

2. The first air raid on Darwin. Burns Philp motor vessel *Neptuna*, loaded with ammunition, blows up after direct hit.   *Photo: Frank Bowen*

3. Blue Funnel cargo liner *Automedon* sunk by German raider *Atlantis* off Sumatra November 1940. She had on board secret papers giving details of defence plan for Singapore.   *Photo: John Clarkson*

4. *Empress of Asia*, 16,909 tons. Bombed and sunk off Singapore while bringing in troops to reinforce garrison.   *Photo: A. Hague*

5. HMAS *Yarra*, the Grimsby-class sloop that saved 1800 men from the burning *Empress of Asia* off Singapore. Later sunk while gallantly defending convoy against Japanese cruiser force.   *Photo: AWM*

6. Injured men from USS *Marblehead* being landed in Tjilajap.   *Photo: Albert Kelder*

7. Leading Seaman Tom Parsons, HMS *Li Wo*, in best whites pre-war.
Photo: South Wales Echo

8. Light cruiser *Mogami*. One of Vice Admiral Takeo Kurita's 7th Cruiser Squadron involved in the Battle of the Java Sea and the massacre of Allied merchant ships in the Bay of Bengal Easter 1942.　　　　　　*Photo: unknown Japanese source*

9. Sister Vivian Bullwinkel shortly after her release from a Japanese prisoner of war camp in 1945.
Photo: Sydney Morning Herald

10. Last allied merchant ship to leave Java, Royal Dutch Mail Line's 9278-ton *Poelau Bras*.
Photo: Frits Noorbergen

11. Royal Dutch Mail Line's *Tawali* embarking refugees in Tjilatjap 3 March 1942.
Photo: H. Dorlas

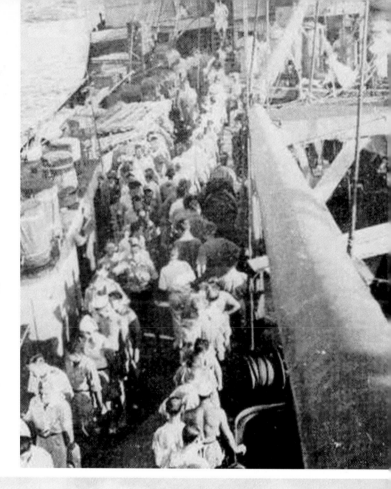

12. Survivors from Royal Dutch Mail Line's *Poelau Bras* after landing on south coast of Sumatra.
Photo: Albert Kelder

13. The old cemetery Tjilatjap, where many of those who fell in 1942 were buried.
Photo: Albert Kelder

14. Vyner Brooke memorial near the spot where 21 Australian nurses were murdered by the Japanese on Banka Island. *Photo: Royal Australian Army Nursing Service*

15. HMS *Li Wo*, ex-Indo China Steam Navigation Company. Sunk while heroically attacking Japanese invasion fleet off Banka Island. *Photo: Indo China Steam Nav Co*

It was fortunate for the remaining survivors of the *City of Manchester* that several US Navy ships were searching in the area for survivors from the old aircraft carrier *Langley*, sunk by Japanese aircraft on the previous day. The first of these to come across the *City of Manchester*'s boats was the minesweeper *Whippoorwill*, then the gunboat *Tulsa*. The *Tulsa* had a doctor on board, and he was able to deal with the casualties in the boats. Unfortunately, two of the seriously wounded died on board the gunboat before she reached Tjilatjap.

Captain Harry Johnson recorded the subsequent fortunes of himself and his surviving crew members:

> As soon as I landed I reported to the Harbour Master and met the commanders of the two American rescue vessels. The Dutch residents arranged accommodation for all the survivors and I arranged with the Harbour Master for the Port Doctor to be sent to the wounded, as the surgeon of the USS *Tulsa* would not agree to move the men to hospital without further medical opinion. There were so many ships in the harbour that I was unable to find the *Tulsa* and much to my grief could not visit the wounded members of my crew. I next reported to the British Vice-Consul, Mr Ross, who arranged accommodation for me in a small hotel. He told me that Java was to be evacuated early next morning and that I must have all my crew ready to board the *Zaandam* (Dutch) and he would give me all instructions later. I tried several times during the night to find out about the condition of the wounded men in hospital, but only succeeded in getting hold of a nurse who could not speak English, and all I could get out of her was, 'The doctor has not been yet'. I was told that one of the hospitals was 40 miles out of town and I knew some of my men were in this hospital. The ship's carpenter came to me at the British Consulate and said that he had the body of the Apprentice at the cemetery but that the officials would not bury him without a certificate from the British Consul with an order for a coffin. I arranged for this with the Consul and hurried off to the cemetery, only to find that the body had already been buried. On my way back to the Consul I saw a Dutch Army officer unloading a truck, I told him about my wounded men being

115

in hospital 40 miles away and asked if I could possibly borrow his truck and drive out to it and he at once offered to drive me himself, and we set off at 0300, arriving back at 0530 with ten of the less seriously wounded men. At 0600 we boarded the *Zaandam*.

For the Norwegian-flag steamer *Prominent*, the order to quit the port of Tjilatjap was just another stage in a voyage that seemed to have no end. It all began in late December 1941, when the 2232-ton *Prominent*, one of Jacob Odland's engaged in their Far East trade, had sailed westwards into the unfamiliar waters of the Middle East to assist in the transfer of the 1st Australian Division from Palestine to Singapore.

At that time, the tide of war in the Western Desert was at last turning in favour of the British and Commonwealth forces, Tobruk having been relieved, and Rommel being on the retreat. Singapore, on the other hand, seemed headed for disaster as the Japanese continued their relentless advance down the Malaysian peninsula. The loss of Singapore would bring the enemy within a short sea voyage of Australia, which had been denuded of its best fighting men by the war in the West. Not without good cause, the Australian Government was becoming increasingly nervous, and had demanded that their troops be moved nearer to home.

The *Prominent*, under the command of Captain Kristen Gjertsen, sailed from the Red Sea in Convoy JS 1 with six other ships, including a fellow Norwegian, the motor vessel *Eidsvold*, later to meet her end off Christmas Island. By the time the convoy reached Colombo it had already become clear that Singapore would fall before the troopships arrived, and that the Dutch East Indies were next on the Japanese list of potential conquests. Consequently, JS 1 was re-routed to Sumatra. The *Prominent* eventually ended up in Tandjong Priok, where she landed her troops on 15 February. While she was in that port, Third Officer Harald Marø, by now a survivor from the *Eidsvold*, joined the ship.

Harald Marø had already been initiated into the horrors of war. Only a month earlier, he had been serving as third officer in the *Eidsvold*, then loading phosphates at Christmas Island, when a storm brewing up obliged her to weigh anchor and move out to sea. For six days she rode out the storm, approaching the land each day

116

to see if conditions inshore were suitable for her to continue loading, but the swell continued to run too high for the lighters to come off. Her master, Captain Samuel Fridvold, began to lose patience.

At 1430 on 20 January, as the *Eidsvold* continued to plod up and down off Christmas Island, Second Officer Sverre Bergendahl, who was on watch on the bridge of the Norwegian ship, reported seeing the track of a torpedo passing down the port side at no more than 300 yards off. Captain Fridvold, called to the bridge, was reluctant to believe that the enemy was active in this remote area, and put the sighting down to the wake created by a passing whale, of which there were many off the island. However, he was a cautious man, and as the *Eidsvold*'s sole defensive armament consisted of just three Marlin machine-guns, he decided to move further inshore under the cover of the fort.

Christmas Island's fort mounted only one gun of indeterminate calibre, but lying within 4 cables of the fort, and with his machine-guns manned and lifeboats swung out ready for lowering, Fridvold felt reasonably safe.

The remainder of the afternoon passed peacefully, and at 1800, with the sun just going down, and not entirely happy about being so close to the shore, Captain Fridvold was making preparations to move back out to sea as soon as darkness came. At 1815 Fridvold was in the starboard wing of the bridge sweeping the horizon with his binoculars, when he sighted what looked suspiciously like a periscope to starboard. He immediately rang for full speed and ordered the helm hard to port.

With a tremendous crash, the incoming torpedo slammed into the *Eidsvold*'s starboard side, just forward of her No. 4 hold, breaking her back. Fortunately, by this time the ship was less than half a mile off shore, and abandoning ship was a simple matter. With the aid of the local pilot boat, all thirty-one crew, with the exception of Chief Engineer Alfred Hoel, reached the shore safely. When it was discovered that Hoel was missing, Captain Fridvold, Third Officer Harald Marø and Mechanic Kare Andersen, returned with the pilot boat to search for him. They discovered Hoel still pottering about in the *Eidsvold*'s engine-room, caring for his beloved machinery to the last. Returning ashore with Hoel, Fridvold made arrangement for his crew to be accommodated in the homes of some of the local families.

When all the activity in the vicinity of the crippled *Eidsvold* had ceased, Lieutenant Yoshimatsu brought I-159 to the surface, but she was immediately spotted from the fort, and a few salvoes from the big gun were enough to make Yoshimatsu dive and beat a hasty retreat from Christmas Island. During the course of the night, the *Eidsvold* broke in two, both halves of the ship sinking in shallow water. As soon as the weather subsided, Fridvold took his men back to the sunken ship to salvage as much as possible from the wreck, most of which was given to the islanders. Their greatest prize was the *Eidsvold*'s wireless equipment, which was dismantled and used to set up a radio station on Christmas Island.

After spending two not unpleasant weeks on Christmas Island, Captain Fridvold and his crew were rescued by the British cruiser HMS *Durban*, and taken to Batavia. Most of them then worked their passage to Sydney in the Australian passenger liner *Marella*. Harald Marø, one of those who opted to stay behind in Java, eventually found a berth as Third Officer in the *Prominent*, a move he was to regret.

Languishing in Tandjong Priok with nothing more achieved than shipping a few tons of coal and topping up with water and provisions, the *Prominent* was finally ordered south to Tjilatjap, where Captain Gjertsen was assured her cargo would be discharged. She reached Tjilatjap on 24 February, and then lay at a buoy with that cargo gathering dust in her holds and Gjertsen biting his nails in frustration, until the annihilation of Admiral Doorman's ships on the 27th.

The *Prominent* joined in the exodus from Tjilatjap early on the 28th, unaware that during the night a fleet under Vice Admiral Kondo, consisting of the cruisers *Atago*, *Maya* and *Takao*, accompanied by the destroyers *Arashi* and *Nowaki*, had slipped through the Sunda Strait. At 0815 next morning, 1 March, Catalina Y66 reported sighting Kondo's ships between 150 and 200 miles south of Tjilatjap. They were lying in wait for any Allied ships attempting to escape from Tjilatjap. The *Prominent* sailed blindly into their arms.

Harald Marø was on watch on the bridge of the *Prominent* when she was attacked by enemy warships, probably the destroyers *Arashi* and *Nowaki*, some 230 miles south of Tjilatjap. Most of the crew of the Norwegian ship and the refugees she carried were on

118

deck when the Japanese ships opened fire on them. Thirteen were killed by the shellfire, among them First Mate/Radio Operator Otto Ottesen, Chief Engineer Nils Nilsen and Second Engineer Johan Stavenes, and several others were seriously injured. The survivors who escaped this bloodbath piled into two lifeboats and set course for Java, which they reached five days later. They landed in a remote part of the island, but the locals helped them carry the five injured men on stretchers made out of lifeboat sails to the nearest town, where the injured were admitted to hospital. All the survivors eventually ended up in a Japanese prisoner of war camp on a small island in the Indies. There, along with 12,000 other prisoners, housed in a camp built for 800, they were put to work to build a dry dock for the Japanese. The conditions they endured while in captivity were horrendous, and several of their number died.

The ageing *Enggano* of the Royal Dutch Mail Line was another of the Dutch contingent on a long voyage without conclusion to be ordered out of Tjilatjap. Commanded by Captain Cor Schoen, the 5412-ton steamer had left London in late September 1941 with a cargo of military equipment for Singapore and other ports in Malaya. Crossing the Atlantic in convoy to Halifax, Nova Scotia, she made her way via the Panama Canal to Melbourne, where she completed her cargo by loading Australian Army vehicles on deck. While the *Enggano* was bunkering at Fremantle, Singapore fell, rendering her voyage unnecessary, and she was diverted to Tjilatjap. She left that port, again with most of her cargo still on board. Third Officer Piet Meek has vivid memories of the dash south:

> On February 27th *Enggano* was ordered to leave Tjilatjap and try to get to either Ceylon or Australia, but first to go 400 miles to the south to wait for orders.
> On March 1st, when about 270 miles south of Java, on the afternoon watch about 1400 local time, we were bombed by a Japanese plane. I was just on deck at No.4 hatch to get some icewater, when the alarm bells rang. I ran to the bridge and saw the first bomb just miss the bridge and drop on the port side next to No.4 hatch, which damaged the hull. In the second run a bomb was dropped in No.2 hatch. This hatch was loaded with explosives and gases, and explosions started

immediately. The impact of the bombs had damaged the deck water lines, so effective fire-fighting was impossible. Around 1500 hours the crew was ordered to board the lifeboats.

Having abandoned ship without casualties, Captain Schoen decided to stay close to the burning ship, hoping that someone would come in answer to his SOS calls. As they lay drifting, a Japanese cruiser passed close by, but for some reason ignored them.

Schoen's calls for help had not gone unnoticed. The *Tawali*, having floated clear of the sandbank at the entrance to Tjilatjap after four hours, was 420 miles south of the port, when Captain Peters received a radio message from the Commander Dutch Naval Forces ordering him to return to Tjilatjap immediately to assist in the evacuation of military personnel. He reversed course immediately, and shortly afterwards the *Enggano*'s SOS was picked up by his wireless operator. The position of the burning ship was plotted, and as she was only just over 100 miles to the north, and near to the *Tawali*'s track, Peters decided to go to her rescue.

As the *Tawali* hurried north, she was spotted by marauding Japanese planes, and came under attack. She fought back with her guns, and although many bombs fell close, and the enemy raked her with machine-gun fire, she suffered no damage or casualties. At about 0130 next morning, 2 March, a glow on the horizon led her to the *Enggano*, which was still on fire, but afloat. Peters carried out a search of the immediate area, which led him to the *Enggano*'s lifeboats containing all sixty-five men of her crew, including Captain Schoen. It is believed that the *coup de grâce* was delivered to the *Enggano* later in the day by the cruiser *Chikuma* and the destroyer *Urakaze*.

The *Tawali* continued on her way north, and around 1000 that morning she came across a lifeboat from the *Toradja*, one of the smallest ships to escape from Tjilatjap on 28 February. The boat contained thirty survivors, four of whom were severely wounded, all that were left of her total complement of ninety. The *Toradja* had been unfortunate enough to cross paths with the destroyers *Arashi* and *Nowaki*, who had blasted the little ship out of the water, killing eleven members of her crew.

The *Tawali* arrived off Tjilatjap late that night, and berthed at 0900 next morning. The *Toradja* survivors then went ashore, but

Captain Schoen of the *Enggano* and his Chinese crew stayed behind to help with discharging the *Tawali*'s deck cargo to make room for the evacuees expected on board. At 1200 Captain Peters was called to Lieutenant Colonel Schokking's office to be told that as many as 600 passengers would board his ship during the day, and that he must leave Tjilatjap for Australia at 1900 at the latest.

Preparations aboard the *Tawali* went ahead at a pace, the hatch coamings being cleared to accommodate the evacuees, and crates containing trucks landed on deck to offer them some protection. Extra stores were taken on board, and in the absence of lifeboats or rafts to take the additional complement, Peters had to make do with bundles of large bamboos lashed together to form makeshift rafts. The passengers when they came on board proved to be a mixed bunch, comprising 359 Royal Dutch Navy personnel from the barracks in Sourabaya, 49 naval dockyard personnel from the same port, 85 British and Australian soldiers, and 20 civilians of Rotterdam Lloyd and JCJL Lines, including 5 women and children.

When she left her berth in Tjilatjap at 2045 on 4 March, the *Tawali* had on board a crew of 97 and 513 passengers. Her accommodation was packed, and every spare square inch of her deck space was occupied by demoralized humans, who saw this ship as their only chance to avoid capture by the advancing Japanese. Two hours later, as she cleared the buoyed channel, the weather closed in, with heavy rain squalls accompanied by thunder and lightning providing a convenient cloak to hide her escape. Even as the *Tawali* reached the open sea, Captain Peters received a radio message changing his destination to Colombo, which, so he wrote in his diary, 'did not please him greatly.' But she reached that port safely ten days later, having picked up on the way fifty-seven survivors from HMS *Anking*, sunk off Christmas Island on 3 March by Japanese cruisers. The Royal Dutch Mail Line ship can be said to have played a significant part in the evacuation of the doomed port of Tjilatjap.

The 8806-ton motor vessel *Modjokerto*, which also joined in the mass exodus from Java, did not enjoy the same good fortune as the *Tawali*. Owned by Rotterdam Lloyd, and under the command of Captain Jack Verhagen, the *Modjokerto* left Tjilatjap on 28 February, leaving behind several members of her crew who were on shore leave when the order came to sail. It is believed that she had on board a total of forty-two men.

Twenty-four hours later, another Rotterdam Lloyd ship, the *Siantor*, also an escapee from Tjilatjap, picked up a radio message from the *Modjokerto* saying she was under attack by enemy aircraft. This was followed half an hour later by another urgent signal reporting, 'warship in sight probably Japanese'. Another thirty minutes elapsed and the *Siantor* listened in to the *Modjokerto*'s final transmission, 'Ship sinking position 12° 40'S, 106° 40'E'.

What really happened to the *Modjokerto* remains a mystery to this day. One theory advanced is that she was damaged by gunfire from the Japanese heavy cruiser *Chikuma*, and was later torpedoed and sunk by a Japanese submarine, either I-154 or I-158. Of the Dutch ship's crew there was no word until the autumn of 1946, when a mass grave was discovered in Kendari (South Celebes). Among the bodies in the grave were some identified as crew members of the *Modjokerto*. An investigation was carried out, which revealed that all fourteen European crew members of the ship had been beheaded on 24 March 1942. What happened to the rest of the crew, twenty-eight Chinese and Javanese ratings, is still not known. The bodies of the Europeans, Captain Verhagen, four deck officers, six engineers, the Wireless Operator, the Lamp Trimmer and the Purser, were later interred in the war cemetery at Batavia.

Chapter Ten

Escape to the South

Holland America's *Zaandam*, a cargo/passenger ship of 10,909 tons, was ordered out of Tjilatjap with the other ships on 26 February, but no sooner was she at sea than she received orders to stand by off the port to take on evacuees. This was yet another bitter disappointment for Captain Stamperius, who had left port with the intention of sailing to Australia.

The *Zaandam* was in San Francisco, and had just completed loading a cargo for Singapore, when the Japanese swooped on Pearl Harbor. The ship and her cargo were immediately requisitioned by the Netherlands Government, and nearly three weeks went by before she was allowed to sail, now bound for Sumatra via New Zealand. Singapore fell while the *Zaandam* was en route from New Zealand, and when she arrived at Lampong Bay, in the south-east of Sumatra, she found the anchorage crowded with ships, many of whom were packed with refugees from Singapore. From there she was sent to Tjilatjap, where she arrived on 10 February, but again the harbour was so crowded that she was unable to discharge her cargo. Once more the Holland America ship was forced to lie idle at anchor.

When on the 26th the order came for all merchant ships to quit the port of Tjilatjap, Captain Stamperius, sensing the urgency of the situation, put to sea without delay. However, the hurried departure proved unnecessary, for within hours of leaving the *Zaandam* received orders to return to Tjilatjap to take on an unspecified number of refugees. As she was approaching the port soon after sunrise on the 28th, Japanese bombers swooped down on her, intent on sinking what appeared to be a defenceless target. Unfortunately for them, while she was in America she had been fitted with a formidable array of anti-aircraft guns, which were manned by a team of eighteen US Navy Armed Guard gunners led by 30-year-old Ensign James Maddox. These men were well trained, and they put up such an accurate barrage that the Japanese planes were forced to keep their distance. Four or five bombs were dropped, but all fell wide of the Dutch ship. Later in the day she berthed in Tjilatjap, and preparations were made to receive her passengers.

In peacetime, when the *Zaandam*, an 18-knot twin-screw vessel built in 1939, sailed on a regular service across the Atlantic from Holland to the Americas, she carried, if not in luxury, then in reasonable comfort, a total of 125 passengers. When she sailed again from Tjilatjap at 2000 on 1 March, her accommodation and decks were packed with no fewer than 1,241 passengers. They consisted mainly of civilian refugees from Singapore, women and children predominating, along with British and Australian soldiers, Dutch Navy personnel, Dutch airline pilots and their families, members of the US and Chinese consulates, and various local officials. Also on board were survivors from the *City of Manchester* and the Dutch ship *Boero*. All were anxious to get away before Java was overwhelmed by the advancing Japanese armies.

Jean Dutilh, a member of the crew of Rotterdam Lloyd's *Kota Gede*, left behind in Tjilatjap in the confusion, and assigned to the *Zaandam*, described the departure of the Holland America ship:

> Lifejackets were only available for the women and children. We had our own, but the majority had nothing. What the authorities did was to bring a couple of hundred bamboo rafts (150 x 50cm) on board.
>
> That Sunday afternoon we did not realise that so many people were aboard the ship. A great number of suitcases came along. But anything bigger than a handbag was, without argument, pushed into the *kali* (river). The Tjilatjap natives went after it in their *prauwen* (canoes). A lot of throwing around of the small suitcases went on and in the confusion some of it went over the side.
>
> We were supposed to leave at 1800, but waited for another train with about 100 women and children. The train never

124

showed up. We heard later that they were stuck at Kroja and so had to stay in Java. In the meantime we had our first meal: in the pantry we could get soup, but no spoon, a thick slice of bread (5cm). The soup had some pieces of potato floating around, some vegetables and a little bit of meat. Still, you had to be lucky to get this nourishment. The absence of a spoon was no big deal.

Darkness did not fall quickly, as the weather was marvellous with a full moon. Around 2100 we left. Once outside the Captain refused to wait for the pilot boat, so the pilot and the harbour master stayed on board. They were not happy. They had nothing with them and left everything, including their families in Java.

Jean Dutilh's report conflicts in places with that of Harbour Master J. Fray, who wrote: 'The evacuees boarded the ship and she left in the evening with Pilot Droste and Assistant Harbour Master van Raalten. The latter had been sent along by me to acquaint himself with the fairway and check the lights. Outside, at sea, the visibility was restricted by driving rain and they missed the pilot boat. As the Master thought it would be too risky to wait for the pilot boat at the roads, and no Navy ships were in sight, the *Zaandam* continued her trip to Fremantle, taking the pilot and Mr van Raalten.'

Captain Stamperius must have been considerably relieved when, as he searched in vain for the pilot boat, the old British destroyer HMS *Stronghold* appeared out of the rain. The *Stronghold*, under the command of Lieutenant-Commander G.R. Preytor-Pinney, one of the few Allied ships to survive the Battle of the Java Sea, had been assigned to carry out an anti-submarine patrol off Tjilatjap until the *Zaandam* and her precious human cargo were clear of the port approaches. Thereafter, Preytor-Pinney was to try to save his own ship by making for Australia at all possible speed.

The *Stronghold* gave the *Zaandam* her protection for a few hours after clearing Tjilatjap, but then, much to the disappointment of those aboard the Dutch ship, the destroyer signalled her farewells and increased speed for the south. The *Zaandam* was a powerful twin-screw motor ship only three years old, but having over 1,300 persons on board in addition to her full cargo, she was carrying a heavy load, and was soon left behind by the destroyer. Some twelve hours later, on the morning of 2 March, she was made very aware of the dangers facing her, when her lookouts sighted a lifeboat from the *Tomohon*, one of the earlier ships to leave Tjilatjap.

The Royal Packet Navigation Company's 983-ton *Tomohon*, commanded by Captain W. Koning, was 230 miles south of Tjilatjap, and making a determined bid for the safety of Australian waters, when she ran straight into the arms of the Japanese destroyers *Arashi* and *Nowaki*. Koning made a gallant attempt to get away, but his little ship was soon overwhelmed by a flurry of 5-inch shells. Much of her accommodation was set on fire, and a number of her crew killed. Accepting the hopelessness of the situation, Koning gave the order to abandon ship, and the survivors got away in three lifeboats.

Fortunately for the *Tomohon*'s survivors, they were ignored by the Japanese destroyers, who suddenly left the scene at speed. They had other fish to fry, for the ships fleeing south from Tjilatjap were coming thick and fast. Captain Koning now called the three boats together, carried out a head count, and then set sail for Java, running before a fresh southerly wind. The boats stayed together for a while, but by the time it was dark No. 3 boat, being the deepest loaded boat with thirty-two people on board, had lost touch with the other two. It was this boat that later in the day picked up the five survivors from the Norwegian ship *Prominent*, and was itself found by the *Zaandam* on the morning of the 2nd. The *Tomohon*'s other lifeboats eventually landed on the south coast of Java, where their occupants fell into Japanese hands.

The *Zaandam*'s voyage to Australia was short, but hardly comfortable for her passengers. Jean Dutilh recalls:

The women and children had cabins. In every cabin there were at least six of them. Sailors, soldiers and Lascars on the hatches and in the fore and aft lower decks. The holds were filled with cargo. Only No.5 hatch had a sun tent. The officers stayed on the promenade deck, boat deck, and the poop. The Dutch flying officers on the deck beneath the funnel. Once it started to get a bit colder everybody withdrew to the inner ship as much as possible, in the lounges, the corridors. Under the deck of the promenade deck it was pitch dark; all windows

126

had been painted black. . . . Although it did not rain during the entire crossing it had been rather cold at night. Everyone tried to find a place in the lounges. In case you wished to sleep comfortable on a sofa you had to start your sleeping arrangements at 6 pm. When I went and looked later in the evening it looked like a battleground. People were sleeping on and under the tables. It was a good thing that Fremantle was not too far away in a fast ship like this.

The *Zaandam* with her large complement of evacuees and survivors on board, reached Fremantle on 6 March, being one of the few ships to escape from Tjilatjap and reach her destination safely. Jean Dutilh remained at sea, sailing in various Rotterdam Lloyd ships. In June 1944, he was in the 7118 ton Willemstad-registered *Garoet* when she was sunk in the Indian Ocean by Kurt Freiwald in U-181. Jean Dutilh lost his life in the *Garoet*. Pilot Droste, a reluctant passenger, landed in Fremantle without his family, and many years would pass before he was reunited with them.

The *Zaandam*'s escort for the first few hours after leaving Tjilatjap, the destroyer *Stronghold*, did not escape the Japanese net. She was under orders to make a run for Fremantle, but had been unable to refuel in Tjilatjap, and her tanks were dangerously low. Consequently, Lieutenant-Commander Preytor-Pinney decided to steam at an economic speed of 12–15 knots, a necessary but unfortunate decision. At approximately 0900 on 2 March, when she was some 300 miles south of Bali, *Stronghold* was sighted by a Japanese reconnaissance aircraft, probably a Type 95 Nakajima float plane. After circling several times out of range of the destroyer's guns, the plane flew away, but no one on board the destroyer, which in addition to her normal complement of ninety-two was carrying thirty-two passengers, Royal Naval personnel, escapees from Singapore, had any illusions as to what would happen next. Guns' crews were brought to first readiness – and they waited.

The hours went by, morning progressed into afternoon with no enemy ship or aircraft appearing, and an air of optimism began to spread through the destroyer as she steadily put the miles behind her. By 1730, with the cover of darkness only an hour away, everyone had begun to relax, savouring the prospect of a hot meal and a quiet night. Then, at 1750, a ship was sighted on the starboard quarter. The speculation was that this was a US Navy cruiser, but Preytor-Pinney was not prepared to tempt fate. He ordered the engine-room to make smoke, and increased to full speed.

In her prime, *Stronghold* had been capable of 31 knots, but she was now in her 24th year, and with a lifetime of gruelling service behind her. She was no match for her pursuer, the Japanese heavy cruiser *Maya*. With her destroyers *Arashi* and *Nowaki* in company, the *Maya* gradually overhauled the British destroyer. When the cruiser had closed the range to 16,600 yards, she opened fire with her 8-inch guns.

Mounting only two 4-inch guns with a maximum range of 10,000 yards, *Stronghold* was powerless to retaliate. Preytor-Pinney's only defence was to run and hope to dodge the hail of shells falling around his ship. This he did with remarkable success for another half an hour, but by 1821 the range was down to 11,300 yards, and the Japanese destroyers had joined in with their 5-inch guns. Now there was no escaping the enemy's fire. The shells began to hit home. Lieutenant Ian Forbes, who had previously survived the loss of the *Prince of Wales* and the gunboat *Grasshopper*, now a passenger on board the *Stronghold*, reported:

She (*Maya*) was far faster than us and wriggle and speed as we did, she inexorably crept up on us, but it was not until she was fairly close that she started to score any hits. When she did we knew all about it. Hit after hit was registered in quick succession. The forward tubes were hit, the ship was slowed down considerably and a terrible carnage began on the decks. Then she lost speed alarmingly – I believe there was a fire in the engine-room – ready-use ammunition was used up and it seemed damage prevented hoisting more. The two undamaged torpedoes were fired, but to no effect, when the *Maya* was lying a mile or two on our starboard bow. The Captain (Lieutenant-Commander G.R. Preytor-Pinney) was severely wounded and the last words I heard him say were 'Pass the word for Commander St. Aubyn'. After which the ship finally stopped and was abandoned.

128

Commander St. Aubyn, who like Forbes was a passenger in *Stronghold*, was killed before he reached the bridge. Lieutenant Forbes's report continues:

> The Commanding Officer then collapsed and the First Lieutenant (Lieut. McFarlane RNR) ordered the ship to be abandoned at 1930 (approx.).
>
> When I had seen the upper deck and bridge cleared of able-bodied men I abandoned ship and within 5 minutes the *Stronghold* was torpedoed or blew up and sank instantaneously.
>
> I could see the calcium flare of a Carley float some distance astern. I swam to this and rallied another float to me which I ordered to remain in company.
>
> I was aware of other men in the water, but I could not see them, although the moon was full, because the sea was rough. From the two floats we shouted in unison and received shouts in reply, but the direction and distance could not be judged.
>
> Shortly after dawn 3rd March a KPM steamer, captured the day before by the Japanese, closed and picked up the personnel of the two floats, numbering fifty, consisting of myself, 47 Naval ratings and 2 Chinese stewards. Later that morning we were transferred to the cruiser *Maya* and conveyed to Macassar, Celebes.

The KPM steamer mentioned by Forbes was the Royal Packet Navigation Company's 1021-ton *Bintoehan*, commanded by Captain H.J. van Dijk. She had been captured on 1 March 400 miles south of Tjilatjap by the destroyer *Arashi*, and was on her way to Bali. After handing over the survivors to the *Maya*, she continued on her way north. For reasons unknown, the Japanese had not put a prize crew on board the *Bintoehan*, and Captain van Dijk scuttled his ship on 3 March when nearing the coast of Bali.

While the *Maya* and her destroyers were pounding the *Stronghold* into her watery grave, just over 100 miles due north HMAS *Yarra*, with the depot ship *Anking*, the fleet tanker *Francol*, and the minesweeper MMS 51 in company, was heading south. Although *Stronghold* had sent out a sighting report, which was picked up by the *Yarra*'s wireless office, she had been overwhelmed before she was able to report she was under attack. Ignorant of her fate, *Yarra*'s commander Lieutenant-Commander Rankin maintained the convoy's course and speed, a modest 8½ knots to conserve fuel. Later in the day, the *Yarra* came across two lifeboats containing Captain P.A. Rentema and thirty-three others, survivors of the Royal Packet Navigation Company's 1172-ton *Parigi*. The *Parigi* had left Tjilatjap on 28 February, bound for Bunbury, Western Australia, but had covered no more than 30 miles before she was torpedoed and shelled by Nakamura in I-153. Six of her crew were killed and a number wounded. The remaining thirty-four, Captain Rentema, two deck officers, one engineer and thirty Javanese ratings, escaped in two lifeboats.

During the remainder of that day the horizon remained empty, and the four ships steamed steadily to the south-south-east. At their reduced speed, they would not reach the safety of Australian waters for another four to five days, but the weather was good, and hopes were running high. The only ominous sign appeared that evening, when two enemy reconnaissance planes were seen in the distance, but when the aircraft appeared to ignore the convoy – perhaps they had not seen them – the optimism returned.

Sunrise on the 4th was a glorious spectacle, the sun rising from a flawless horizon to welcome the little convoy to the day. But, unfortunately, as the sun rose, it revealed the topmasts of enemy cruisers bearing down from the north-east. Able Seaman J.R. Archibald of HMAS *Yarra* wrote a vivid account of what followed, which merits quoting in full:

0630   We went to dawn action stations at 0539 and remained there until 0630, by which time it was daylight. 'Hands to Breakfast' was piped and we were standing by awaiting orders from the bridge to carry on. Then the alarms sounded and we looked to see what it was. A force of ships was observed astern of us distance about 8 miles. It had been first sighted, I think, from the bridge. At the same time as the alarms were sounded the convoy was ordered to disperse and a smoke screen was laid.

0635   The force astern was overtaking us very rapidly and at about 0635 fired its first salvo which fell about 200

130

yards astern. *Yarra* was put about and opened fire immediately. One round from *Yarra* struck an 8-inch cruiser on the bridge. *Yarra* then followed the rest of the convoy into the smoke screen and was able to remain hidden from the enemy and free from damage by their shells, which were dropping all around, for ten minutes. During these ten minutes orders were given from the bridge to prepare to abandon ship and hands were busy turning out seaboats and lowering them, cutting lashings on rafts, getting sails for the seaboats, provisioning boats (no food unfortunately was got into the Carley floats), and a variety of jobs associated with the saving of as many lives as possible in what we well knew was going to be the end of our ship.

0645　At 0645 *Yarra* became discernible in the smoke screen and we were immediately hit with a heavy salvo which struck just ahead of the starboard waist demolishing the sick bay. Probably lost by this hit would be Surgeon-Lieutenant W.J. Maclaren-Robinson RAN, SBAR Miekle and a sick bay PO whose name I cannot remember. In addition, approximately 30 Javanese seamen, survivors of the Dutch merchantman *Tarangi* (*Parigi*), which with her captain and two deck officers and one engineer officer had been picked up at 1800 on Sunday 1 March in the Indian Ocean about 24 hours out of the Sunda Strait, were accommodated in the sick bay passageway, and the likelihood is that they all perished with this salvo.

0647　The second salvo was the worst actually encountered throughout the whole action, and it struck and carried away the bridge and surrounding superstructure. The impact was so severe that it practically stopped the ship. Lost by this would almost certainly be the commanding officer, Lt. Cmdr. R.W. Rankin, RAN, the navigating officer, Lt. Dawson, RANR, Lt. N.M. Anderson, RAVR, Lt. G.L. Wright, RAVR, Commander (Gunner) W.D. Bull, PO Josh (Gunner's Mate), Petty Officers

W.E. Smith and R. Parsons, Yeoman of Signals ——,
Leading Seaman ——, Leading Cook W. Briggs, Tel. C.
Simpson and A.B. Peterson. Lost also would be two RN
telegraphists who would be with Tel. Simpson in the
wireless room.

0650 It would be difficult for me to say just how many
salvoes hit the Yarra after the second. Two heavy
cruisers were concentrating on Yarra from a distance of
about 2 miles. Shells were falling in every direction and
the ships we were escorting were being attacked by the
force, which had now spread out. The cruisers had put
up three of their planes, one of which dive-bombed and
sank the motor minesweeper. There were, I believe, 14
survivors and they were picked up and brought to
Fremantle. By what ship I do not know.

Most of the salvoes hit the *Yarra* in the bridge area
and forward of this. Then a salvo hit the engine-room
stopping the engines and putting out all the lights.
Another salvo took No.3 gun, the mainmast and our
after 5-inch. Seaboats were all lost by this gunfire.
Casualties in this phase of the action would probably
include ABs W. Giles, G. Lloyd, K. Banks, R. Oliver, W.
Rushton, E. Moffat and Johnson, three ABs whose
names I cannot remember and the PO in charge of the
after part of the ship.

The *Francol* sank from gunfire about this time. I do
not know if there were any survivors from her.

0655 *Anking* was next to go. She was sunk by gunfire from
the cruisers and destroyers. She sank at about 0655.
There were a few survivors, who I afterwards learned
were picked up by the *Tawali* and taken to Colombo. A
few more were picked up by the Dutch submarine K 11
and taken to Colombo. I have no knowledge of the fate
of any others of the *Anking*'s personnel.

0700 At 0700 orders to abandon ship were given by the 1st
Lt., Lt-Cmdr F. Smith. Two Carley floats were thrown

into the water and 33 of us went over the side and climbed into the floats. Lt-Cmdr Smith did not jump into the water as far as I know and was not saved, my last recollection of him being of him standing on the deck giving orders and getting the men away.

0705   Thirty-three of us managed to gain the two Carley floats. One of the destroyers, similar to the *Hikiki* class, approached to within 100 yards of us. An officer on her bridge had his binoculars on us. I think he was looking for officers. A rope ladder was then lowered from her port waist and one seaboat was turned out. We made no effort to approach them and the destroyers steamed off in the direction of the *Yarra*, which was still afloat. The destroyers then stood off at a distance of about 200 yards from *Yarra* and poured salvo after salvo into her for almost three hours.

0930   The destroyers ceased fire at 0930 with the *Yarra* still afloat. A seaplane from one of the cruisers then dive-bombed *Yarra* from masthead height, dropping one bomb which was a near miss. We all thought that they were rotten shots if they could not hit a stationary ship with no protection from masthead height.

1000   Finally HMAS *Yarra* sank after having withstood almost three hours of battering. The time would be approx 1000. Incidentally, it is desired to add that the seaplane that dropped the bomb seemed to have retractable floats. These matters are very hazy to me now but I have the impression that those of us in the raft commented on this at the time.

1005   The enemy force steamed off. I cannot state on what course. Thirty-three men were then on the two rafts. The rafts remained together for four days and were eventually both picked up by the Dutch submarine K 11. During the course of the five days we were adrift 20 of the 33 men died from exposure. On the afternoon of

Sunday 9 March at 1430 K 11 surfaced near us and took us on board. Those who to my knowledge died whilst on the Carley floats are: on the 3rd day Ldg Sea J. Milling, OS Powell, 4th day OS Weitzerman, the Dutch merchant captain, two Dutch MN officers, CPO W. Holmes, Stoker I. Edwards. 5th day Chief Writer L. Whare, AB J. Oakes, Chief Stoker P. Ryan, Stoker PO C. Prater.

Landed from K 11 at Colombo 18.3.42 at 1000.

General   It is not my opinion that there will be any other survivors besides those already saved. Gunfire destroyed all our boats and we were on the only available rafts. There was nothing else on the ship that would float. The only officer I have not mentioned previously is the Engineer Officer and I think that he would go when we got hit in the engine-room. With him would go whatever other engine-room staff I have not otherwise mentioned. AB Oakes, who was on No.2 gun, told me before he died that Ldg Sea Taylor would not leave his post on the gun and had refused to abandon ship, saying that he would fire the gun on his own. It would not be possible to say whether he was able to do this as there was such confusion in the noise of the salvoes but Oakes said to me 'Buck (Taylor) has got too much guts for these Japs altogether'. Also I would like to mention the courage and determination of Signalman G. Bromilow who although badly wounded in the right leg and from shoulder to shoulder stuck out five days on the raft without a whimper, and would not take an extra ration of water when offered to him.

I would like to conclude by saying that my memory is somewhat hazy on some points but to the best of my knowledge what I have related is correct.

The survivors from HMS *Stronghold* taken aboard the cruiser *Maya* were brought up on deck to witness the end of HMAS *Yarra*. One of them, Able Seaman John Murphy, later commented:

About twenty minutes or half an hour after the commencement of the action we were taken on deck and shown, as they tried to impress us, the might of Japan's Navy. Silently we stood and watched the little sloop, White Ensign flying and guns blazing against the hopeless odds. The *Yarra* was the only ship left afloat, and we could see flames and a great deal of smoke. The two destroyers were circling *Yarra*, which appeared to be stationary, and were pouring fire into her. She was still firing back, as we could see the odd gun flashes. The three cruisers formed line ahead and steamed away from the scene. The last we saw of *Yarra* was a high column of smoke but we were vividly impressed by her fight.

The gun the *Stronghold* eyewitnesses saw firing up to the end of the *Yarra* was manned by 18-year-old Leading Seaman Ronald 'Buck' Rogers, who had refused to abandon ship when the order came. Incensed by what the Japanese had done to his ship, Rogers was loading, aiming and firing one of *Yarra*'s 4-inch guns on his own, a remarkable and brave action that cost him his life. In reality, for all the courageous fight put up by her crew, the *Yarra* had been doomed from the start. The *Maya*'s 8-inch guns, firing at the rate of thirty shells a minute, had merely used her as target practice.

The motor minesweeper MMS 51 was armed only with a few machine-guns, and took no part in the fight, but the depot ship *Anking* and the tanker *Francol*, each armed with a single 4-inch gun, put up a valiant defence. MMS 51 was first to go, blown to pieces by the the Japanese dive-bombers. *Anking* came under fire from one of the cruisers, and was soon on fire and sinking. Her crew abandoned the ship when her decks were awash, getting away in two lifeboats, both of which were damaged by shellfire. In the mêlée, one man, Petty Officer Cook Morgan, was left behind. As the ship went down under him, Morgan decided to swim to the nearest destroyer. He reached the enemy ship, but as he tried to climb aboard, the Japanese sailors, seeing that he still carried a revolver strapped around his waist, tried to stop him by stamping on his fingers as he attempted to lift himself over the gunwale. Morgan lost his temper, drew his gun and fired at them. The ferocity of his response took the Japanese by surprise, and they allowed Morgan to board. As soon as he was on deck, he threw his revolver over the side and surrendered. Thereafter, he reported that he was well treated.

The *Francol*, meanwhile, had been attacked by a formation of Japanese bombers, and was soon reduced to a blazing hulk. Her crew abandoned ship in four boats, which were approached by one of the destroyers. The boat containing *Francol*'s captain was ordered alongside, and its crew taken prisoner. The other boats were allowed to row away.

When the gallant little *Yarra*, on fire and broken in two, finally gave up the unequal fight and sank, the victorious Japanese ships made off to the north-east. Behind them they left a sea covered in wreckage, on which floated a pathetic fleet of heavily loaded boats and rafts containing more than a hundred men.

Later in the evening, the Dutch merchantman *Tawali* rescued fifty-seven men from the *Anking*, but failed to see the two Carley floats from MMS 51, which contained fourteen men. For the next two and a half days the floats drifted at the whim of the currents, their occupants, many of them wounded, scorched by the sun during the day and racked by the cold at night. They were fortunate that on the afternoon of 7 March they were sighted by another Dutch steamer, the *Tjimanoek*, southbound from Tjilatjap.

The *Yarra* survivors, thirty-three men distributed between two Carley floats, including Captain Retema of the *Parigi* and two of his officers, set out to reach Christmas Island, 300 miles to the north-west, but with only two gallons of water and a tin of biscuits between them, they were doomed. One of their number, Bill Witheriff recalled: 'During those five days all except thirteen of us either went mad, died of exhaustion or the sharks had a meal . . . Poor old Charlie just couldn't take it and after three days went silly through drinking salt water and finally jumped over the side.'

They all would have died, had not the Dutch submarine K 11, quite by chance, crossed their path on 9 March and taken on board the thirteen men, all that remained of HMAS *Yarra*'s total complement of 151. Lieutenant-Commander Robert Rankin and all his officers, along with all the other *Parigi* survivors, perished with the *Yarra*.

On being landed in Colombo by K 11, the *Yarra* survivors were fêted as heroes, but it was not until 25 March that the story of the little sloop became known in Australia. At the time, Prime Minister

John Curtin was lavish in his praise, saying, '*Yarra* established for herself and her ship's company a place in naval history alongside such ships as HMS *Jervis Bay* and other ships which have written the epic stories that star our naval history.' Otherwise, the gallantry and sacrifice of Lieutenant-Commander Rankin and his men went unrecognised. No medals were recommended or awarded for this action.

Chapter Eleven

The Flight from Sumatra

Amongst the little ships taking part in the hurried exodus from Singapore on 14 February was the yacht *Cecilia*, owned and sailed in the far off days of peace by Captain Mike Blackwood of the Argyll and Sutherland Highlanders. With Blackwood were forty-three British soldiers, most of them from his own regiment, which had fought a gallant but hopeless rearguard action on the Malaysian peninsula. The senior man on board the *Cecilia* was Brigadier Archie Paris, MC, who had commanded the 12th Indian Brigade in Malaya.

Running the gauntlet of attacking Japanese aircraft, and dodging from island to island, the *Cecilia* reached the east coast of Sumatra unscathed, and on the morning of the 15th entered the mouth of the Indragiri River. Blackwood took his little craft 70 miles up river to Rengat, where he and his passengers went ashore and joined up with a number of other Argylls who had also made good their escape from Singapore.

When the *Cecilia* reached Sumatra, the island was already lost. The island's oilfields, mainly around Palembang in the south, were reputed to produce the finest crude oil in the world, and in great quantities. This made Sumatra a priority target for the oil-starved Japanese, and even as the defences of Singapore crumbled, a large seaborne invasion force was heading for the entrance to the Moesti River, which gave access to Palembang. It was this force that the unfortunate *Li Wo* ran into on the morning of the 13th.

The defence of Palembang and its oilfields was in the hands of about 2000 Dutch troops, mainly native Sumatrans led by

European officers, while the two airfields in the area were defended by men of the 6th RAF Heavy AA Regiment. Despite the Japanese landing being supported by some 270 paratroopers dropped near the airfields, the defenders put up a magnificent fight, with the RAF men depressing their 40mm Bofors guns to the horizontal and firing over open sights. But the Japanese had overwhelming superiority in guns and men, and Palembang, its oilfields and airfields were soon in their hands.

When he became fully aware of the situation to the south, Brigadier Paris decided the time was long past when he and his ragged band of Argylls might have been able to influence the outcome of the battle for Sumatra. The only option open to them was to escape from the island and to find a ship to take them to Australia, Ceylon or India, so that they might fight another day. Paris led his men across the waist of Sumatra, 130 miles by road and rail, to the port of Padang on the west coast.

They arrived in Padang to find the port in a state of complete chaos. The town was packed with military and civilian refugees from the debacle of Singapore, all without leadership and with the same object in mind, escape from Sumatra. The confusion in Padang was made worse by Japanese bombers being almost continuously overhead, raining down death and destruction. Much of the town was in ruins, and the harbour and bay were littered with sunken ships. Very few ships were now calling at the port, and Brigadier Paris and his men, being late arrivals, had a long wait ahead of them.

It was not until 26 February, when the mass exodus from the Dutch East Indies was at its height, that the Argylls found a means of escape from Sumatra. She was the 1035-ton *Rooseboom*, a small inter-island steamer owned by KPM. Built in 1926, the *Rooseboom* had a maximum speed of 10 knots, and accommodation for sixteen 1st Class and thirteen 2nd Class passengers. She was also certified to carry 407 deck passengers. In command was Captain M.C.A. Boon, who had a crew of Dutch officers and Javanese ratings. When she received orders to call at Padang to take on refugees, the *Rooseboom* was on her way from Tandjong Priok to Ceylon.

When the *Rooseboom* sailed from Padang on the evening of the 26th, she had on board, in addition to her crew, a total of 500 evacuees, mainly British military personnel and civilians from Malaya, including the *Cecilia* party. Her accommodation was full, and on deck troops were packed shoulder to shoulder, covering every available square inch. For such a small ship – she was only 230 feet long by 38 feet in the beam – she was grossly, if not dangerously, overloaded, so low in the water that the waves were almost lapping at her rails. More significantly, and this probably escaped the notice of the majority of her passengers, who were grateful to have found a means of escape from the Japanese, the *Rooseboom* carried only four lifeboats, each with a capacity of twenty-eight persons. There were no life-rafts on board.

The *Rooseboom* was under orders to proceed at all speed to Ceylon, 1300 miles to the north. There was, as yet, little sign of Japanese surface ships in the Indian Ocean, but it was believed that several enemy submarines were operating in the vicinity of Sumatra and, of course, there was a real threat from carrier-borne aircraft. With this in mind, one of the first acts of Brigadier Paris and his Argylls was to set up their Bren guns on deck to meet any attack from the air.

In her peacetime voyaging between ports in the Dutch East Indies the *Rooseboom* was rarely pressed for time, and her four-cylinder steam engine had not been pushed beyond a leisurely 10 knots. On this occasion, given the need to move out of range of the Japanese as quickly as possible, Captain Boon prevailed upon his chief engineer to achieve the impossible – which he did. The weather was calm, and with every well-worn plate and rivet in her hull vibrating madly, the gallant little ship worked up to an unheard-of speed of 11 knots.

Two nights passed without incident, and on the morning of the 28th Boon felt confident enough to pass word around the ship that she was now out of range of Japanese land-based bombers, and therefore reasonably safe. This lifted a cloud of uncertainty that had been hanging over the ship, and even those unfortunates packed on the open deck, who had endured two days of extreme discomfort, raised a cheer. That night, Brigadier Paris invited a number of his officers to share a warm beer with him. Like so many men who had come through so much danger and hardship fighting ashore, they had supreme confidence in the ship that was taking them to safety, and they drank a toast to arrival in Colombo, then less than forty-eight hours steaming away. Five hours later, just as midnight approached, the torpedo struck.

Since torpedoing the Norwegian ship *Eidsvold* off Christmas Island on 20 January, I-159 had cruised south of Java and Sumatra without further success, and with her fuel and provisions running low, Lieutenant Yoshimatsu had been forced to take her into the new Japanese submarine base at Penang. Back at sea in February, with orders to sit astride the escape route from the Dutch islands to Ceylon, I-159 spent most of the month patrolling in mid-Indian Ocean, and in spite of the number of Allied ships fleeing north-wards, failed to find a single target for her torpedoes. Yoshimatsu was on the point of requesting permission to hunt elsewhere when, late on the 28th, the *Rooseboom* came over the horizon.

It took only one torpedo in her engine-room to bring the heavily laden *Rooseboom* to a sudden halt. She heeled over to port, and began to sink at once. Panic broke out on her crowded decks, men, women and children, who moments before had been settling down for the night, scrambling in all directions, their screams and shouts drowned out by the loud hiss of escaping steam and the rush of water as it poured into the breached hull. Captain Boon and his officers went immediately to the boat deck, where they discovered that the two lifeboats on the port side had been destroyed by the blast. On the other side of the deck, a crowd of frightened humanity surged around the remaining two boats, one of which was already full. As Boon watched in horror, the forward falls of this boat parted under the weight, and the bow dropped, catapulting most of the occupants into the sea. The other boat was lowered in a rush, and it was holed in the bow when it slammed against the ship's side.

When dawn came on 1 March, all that was left of the *Rooseboom* was a sea of broken wreckage, in which floated one leaking lifeboat, so crowded that the waves were lapping over its gunwales. Surrounding the drifting boat was a mass of humanity engaged in a grim struggle to stay alive, some hanging on to the boat, others treading water determinedly. Around them floated the dead bodies, already bloated and obscene. It was a pathetic sight with which to greet the new day.

The only lifeboat to survive the sinking of the *Rooseboom* resem-bled her mother ship as she had been a few hours previously, packed with humanity. Measuring only 28 feet long by 8 feet in the beam, and certified to carry twenty-eight people – and at that it would be overcrowded – the boat had on board no fewer than

141

eighty survivors. There was no room to sit down, and the occupants were forced to stand shoulder to shoulder. As uncomfortable as that may have been, they were far better off than the fifty-five unfortunates still in the water and hanging on to the sides of the boat to keep afloat. In the boat were Captain Boon, his Chief Officer, Chief Engineer and twelve Javanese ratings, Brigadier Paris and sixty-one troops, and only three women. These were Gertrude Nunn, wife of the Director of Works in Singapore, the Chief Officer's wife, and a young Chinese girl, Doris Lim. Boon and his senior officers, who were on the bridge when the torpedo struck, were the only ones fully clothed, the others being naked or nearly naked. As to provisions, the boat contained forty-eight 12oz tins of corned beef, two 7lb tins of fried spiced rice, forty-eight tins of condensed milk, and six one-litre bottles of fresh water, which at some time had been put in the boat as extra rations. The bulk of the food and fresh water, along with most of the small gear, had been washed overboard when the boat was swamped on launching. What remained, shared amongst a total of 135 survivors, was unlikely to last long.

The situation could not have been more hopeless. The boat was adrift 500 miles from the nearest land with little hope of rescue, the *Rooseboom* having gone down so fast that no SOS went out, and it was unlikely that any passing ship would come upon them. Nor could they hope to do more than drift at the mercy of wind and current, the boat being too crowded to allow sails to be hoisted, or what few oars remained to be shipped. But although their plight was obvious to everyone, there was an air of determination in the boat. Brigadier Paris, suffering from internal injuries received when he was dragged down by the sinking ship, and clad only in a borrowed shirt, took command of the troops and instituted a rota system, whereby all uninjured men would take a four-hour spell in the water each day to relieve those clinging to the sides of the boat. He also supervised the construction of a raft made from pieces of wooden debris lashed together. When completed, the raft supported twenty men. It was submerged under their weight, doing little more than keeping their heads above water.

Captain Boon did his best to raise morale by assuring everyone that, although no SOS had been sent out, Colombo must be aware that the *Rooseboom* was due to arrive on the 3rd, and a search would be set in motion when she failed to turn up. For this reason, he said, they should remain in the vicinity of the sinking, and not attempt to make for the land – not that, if the facts were faced, there was much else they could do. Knowing full well in his own mind that they might be in for a long wait, Boon set the daily ration of a tablespoonful of water at sunrise, a similar amount of condensed milk mixed with water at night, and one tin of corned beef to be shared between twelve each day. At this early stage, no one had much appetite for the spicy fried rice.

And so the long, agonizing wait began. At first, there was optimism, and every imagined speck on the horizon was hailed as a rescue ship coming for them. But as the days went by, and then the weeks, a merciless sun beating down during the day, and the chill of the nights taking their toll of the naked and half-naked wretches in and around the boat, hope was replaced by abject despair. The dying had begun early on, first those in the water, some taken by sharks, others quietly going mad and allowing themselves to drift away and sink slowly into the deep and strangely welcoming sea. Those lucky enough to be inside the gunwales of the crowded boat fared only marginally better, and as the food and water ran out, most succumbed to the effects of drinking sea water, which in its turn drove them mad. Violence broke out, which at times resulted in murder and, it is said, cannibalism. When, twenty-six days after the *Rooseboom* sank, the boat reached land, only five out of the original 135 survivors were still alive. They were Corporal Walter Gibson of the Argyll and Sutherland Highlanders, the Chinese girl Doris Lim and three Javanese seamen.

Borne on the Equatorial Current, the *Rooseboom*'s lifeboat had drifted first to the east, then south-east for nearly 800 miles, until one night it was thrown ashore on Sipora Island, only 80 miles from the port of Padang, which the ill-fated ship had left twenty-six days earlier.

As soon as the boat grounded on the beach, the three Javanese seamen disappeared into the mangrove swamps fronting the shore without a backward glance. Walter Gibson and Doris Lim, too weak to move far, crawled up the beach until they thought they were safe from the breaking waves, and collapsed into a deep sleep. It was still dark when they awoke – perhaps the same night, or perhaps twenty-four hours later, they had no means of knowing.

143

They crawled further inland, until they found water. It was muddy and it stank, but it was fresh. They drank and fell asleep again.

It was full daylight when they came out of their drugged sleep to find themselves surrounded by savage-looking natives armed with bows and arrows and machetes. They fully expected to be hacked to pieces, and their fear turned to amazement when they received not blows but green coconuts. They gorged themselves on the cool milk and sweet white flesh of the nuts, the first real sustenance they had enjoyed for so many weeks. Later, they were taken by canoe some way along the coast, and left on the beach near a village.

The village turned out to be inhabited by Malays, brought there as transportees in the days when the island of Sipora was a Dutch penal settlement. They were well cared for by the Malays, and they stayed six weeks in the village, during which time they steadily regained their strength. It was in these long idle days that Gibson discovered that Doris Lim had worked for British Intelligence in China, and was on the Japanese wanted list.

The idyll came to an end with the arrival of the Japanese in the village. With no escape avenue open to them, the two survivors were arrested by the Japanese and were taken back to Padang, arriving there on 18 May, seventy-nine days after they had set sail from the port in the *Rooseboom*. When they arrived in Padang they were separated, Gibson being subjected to a prolonged and brutal interrogation, his captors being not so much interested in him as in the espionage activities of Doris Lim, about which Gibson was totally ignorant. The two met again briefly, but after that Gibson did not see the Chinese girl again. Later, he said he was told that she had been shot by the Japanese. Another version of her disappearance emerged after the war, a report that she had married a Chinese peasant farmer in Sumatra who had murdered her in early 1945. Whatever happened to Doris Lim may never be known, but it seems certain that she survived the sinking of the *Rooseboom*, only to die an untimely death somewhere in the Indies before the end of the war.

Gibson spent a month in Padang, before being moved with other prisoners to a camp at Medan, in the far north of Sumatra. In June 1944 he was one of over 700 Allied prisoners of war who were herded aboard the transport *Harrikuku Maru*. Originally the 33-year-old *Van Waerwijck*, another of KPM's fleet of inter-island steamers, scuttled in Tandjong Priok harbour ahead of the Japanese invasion in March, the *Harrikuku Maru* was in a sorry state, running with red rust and crawling with rats. Two days out of Medan in a convoy of eight ships escorted by four river gunboats, she was torpedoed in the Straits of Malacca by the British submarine *Truculent*. For the second time in two years, Walter Gibson found himself struggling in the water as his ship went down. This time he was more fortunate in that he was picked up within an hour or two by one of the other ships in the convoy. He ended the war in a prisoner of war camp in Singapore. Walter Gibson was the only survivor of the *Rooseboom*'s final voyage capable of writing an account of what happened to the ship, her passengers and crew. His account was a lurid one, containing tales of murder and cannibalism, and portraying himself as the only man able to exercise control in the lifeboat in the later days of its long voyage. It has been revealed in recent years that he was known by reputation in the Argyll and Sutherland Highlanders as a 'Walter Mitty' character, much given to fantasizing. His rank at the time of his capture was corporal, but he is said to have 'promoted' himself to sergeant when interviewed by the Press after the war. He later claimed to have been commissioned in the field as lieutenant, and posed as an officer wearing the ribbon of the Military Cross, to which he was not entitled.

The last ship out of Padang, sailing on 10 March with the Japanese at the gates of the port, was British India Line's 4360-ton passenger/cargo ship *Chilka*. Taken into service by the Admiralty as a troopship after Pearl Harbor, she was on this occasion carrying no troops, most probably because by this time all Allied troops had either been taken prisoner, or had already fled the island in other ships. She had on board a total complement of 16 British officers, 3 gunners, 104 Lascar ratings, and 4 passengers. In command was Captain W. Bird.

In the absence of any orders to the contrary, Captain Bird had decided to make for Colombo, calculating that at the *Chilka*'s best speed of 13½ knots they would reach Ceylon in just over four days. It seemed unlikely that his ship would come to any harm on such a short passage. He was proved to be wrong.

Lying in wait for escaping ships like the *Chilka* was one of the Imperial Japanese Navy's most formidable submarines. Displacing nearly 2000 tons, mounting two 12-cm guns, and with a surface speed of 24 knots, I-2, commanded by Lieutenant-Commander Hiroshi Inada, was at sea and hungry for her first victim.

On the morning of the 11th, the *Chilka* was just seventeen hours out of Padang, when the gunners manning their 4-inch on the poop reported a submarine coming up fast astern, and already within 2000 yards of the ship. Without hesitation, Captain Bird ordered his gunners to open fire. A running fight followed, with the *Chilka*'s 4-inch gamely hitting back at the superior firepower of I-2's big guns. But it was all over in twenty minutes. Japanese shells hit the ready-use ammunitions lockers on the poop, and the resulting explosion knocked out the 4-inch, killing one of the gun's crew. By this time, the *Chilka*'s accommodation was burning fiercely, nine of her fourteen lifeboats had been wrecked, two Lascar seamen lay dead, and three officers were wounded.

It was now obvious to Captain Bird that further resistance would only result in more loss of life, so he stopped the ship, signalled the submarine by lamp that he was abandoning ship, and ordered his crew to take to the boats.

Uncharacteristically for a Japanese submarine commander, many of whom were already acquiring a reputation for murdering survivors of merchant ships, Hiroshi Inada ordered his guns' crews to cease fire, allowing the evacuation of *Chilka*'s crew without further casualties. Once clear of the ship, Captain Bird stood off and watched his command sink. When the submarine had moved off, he set course for the nearest land, the islands off the coast of Sumatra, some 200 miles to the east. Five days later, the boats came ashore on Nias Island, which lies 50 miles off Sumatra, and 220 miles north of Padang.

After a short trek overland through swamp and jungle, the survivors reached an isolated mission hospital, where the wounded were able to get attention. It was while they were at the hospital that Captain Bird learned that the Japanese had landed on the island and were advancing towards the station. He had no intention of spending the rest of the war in a Japanese prison camp, so he called for volunteers to take a boat to Ceylon. The response was not enthusiastic; only Chief Engineer Button, Second Engineer Sanderson, Third Engineer McCauley, Fourth Engineer Stacey, the ship's doctor, H. Mason Dixon, and Seaman Gunner Adams were willing to attempt the voyage.

Thirty-five days after setting out from Nias Island in a steel lifeboat provided for them by the Dutch District Officer, Bird and his volunteer boat's crew were picked up by the Greek vessel *Pipina* in the Bay of Bengal, in the vicinity of Madras. They had covered a distance of 1,160 miles under oars and sail, and all seven men were little the worse for their long voyage when they stepped ashore in India.

The remainder of the *Chilka* survivors, who had been left behind on Nias Island, were taken prisoner by the Japanese and spent the rest of the war in a prison camp in Malaya. It emerged later that one officer earlier reported as taken prisoner, Assistant Purser H.W. Munroe, had been lost when the *Chilka* went down. Two others, Third Officer George Hodges and Fourth Engineer John Kerr, suffered the worst of all fates, being lost on 26 June 1944 when the Japanese ship transporting them between camps was sunk by an American submarine.

Royal Dutch Mail Line's *Poelau Bras*, under the command of Captain P.G. Crietee was among the mass exodus of ships from Tjilatjap on the night of 27/28 February. She was a big, powerful motor ship, 9278 tons gross, with twin screws driven by 1450nhp Sulzer diesels, giving her a sea speed of 15 knots. Making use of her superior speed, by the morning of 2 March she was already nearly 700 miles into the Indian Ocean, and in the opinion of Captain Crietee, out of range of Japanese land-based aircraft. Freedom was beckoning, until a message was received from Bandoeng ordering the ship to return to Tjilatjap to pick up refugees. Having come this far, Crietee might have been forgiven for turning a deaf ear to the recall, perhaps pleading a weak signal misunderstood over such a long distance. But this was not just a routine call to pick up cargo. Lives were at stake. The *Poelau Bras* reversed course and retraced her steps.

Within sight of Tjilatjap harbour, Crietee received another radio message diverting him to Wijnkoop Bay, also known as Pelabuhan Ratu, 150 miles to the west, near the Sunda Strait, where she was to take on board senior Army and Navy officers, and Shell employees with their wives and children. The mission was urgent.

The diversion proved providential for the *Poelau Bras*, for soon after she reached Wijnkoop Bay, Japanese planes attacked Tjilatjap in force, laying waste to the port and sinking any ships remaining in the harbour. Captain Crietee realised that the whole of Java was about to fall into enemy hands, and he lost no time in embarking his passengers. No accurate figure survives of the number of refugees the *Poelau Bras* took on board, but the best estimate is 150, consisting of high ranking Army and Navy officers, including Rear Admiral J.J.A. van Staveren, second in command of the Royal Netherlands Navy in the Dutch East Indies, senior employees of the Shell oil company and their families, and about eighty other Navy personnel. When she sailed from Wijnkoop Bay, on the night of 6 March, she had on board a total complement of between 240 and 260 persons, among them a number of crew members from her sister ship *Poelau Tello*, bombed and sunk off Sumatra some days earlier.

The *Poelau Bras* was the last Allied merchant ship to leave Java, which was soon to surrender to the Japanese. She had orders to make for Colombo with her precious cargo, first steering to the south for 200 miles to ensure that she was well clear of the coast of Sumatra before altering course to the north-west. She might well have got away, if the bad luck she appeared to be trailing in her wake had not again taken a hand. It so happened that, on the morning of the 7th, when the *Poelau Bras* was some 50 miles to the north-west of Christmas Island and about to alter course for Colombo, the battleships *Haruna* and *Kongo* were shelling the lonely island outpost. Aircraft from the carrier *Soryu* joined in the bombardment, and it was one of these that, quite by chance, sighted the *Poelau Bras*.

The Dutch merchantman was zig-zagging at the time, for Captain Crietee, believing she was well out of range of land-based aircraft, was anxious not to present an easy target for Japanese submarines. The single high-flying aircraft passed over at 0900 without apparently paying much attention to the *Poelau Bras*, but an hour later the heavy drone of engines in the east announced the arrival of a flight of nine Japanese 'Val' dive bombers. The 'Vals', each carrying an 800 lb bomb load, and veterans of the attack on Pearl Harbor, came in from the sun in line astern, stopping the fleeing ship with a well-aimed bomb straight down her funnel.

Within minutes she was on fire and sinking by the stern. Captain Crietee gave the order to abandon ship.

Four of the *Poelau Bras*'s seven lifeboats had been destroyed, and one could not be launched. The remaining two boats and two rafts left the sinking ship carrying 116 survivors. Those who were left, between 120 and 150, depending on how many were on board, were either dead, or lying wounded on deck as the ship sank under them. A survivor, Franciscus Zantvoort, a seaman in the Royal Dutch Navy, later wrote:

> After four days in a lifeboat, we came ashore near Kroe (now Crui), the people were reservedly friendly, we heard that a village head had informed the Japanese about our presence. After about a week the Japanese arrived with trucks, they made quite a show of it, surrounding us with machine-guns and a lot of shouting, which made it all very frightening; a funny part was that the village head who wanted to show off as the man who had informed them, got quite a beating because they found him to be in their way.
>
> The treatment by the Japanese in the POW camps was atrocious, we had to work hard under abominable conditions with a minimum of food, beatings were common. Other punishments for the slightest trespass were, e.g. standing at attention for hours in the merciless sun or the prisoners standing in line opposite each other and then beating each other, and you better beat hard the first time, otherwise the Japs would give you a lesson how it was supposed to be done . . .

Frans Zantvoort spent the remaining years of the war in various Japanese camps in Sumatra, surviving despite the most horrendous conditions. His summing up of the final days of his captivity contained some simple logic:

> . . . The situation became very desperate, towards the end there were about 300 prisoners left and people were dying at the rate of sometimes eight a day, we did not have the strength anymore to give them a proper burial, they were rolled in a mat and dragged to the edge of the camp and shoved under the barbed wire and left lying in the jungle. And then our

rescue came because of the A-bombs on Nagasaki and Hiroshima, which also cost the lives of thousands of Japanese, but the alternative would have been an extensive bombing and invasion of Japan to end the war, which was averted and thus saved the lives of millions of others, both Americans and Japanese and prisoners such as me. As a matter of fact, right after the war, documents were found which showed that the Japanese were about to kill all remaining prisoners anyhow.

With the sinking of the *Poelau Bras* Admiral Nagumo's ships had come to the end of their task in Dutch East Indies' waters, leaving the islands totally under Japanese control. The fleet now returned to its base at Staring Bay in the Celebes. Very soon, it would move westwards into the Indian Ocean, where the Royal Navy still held sway.

Chapter Twelve

The Net is Spread Wider

At the end of May 1942, with no suitable targets remaining in the East, the submarines of the Japanese Imperial Navy were obliged to look elsewhere. Five boats of the 8th Submarine Squadron, I-10, I-16, I-18, I-20 and I-30, were sent west to try their luck in the Mozambique Channel, the route used by Allied merchant ships sailing to and from India. In the van was I-20, commanded by Lieutenant-Commander T. Yamada, who on the night of 30 May made an audacious attack on the British base at Diego Suarez in northern Madagascar. Yamada launched a midget submarine, which penetrated the harbour defences and torpedoed the old battle ship HMS *Ramillies* and the tanker *British Loyalty*. *Ramillies* was able to limp down to Durban for repairs, but the tanker was sunk. This audacious attack set the alarm bells ringing in the Admiralty, who had not expected the Japanese to penetrate so far to the west. The bells rang even louder when Yamada moved into the Mozambique Channel and followed up his initial success by sinking no fewer than seven merchantmen, totalling more than 35,000 tons, in just over three weeks. The first of his victims was the Panamanian motor vessel *Johnstown*.

The 5086-ton *Johnstown*, ex-Danish ship *Neil Maersk*, had been taken over by the US Government in July 1941 and given to Isthmian Lines of New York to manage. She remained under the command of Captain Adolph U. Rorup and was manned by her original thirty-seven man Danish crew, supplemented by a team of six US Navy Armed Guard gunners led by Ensign Henry A. Robertson.

151

At dawn on 5 June 1942, the *Johnstown* was at the northern end of the Mozambique Channel and bound south on a voyage from Karachi to a US port via Lourenço Marques in ballast. She was sailing unescorted, making good a speed of around 12 knots, and at that time not zig-zagging. It was reported by Ensign Robertson that the ship's navigation lights had been switched on for much of the night. If this was correct, then it was a grave dereliction of duty by those on watch on the bridge, and almost certainly led to the loss of their ship. Certainly, if the lights were burning, Lieutenant-Commander Yamada would have had no difficulty in finding and following the ship in the darkness. As the sky lightened in the east, he moved in.

At 0600 the bridge telephone rang, rudely disturbing the peace of the early morning. It was the Armed Guard gunners on watch on the poop reporting that they had seen a torpedo passing within 600 yards of the stern.

The Officer of the Watch hit the alarm bell, bringing the *Johnstown*'s crew tumbling from their bunks, but few of them had reached the deck before Yamada's second torpedo ploughed into the starboard side amidships. The explosion ripped open the main deck, destroyed the starboard lifeboat, and started a number of serious fires. The *Johnstown* listed heavily to starboard, and slowly lost way through the water. Captain Rorup gave the order to abandon ship.

The two Armed Guard gunners stationed on the poop had been blown in the air by the explosion of the first torpedo, and were seriously injured when they landed on the deck below. Otherwise, only Captain Rorup and two crew members were slightly injured. All forty-three men were later picked up by the British ship *Tasmania* and the New Zealand hospital ship *Maunganui*.

Yamada went on to sink the 5209-ton Greek ship *Christos Markettos*, the British steamer *Mahronda* of 7926 tons, the 2052-ton Panama-flag *Hellenic Trader*, the 5063-ton British motor vessel *Clifton Hall*, the Norwegian steamer *Goviken*, 4854 tons and the 5311-ton British tanker *Steaua Romana*.

With all American naval forces occupied in the Pacific, and the Royal Navy unable to spare ships from its tiny Eastern Fleet for escorts, the Japanese submarines soon found they had a free hand in the Indian Ocean. In June 1942 they sank another 74,678 tons in the Mozambique Channel alone. Among that total was the British steamer *Mundra*, a 7341-ton ship registered in Glasgow.

The *Mundra*, a 13-knot passenger/cargo ship owned by the British India Steam Navigation Company, on a voyage from India to the United Kingdom via Durban, sailed unwittingly into the mayhem of the Mozambique Channel and immediately became heavily involved. On 2 July she was in the vicinity of Juan de Nova Island when a lifeboat was sighted. This contained the Captain, Third Officer and three ratings from the Swedish ship *Eknaren*, sunk by I-16 on 1 July, and the Captain and four Chinese ratings from the Norwegian steamer *Goviken*, sunk by I-20 on 30 June, and picked up by the *Eknaren* on the same day. Three days later, when she was near the coast just south of Lourenço Marques, the *Mundra* came across another lifeboat. This carried the Captain and two ratings from the Dutch ship *De Weert*, sunk by I-18 on 1 July. Second Officer J.W. Killan, of the *Mundra*, takes up the story:

> Keeping close to the coast, the vessel passed close to Cape St. Lucia Light, abeam at eight miles at about 2330 on the 5th. The moon rose shortly before 1 o'clock and the vessel proceeded on 220° course and was not zig-zagging. At 0100 a shot was fired at her from the starboard quarter at close range, estimated 800 yards. A second shot followed immediately. The Captain came on the bridge instantly, ordered emergency stations and hard a' starboard helm, and gun's crew to open fire.
>
> Two shots were then fired in quick succession which struck the amidships accommodation on the port side setting the whole lot blazing furiously and completely enveloping the top of the engine-room. Meanwhile the helm was put hard a' port and a double ring for best possible speed given on the engine-room telegraph. The Radio Officer was then instructed to despatch an SSSS message.
>
> The submarine had still not been sighted from the bridge and no reports had come through the lookouts.
>
> By this time the native crew had panicked and commenced lowering lifeboats themselves. No order was given to abandon ship. The fire spread to the whole of the amidships accommodation and into No.4 hold, the tween deck of which was full

of safety matches. Aided by a north-westerly wind force 4, freshening, the blaze took good hold. Further shots demolished the radio room and the bridge was collapsing. Some boats by this time had been launched or had been rendered useless by fire or the results of the panic handling by the native crew. The vessel was then almost stopped.

I proceeded to the foredeck and launched the starboard liferaft. The Captain then shouted down from the bridge to know if anyone was launching the forward rafts, to which I replied that I was in the act of doing so. I got on to this raft which drifted astern of the vessel and had been overladen with survivors swimming around in the water. The raft then drifted forward of the ship and shortly after passing amidships a dull explosion took place, the ship's side was seen to buckle and her back broken. No track of the torpedo was seen by me. The explosion occurred approximately twenty-five minutes after the commencement of the attack. The raft was abreast of No.1 hatch at the time that the bow came upright out of the water and the vessel sank. The wind, sea and swell got up but the raft kept us just afloat until a lifeboat was sighted when dawn came in. We paddled to the boat, reaching it at about 2 pm and boarded to find three survivors, one European and two natives were there. The European 5th Engineer had baled this boat from the waterlogged state and we were thus able to make use of it. Another raft was in sight and we proceeded towards them eventually taking them in tow owing to the excessive numbers already in the boat. At about 1500 a vessel was sighted which proved to be the *Dundrum Castle*. We had taken the towed raft party on board the lifeboat for the night. We were all picked up by the *Dundrum Castle* at 5 pm approx. on the 6th, proceeded to Durban and landed on the morning of the 7th.

The *Mundra* was a victim of the Japanese submarine I-18, commanded by Lieutenant-Commander K. Otani. I-18, a large submarine of 2180 tons displacement, was armed with a 5½-inch deck gun, which she used with devastating effect. It was the bursting of these large calibre shells that caused much of the panic amongst the *Mundra*'s Indian crew members. As a result of their

154

premature launching of the lifeboats, ninety-three of them are said to have lost their lives. Only one officer was lost.

The Japanese submarines remained in the western part of the Indian Ocean until October 1942, by which time, with increased British naval and air activity in the area, they were finding it increasingly difficult to carry out their unrestricted warfare against Allied shipping. At the same time, the Americans had recovered from the shock of Pearl Harbor, and their Navy was hitting back in the Pacific. The I-boats were needed elsewhere, and by the middle of the month most had retired eastwards. However, there was no respite for the Allied merchantmen, for the Japanese boats were replaced in the Indian Ocean by a far greater menace, German Type IXC U-boats.

The Type IXCs were large long-range submarines, 1144 tons displacement, 77 metres long, and with a cruising range of nearly 14,000 miles. They were armed with twenty-two torpedoes and a 105mm deck gun. Their success in the Indian Ocean was immediate. Others of their ilk were at work in the Atlantic in the region of the Equator. It was one of these that brought an untimely end to the career of the *Zaandam*.

In October 1942 the war in North Africa was rapidly moving to a mighty crescendo. The advance of the Afrika Corps into Egypt had been decisively halted at El Alamein, and preparations were well in hand for a last great battle, which would push Rommel westwards into the hands of British and American forces soon to land on the beaches of Morocco and Algeria. In order to sustain this battle, which would be fought over 1,500 miles of difficult desert terrain, a vast amount of arms and ammunition was needed. This was already on its way across the Atlantic from America.

At 8 o'clock on the morning of 7 October, the 4700-ton *Firethorn*, loaded dangerously near to her marks with tanks, guns, ammunition and stores, was 60 miles to the west of the Cape of Good Hope, and heading for Cape Town to refuel, before rounding the Cape for Suez. The *Firethorn*, flying the flag of Panama, was the Danish motor vessel *Norden*, taken over by the American War Administration on the fall of Denmark, and now under the management of the United States Lines of New York. In command was Captain Paul F. Schultz, who headed a cosmopolitan crew hailing from Denmark, Holland, Belgium, Portugal, Russia, China and Canada. Her guns were manned by twenty-one US Armed Guard gunners, led by Lieutenant (Jg) Robert H. Berkley, USNR.

Nearing the end of a twenty-two day passage from New York, which had been without incident, Captain Schultz was of the opinion that the worst of the danger was past. He was not to know that Carl Emmermann, in U-172, was lying in wait for an easy target like the heavily-laden *Firethorn.*

At precisely 0830 Emmermann fired a spread of two torpedoes, one of which hit the *Firethorn* on the port side directly below her bridge, blowing a huge hole in her hull. Moments later, Emmermann's second torpedo exploded in the Danish ship's engine-room, effectively delivering the *coup de grâce.* The *Firethorn* took on a heavy list to port, and sank in less than two minutes.

The order to abandon ship was given soon after the first torpedo struck, but reality proved to be far removed from the practice drills carried out during the voyage. The port lifeboat had been destroyed in the explosion, and the ship had developed such a heavy list to port that the starboard boat could not be launched. Captain Schultz and nine of his crew, including two Armed Guard gunners, were dead, and those who survived jumped over the side before the ship went down. Fortunately, four life-rafts and a small work boat floated off the *Firethorn* as she sank. The boat was found bottom up, but was righted and used to pick up those in the water and put them aboard the rafts. The rafts were lashed together, and six men then set off in the work boat to reach the coast. They were picked up later in the day by the corvette HMS *Rockrose.* Next day, *Rockrose* and a minesweeper searched the area and found the life-rafts.

In all, fifty-one survivors from the *Firethorn* were landed in Cape Town on 9 October. There they joined 118 survivors from four other US merchant ships, the *Chicksaw City, Coloradan, Examelia* and *Swiftsure,* all sunk off the Cape by U-boats within days of the *Firethorn,* who were waiting for a ship home.

Following her epic voyage from Tjilatjap to Fremantle carrying more than 1,200 refugees earlier in the year, the Holland America motor vessel *Zaandam* was back in more familiar waters, trading between Africa and the Americas. On 24 October 1942, under the command of Captain J.P. Wepster, she sailed from Cape Town, bound for New York with 8000 tons of chrome and copper ores and 600 tons of general cargo. Her crew numbered 130, including eighteen US Armed Guard gunners, and once again she carried refugees from the war, in this case the 169 men who had lost their ships to the U-boats off the Cape, among them the *Firethorn*'s crew.

Once clear of Table Bay, the *Zaandam* worked up to full speed and began to zig-zag around a north-westerly course which would take her south of the islands of St. Helena and Ascension, and thence midway between the rocky islets of Fernando de Noronha and St. Paul, which stand sentinel off the coast of Brazil. The long passage up the South Atlantic passed without incident, and the *Zaandam*, making good a speed of nearly 17 knots, passed between the islets on the first day of November.

Morning star sights on Tuesday put the ship just over seven days away from New York. She would soon come under the umbrella of long-range Catalinas flying from the West Indies and, partly induced by the sweltering heat – they were less than a degree north of the Equator – both crew and passengers had settled into a relaxed routine. This proved to be a costly mistake. Lurking beneath the calm blue sea was the long-range U-cruiser U-174. At the periscope of U-174 was Fregattenkapitän Ulrich Thilo, who like his command was new to this deadly game of cat and mouse. Thilo had opened his score only twenty-four hours before with the sinking of the small British cargo steamer *Elmdale*, and was looking for more successes. In the case of the *Zaandam*, she was a large ship and travelling fast, unusual for the run-of-the-mill Allied merchantman. Thilo suspected she might be a Q-ship or armed raider. He approached her with caution, patiently stalking her throughout the day, and by late afternoon had finally manoeuvred his boat into position for a clear shot. His aim was true, and at 1627 his first torpedo found its mark in the *Zaandam*'s vitals, blasting open her engine-room. The force of the explosion completely destroyed the main engines, put the steering gear out of action, and demolished much of the accommodation above the engine-room. Seaman Second Class Basil D. Izzi, one of the *Zaandam*'s Armed Guard gunners, wrote many years later:

I was torpedoed on November 2nd on a Tuesday afternoon about 4 o'clock. It was a clear day and the sun was shining bright. About 4.15 we were in my cabin playing cards, four of the fellows besides myself. Our radio man walked in and told us our position, where we were and everything. He just walked out and as soon as he walked out our first torpedo struck us. We got up and ran out to the door, we were trying to get to the guns but the shortest way was blocked by the wreckage from the torpedo from topside, so we had to go back inside the ship and through the lounge up on the next deck, the easiest way we could get to the guns. When we were getting there we saw the ship's crew was letting the rafts get underway . . .

The gunners met a great deal of confusion on deck. Most of the *Zaandam*'s crew were preparing to abandon ship, but Captain Wepster had other ideas. It was his opinion that the explosion in the engine-room was not that of a torpedo, but a cylinder head blowing on one of the diesel engines. He was unable to stop the life-rafts being launched, which was premature anyway, for the ship was still under way, but he did call a halt to the boats being lowered. He also countermanded the orders of the Gunnery Officer, Ensign James Maddox, who had sent his men to the guns. What prompted Captain Wepster's decisions cannot be explained, for it was obvious to everyone that his ship, her engine-room flooded, was already sinking.

The situation was clarified beyond doubt a few minutes later, when Ulrich Thilo put a second torpedo into the *Zaandam*, and dragged down by the sheer deadweight of her cargo of ores, she sank bow-first in less than two minutes. Those who were able to jumped over the side, but some, in that brief opportunity afforded them, succeeded in launching the three lifeboats that were still intact – three others had been destroyed by the explosions. Unfortunately, No. 2 boat capsized on hitting the water, and Chief Engineer Ebbeler and a Javanese steward from the *Zaandam* were lost, but when this boat had been righted by several survivors, they began picking up others from the water and from rafts in the vicinity. Eventually, a total of sixty survivors were on board. Nos. 1 and 4 boats held seventy-two and thirty-four respectively.

After the *Zaandam* had gone down, Ulrich Thilo brought U-174 to the surface and approached the drifting lifeboats, mainly to satisfy his curiosity about his victim's identity. He questioned Second Officer Karssen, who revealed only the name of his ship, her last port, and her destination. Thilo then left the survivors to their fate. U-174 sank only two more ships, before meeting her end at the hands of American aircraft off Nova Scotia in April 1943.

Of the *Zaandam*'s lifeboats, Nos. 1 and 4 were picked up by the American tanker *Gulfstate* on the morning of 7 November, and landed at Belem next day. Unfortunately, two badly injured survivors died on board the *Gulfstate* before she reached port. No. 2 boat, with Second Officer W. Broekhof in charge, landed on a deserted part of the Brazilian coast on the 10th. Shortly after she reached the shore, two of the injured men died. With the help of some local fishermen, Broekhof and Captain Matthews of the *Swiftsure* sailed to the nearby village of Pharo, but could find no one to help them. Broekhof then borrowed a horse and rode to the nearest police station, from which he sent a message to the British Consul in Paranaiba, who then informed the American Consul in Belem. The survivors were eventually taken to Sao Luis, where they were hospitalized. When the final count was made, it was established that of the 299 men on board the *Zaandam* 162 had survived, while 137, including Captain Wepster, had died. But that was not the end of the story.

Twenty-year-old Armed Guard gunner Basil Izzi, whose card game was so violently interrupted by Ulrich Thilo's first torpedo, ran aft to his gun station on the poop as soon as he reached the deck. He was joined there by Ensign Maddox and the rest of the 4-inch crew. The gun was loaded and ready to fire within seconds, but remained silent, as there was no target visible. When the second torpedo struck, and the lifeboats began to leave the *Zaandam*'s side, Izzi followed his fellow gunners over the side, leaping from the high stern as the ship foundered.

Hitting the water from a great height, Izzi was winded, and sank half-conscious into the depths. His lungs were on the point of bursting when he came to his senses and struck out for the surface. When he finally reached the surface, he found a piece of wreckage which kept him afloat while he looked around him. He appeared to be completely alone. There was no sign of the *Zaandam*'s boats or rafts, nor could he see anyone else near him in the water.

With the dreadful feeling that he might be completely alone – perhaps the only survivor – growing, Basil Izzi, clinging to his scrap of wreckage, drifted throughout the rest of the afternoon and the long night that followed. During the darkness he heard the voices of other men drifting nearby, but he could not contact them. At times his nightmare was filled with the screams of men as they were taken by sharks. When the daylight came again, he was still alive, but his spirits were at a very low ebb. Then he saw the raft. And there were four men on it, whom he was unable to recognize at the distance.

Making a great effort, Izzi kicked out for the raft, and when he finally reached it, the others helped him aboard. They were Ensign James Maddox, Cornelius van der Sloat, one of the *Zaandam*'s engine-room ratings, George Breezely, an Armed Guard gunner from the *Examelia* and Nico Hoogendam, a 17-year-old seaman from the *Firethorn*. These men had also spent the night in the water, and had found the life-raft only a few hours before Basil Izzi came across it.

After a small meal of chocolate, condensed milk and a mouthful of water, Izzi began to recover from his ordeal of the night. He later wrote:

> We slept pretty well that day, and we didn't see anything at all, we didn't see any more bodies, no planes or ships coming out. The next day came and we thought we would have to start pulling watches day and night. In the day time we pulled watches for about 10 minutes, and in the night time maybe an hour or two hours. We did that until about the 35th day when we got so weak that we couldn't pull watches anymore. Our food lasted for 16 days, we rationed it out in very small pieces, chocolate and very small rations of water. For a while they were feeding these hardtack biscuits to the birds as we thought for a while that we would get picked up. After our food ran out we still had a little water but we had to get some food somewhere, so we had a line about 12 feet long and we made it into a running bowline like a lasso, and we hung it over the side and we knew that the sharks would come under the raft to attack us. We hung our toes or feet in the water. So, we did that for a while and we didn't succeed

at first, but the second time a shark did go through the rope and we pulled it and caught it by its tail. We took that shark aboard and hit it with everything we had, we hit it with the paddle, we had a knife and we took its heart out and liver, and still the heart was beating for 15 minutes after we took it out. We ate the heart and liver first, after that we cut some of the white meat off its back. Well that was tough and it was very dry, but we ate a little of that anyway. We cut some more off and we put it in a food container, which by this time was empty, to try to see if it would be good tomorrow, the next day. We got up the next morning and we found that the meat wasn't any good and it wasn't fit to eat so we had to throw that overboard. That was the first fish that we caught. At night time there were a lot of birds fishing around, and they would come and roost on the raft on account of the water being so rough they couldn't ride the waves so they would come onto the raft and rest, so we would just creep up behind them and catch them. We caught about 25 of those birds the same way. One day we caught about eight little fishes, like sardines . . .

The days came and went, during which the raft, carried on the South Equatorial Current, drifted in a north-westerly direction at the rate of a few miles a day. Throughout, the raft was in warm waters that teemed with fish, while birds, oblivious to the danger, hovered overhead and often alighted on the raft. The survivors rarely went hungry, but water was a problem. Then, on their twentieth day adrift, they saw their first ship. Basil Izzi wrote:

We burned flares and we waved our hands and waved our shirts, but the ship, I guess, didn't see us so we felt kind of bad but still we thought that probably another ship would come by, and a ship did come by the next day. It was late in the afternoon about 4.30. We did about the same thing, we also burned flares, we had four left and we burned three. We waved a flag and our shirts. We had a yellow cloth there that we used to wave so that the ship might have seen that bright color. That ship stuck around a good time but finally went off. About three weeks later we saw a large ship but it was so far away that we didn't even attempt to try to let them see us.

The days would go on and sometimes we would be without food for two or three days, sometimes without water for four and the longest we were out of water was for six days. On the sixty-sixth day one of the sailors died on the raft. Before he died he was sick a long time, somewhere around a month or five weeks. He was very sick, complained of pains in his stomach, he went blind in one of his eyes, and he couldn't hear out of one of his ears. He suffered quite a bit and on the night of the 65th day he was groaning and he talked out of his mind, people we didn't know he talked about. We put him in a dry spot on the raft for that night and when we woke up the next morning he was dead. My gunnery officer was sick at the same time but not as bad and he said that he hoped that he wasn't next, but he was the next. We said prayers for them and we buried them at sea. Well, the three of us were left and we hoped that if anybody else was going to die that all three of us would die together.

On the eighty-second day we saw our first airplane and it was so high that we didn't think that they saw us. But early the next morning this same type of plane came back again. It was not as high but was at a far distance. So, then we knew that we were near land and we thought probably some convoy was coming out of some port. About an hour later we saw smoke at the horizon then it disappeared. Later on it came back and then more smoke and more. That went on for about one hour and finally we could see the masts of all those merchant ships and we saw one destroyer and we saw another which we thought was a destroyer which was a PC boat that picked us up.

Although they were not aware of it, Basil Izzi and the other remaining survivors, Cornelius van der Sloat and Nico Hoogendam, had drifted into the path of a newly instituted convoy route, from Trinidad to Recife, the first of these convoys, in fact. Izzi describes the never to be forgotten scene when these three men, who had been drifting on a tiny wooden life-raft, exposed to wind and weather, without adequate food or water, for eighty-three days, were finally rescued:

162

We had one of the Dutchmen stand up, we held him by his knees so he wouldn't fall down while he was waving his flag. He waved this flag and we saw this ship would turn around and head one way and then it would head the other way. One time he said – 'Well, it looks like it is not coming to pick us up', but we told him not to give up, to keep on waving that flag. The fellow on the starboard watch said he spotted us at about 5000 yards. He said he then called the Skipper up and the Skipper looked through his binoculars and said it was a liferaft, so he signalled to the commander escort vessels and said he was going to investigate a raft. They were coming full speed ahead for us and a gush of smoke came from the starboard side of the ship and the Dutchman thought they got hit by a torpedo and he says – 'Gee, they got hit by a torpedo'. I turned around and looked , there was smoke over the side but I knew it wasn't a torpedo, the ship kept going on. They were blinking their lights and the fellows waving flags, and then we knew that they had spotted us. They pulled alongside and they dropped the ladder off the side and they helped us climb aboard and the first thing they gave us was peaches. That Dutchman hollered for beans but they said beans were kind of heavy so they gave him some peaches. It started raining after that . . .

Basil Izzi, Cornelius van der Sloat and Nico Hoogendam were picked up by the American submarine-chaser PC 576, one of the escorts of the Recife-bound convoy. They were all suffering from exposure and dehydration, and had lost nearly half their normal weight when taken aboard the rescue vessel, but after a spell in hospital at Pernambuco, all three were fit enough to be flown home.

Chapter Thirteen

The Easter Debacle

With Malaya, Singapore and the Dutch East Indies overrun, Britain now looked to the defences of the last remaining bulwark of her Empire in the East, the sub-continent of India. The main threat was from the sea, and after the staggering loss of the battleships *Prince of Wales* and *Repulse* to Japanese aircraft four months earlier, Vice-Admiral Sir James Somerville had a considerably weakened Eastern Fleet to guard 28 million square miles of ocean and a coastline 3000 miles long. The Somerville command comprised the battleships *Ramillies, Resolution, Revenge, Royal Sovereign* and *Warspite*, the aircraft carriers *Formidable, Indomitable* and *Hermes*, the heavy cruisers *Cornwall* and *Dorsetshire*, the light cruisers *Caledon, Dragon, Emerald, Enterprise* and *Jacob van Heemskerck*, and nine destroyers.

On paper, this was an impressive array of naval might, but the majority of Somerville's ships were elderly First World War veterans and ill equipped for modern sea warfare. The three carriers, key elements of the fleet since the recent demonstration of the value of air strikes by the Imperial Japanese Navy, carried between them nine Sea Hurricanes, sixteen Martlets, twelve Fulmars, forty-five Albacores, and thirteen Swordfish. Of these, only the Hurricanes were a match for the Japanese Zeros, while the Martlets and Fulmars might put up a credible performance, but the antiquated Albacores and Swordfish biplanes were so much window dressing when it came to a fight.

Somerville first heard of the impending Japanese sortie into the Bay of Bengal on 31 March. His opponent, Vice-Admiral Chuichi

Nagumo, who had commanded at Pearl Harbor, had in fact left his base in the Celebes on the 26th with a powerful fleet of thirty-two ships. The heavy guns were provided by the fast battleships *Haruna*, *Hiei*, *Kirishima* and *Kongo*, and in company were the aircraft carriers *Akagi*, *Ryujo*, *Hiryu*, *Soryu*, *Shokaku* and *Zuikaku*, the heavy cruisers *Chikuma*, *Chokai*, *Kumano*, *Mikuma*, *Mogami*, *Suzuya* and *Tone*, the light cruisers *Abukuma* and *Yura* and thirteen destroyers. Although Nagumo's battleships were just as old as Somerville's, they were 4 knots faster, his heavy cruisers were all modern 33-knotters, and his carriers had on board 350 front-line aircraft piloted by battle-hardened veterans who had already seen action in the raids on Pearl Harbor and Darwin.

Throughout 1st and 2nd April, Somerville combed the southern approaches to the Bay of Bengal, steaming west by day and east by night, but the horizon remained empty, and reports from his reconnaissance planes were negative. Late on the 2nd, in the absence of any sign of a Japanese fleet, and with some of his ships running short of fuel and water, the Admiral decided to return to his base at Adu Atoll, in the Maldives. The heavy cruiser *Cornwall* was sent south to meet a troop convoy then northbound from Australia, while her sister *Dorsetshire* returned to Colombo to continue her refit, which had been interrupted by the emergency. The carrier *Hermes*, escorted by one destroyer, was despatched to Trincomalee.

On the afternoon of the 4th, some hours after Somerville's ships reached Adu Atoll, the Admiral received a report that a large Japanese fleet had been sighted 360 miles south-east of Ceylon, and was steaming towards the island. The sighting report came from a Catalina piloted by Squadron Leader Leonard Birchall, who had taken off from Koggala Lagoon, in the south of the island, before dawn on the 4th. Birchall's orders were to set up a patrol 250 miles south of Ceylon, but as the day wore on he was told to move further south. That night, in the light of a brilliant moon, the Catalina's crew sighted the Japanese ships far below, four battleships, five carriers, and a number of cruisers and destroyers, their wakes streaming behind them as they hurried northwards. Birchall went lower to investigate, but as he did so, a swarm of Zero fighters pounced on his flying boat, riddling it with bullets. Fortunately, Birchall's wireless operator was able to get off a sighting report before the Catalina crashed into the sea.

Birchall's report reached Admiral Somerville in the early hours of the 5th, leaving him in a quandary. The Japanese ships were nearly 600 miles east of Adu, and with his own ships in the middle of refuelling he could not hope to intercept the enemy fleet before it was within striking distance of Ceylon. However, he decided to sail at once with his fastest battleship, the 37,000-ton *Warspite*, accompanied by the carriers *Indomitable* and *Formidable*, two cruisers and six destroyers, hoping that he might be able to bring the Japanese to battle as they returned from their attack on Ceylon. The slower ships would follow as soon as they had completed refuelling.

Meanwhile, in Ceylon, Admiral Layton, who commanded the defences of the island, was preparing for the worst. All ships able to put to sea were cleared from the two main harbours, Colombo and Trincomalee. *Cornwall* and *Dorsetshire*, which had just arrived in Colombo, were sent at full speed to join Admiral Somerville, and the *Hermes*, which had no aircraft on board, sailed from Trincomalee and was told to keep clear to the north-east.

Easter Sunday, 5 April 1942, dawned miserably, with the first rain-swollen clouds of the south-west monsoon gathering over Colombo. Thanks to the sacrifice of Leonard Birchall and his crew, anti-aircraft gunners were standing to at their guns, and the fighters were in the air, thirty-one Hurricanes of 30 Squadron and 258 Squadron RAF, and six Fairey Fulmars from 803 and 806 Squadrons of the Fleet Air Arm. When at 8 o'clock the Japanese planes, launched from Admiral Nagumo's carriers, then only 120 miles to the south, appeared overhead, their reception was a hot one.

In the dogfight that raged over Colombo, the attacking force, consisting of fifty-three 'Kate' bombers and thirty-six 'Val' dive bombers, escorted by thirty-six Zero fighters, found that, probably for the first time, they were up against powerful, modern fighters. The Hurricane IIs that took off from Ratmalana airfield claimed twenty-two enemy planes shot down for the loss of fifteen of their own aircraft. The much slower Fulmars of the Fleet Air Arm lost four of their number for only one kill, while six Swordfish, unsuspectingly arriving from Trincomalee at the height of the battle, were all shot down. However, a number of Zeros were said to have run out of fuel on their way back to the carriers, and crashed into the sea.

The Japanese bombers caused little damage to the town of Colombo, other than bringing home to the inhabitants with brutal force that they were no longer isolated from the war. Admiral Layton, who had witnessed the chaos at the fall of Malaya and Singapore, ordered all European women and children to be evacuated, which perhaps helped to keep the civilian casualty rate low. In the port, it was a different story. Some of the installations were damaged, but the brunt of the attack was taken by those ships remaining in harbour. The 11,198-ton armed merchant cruiser *Hector*, under repair and about to be handed back to her owners, Alfred Holt's Blue Funnel Line, after two and a half years Admiralty service, became a prime target for the bombers. She was repeatedly hit, her fuel tanks exploded, and she was soon ablaze from end to end. The crew of the tanker *British Sergeant*, berthed nearby, helped with the fire-fighting, but the *Hector* was gutted and sank at her moorings, where she burned for another two weeks. One hundred and fourteen of her crew lost their lives.

Other Royal Navy ships in the harbour were the old destroyer *Tenedos* and the submarine depot ship *Lucia*, both under repair. The *Tenedos*, having narrowly escaped destruction when Japanese planes attacked the *Prince of Wales* and *Repulse* in the opening days of this bitter war, ended her long career resting on the bottom of Colombo harbour, while the *Lucia* sustained heavy damage. Of the merchant ships still in port, the 6000-ton cargo liner *Benledi* was set on fire, and Cayzer Irvine's *Clan Murdoch* sustained minor damage. The 23-year-old Clan liner had arrived in the harbour only a few hours earlier, having completed the 1,200-mile passage from the Burmese port of Akyab in four days. For an undeniably ageing steamer normally hard pressed to make 7½ knots with a fair wind, this was a record indeed. But necessity had lent her wings, for with no extra food and water on board, and her decks crowded with over 1000 men, remnants of the British forces retreating in chaos before the Japanese non-stop advance up the valley of the Irrawaddy towards the Indian frontier, time was of the essence. Also in harbour was the tanker *British Judge*, still under repair after being bombed and torpedoed when escaping from Java. In all, 600 seamen lost their lives in Colombo on that day.

Despite the ships and men lost, and the damage inflicted on the port, it can be said that Colombo was the first bloody nose inflicted on the Japanese by the Allies. Of the raid Winston Churchill wrote: 'The stubborn resistance encountered at Colombo convinced the Japanese that further prizes would be dearly bought. The losses they had suffered in aircraft convinced them that they had come in contact with the bone.'

Two hundred miles to the south of Colombo on that Easter Sunday morning the weather was in a kinder mood. Only a few fair weather cumulus clouds moved lazily across a sky of purest blue, the wind was light, the sea untroubled, and the visibility unlimited. The two cruisers *Cornwall* and *Dorsetshire* were sailing in company, their feathered wakes stretching straight and true to the horizon as they surged ahead at their best speed of 27½ knots on a south-easterly course towards their rendezvous with Admiral Somerville's ships. *Dorsetshire* (Captain A.W.S. Agar, VC) was in the lead, with *Cornwall* (Captain P.C.W. Manwaring) following in her wake. Both Agar and Manwaring were only too well aware that the Japanese fleet was very near – perhaps only just out of sight over the horizon – and without air protection they felt very vulnerable. They had been steaming with their ships closed up at action stations since before dawn.

The first sign of the enemy came at 1100, when lookouts aboard the *Dorsetshire* sighted a single aircraft estimated to be at least 20 miles astern. The plane disappeared before it could be positively identified, but there was little doubt in anyone's mind that it was a Japanese reconnaissance aircraft. The question was, had it sighted the two British ships?

Two hours passed, and the sky remained empty. The tension that had built up in the two cruisers was slowly easing. Then, at 1300, two other aircraft appeared, one ahead and one astern, and both about 14 miles off. The one ahead was identified as a friendly Catalina, but the one astern was considered hostile. It now seemed certain that the cruisers were in danger. This was confirmed forty minutes later, when the *Dorsetshire* sighted three aircraft passing overhead at high altitude. They could not be positively identified, but Captain Agar was not leaving the defence of his ship to chance. He ordered his 4-inch AA guns to open fire. *Cornwall* joined in, and the ships' combined firepower of sixteen 4-inch guns filled the sky around the high-flying aircraft with puffs of dirty grey smoke.

This was the signal for the attack to begin. The three planes already seen – they were 'Val' dive bombers – went into a steep dive and screamed down on the *Cornwall*, ignoring the hail of shells thrown at them by the cruiser's 2-pounder pom-poms. They released their 500lb bombs at low altitude, the first hitting the *Cornwall*'s after hangar, the second scored a near miss forward on the port side, the third missing altogether.

As the *Cornwall* staggered under the blast of the first strike, a second flight of three 'Vals' appeared out of nowhere and swooped on the *Dorsetshire*. Although Captain Agar took immediate avoiding action, the 'Vals' came in at mast-top height before releasing their bombs, and could not possibly miss. The first bomb hit the cruiser's quarter deck, pierced her armour, and exploded in the steering gear deck, putting the gear out of action. The second bomb landed just abaft the after funnel, its blast demolishing the catapult and both wireless offices, while the third landed on the port side amidships, knocking out all the 4-inch AA guns on that side. This was the signal for a succession of attacks on the *Dorsetshire* by flights of three 'Vals', each following seconds after the other. In this devastating assault Agar's ship was hit again and again. All her pom-poms were put out of action, the boiler-room received a direct hit, X turret was disabled, and the after funnel demolished. The same bomb caused the after magazine to blow up, dealing the final crippling blow to the already hard-hit ship. The *Dorsetshire*'s after deck was a mass of flames, all communications from the bridge to the rest of the ship had been cut, and she was taking on a heavy port list.

The cruiser took another four direct hits and several near misses, from the Japanese bombers, by which time Captain Agar conceded that his ship was sinking. He called all hands up on deck, and then gave the order to abandon ship. The order was none too soon, for the *Dorsetshire* was slowly capsizing, and as her surviving crew members dived over the side, the Japanese planes came in low, spraying the water with their machine-guns. The cruiser sank stern first minutes after the order to abandon had been given, and soon there was only a sorry mess of oil-soaked wreckage, bodies, and struggling survivors to mark her passing.

HMS *Cornwall* had been subjected to an even more concentrated attack by the Japanese dive bombers. For two full minutes the bombs rained down on her like hailstones in a thunderstorm. Most were near misses, only eight direct hits being scored, but the *Cornwall*, like her fellow cruiser, suffered mortal damage. One of the first bombs to fall was a near miss abreast the port side of the bridge, which flooded the port bilges and caused a complete failure of electrical power throughout the ship. Another near miss, amidships on the starboard side, is believed to have killed all those in the after engine-room, while other near misses flooded both boiler-rooms, which had to be evacuated. Splinters from a direct hit nearby killed and injured many of those on the bridge. Other bombs found their target, between the two after gun turrets, near the dynamo-room, in the sickbay, and in the recreation space, causing heavy casualties. An oil bomb was dropped to complete the carnage, setting fire to much of the forward superstructure on the starboard side. In the words of one survivor: 'In less than five minutes after the attacks started all power had failed, and both boiler-rooms and both engine-rooms were flooding rapidly. The port gunwale of the ship was awash, and the starboard outer propeller was breaking surface, the ship being slightly down by the bows. Thick black smoke was issuing from the foremost funnel uptake casings on both sides of the upper deck.'

By 1351, eleven minutes after they had first appeared, the Japanese bombers had withdrawn, presumably because they had used up all their bombs. Their attack had been carried out with clinical precision, the planes coming in from right ahead with the sun behind them, releasing their bombs from about 500 feet, and pulling up before the AA guns could be brought to bear. Their bombing was accurate, and as the planes came in, nose to tail, one after the other, their bombs exploded within seconds of each other. They left below them a scene of complete destruction, once again demonstrating the superiority of the carrier-borne aircraft over the big-gun ships. It was a lesson that, even after Pearl Harbor and the loss of the battleships *Prince of Wales* and *Repulse*, the Royal Navy was still reluctant to learn.

The bombers came back after a short interval, but this time contenting themselves with circling the scene of their triumph, and not, as many of those below feared, machine-gunning the men in the water. The *Cornwall* was still afloat, and desperate attempts were being made to correct her growing list by transferring ballast. But it was to no avail. The British cruiser was finished, already sinking, and Captain Manwaring who, although severely wounded, had remained on the bridge in command, could do no more than order his men to abandon ship. Four minutes later, the *Cornwall*, now listing 70 degrees to port, finally gave up the struggle, and slipped beneath the waves bow first.

The two British cruisers, mounting between them sixteen 4-inch AA guns and twenty-eight 2-pounder pom-poms, made little impression on the estimated twenty-seven Japanese dive bombers that attacked and sank them. It was claimed that one aircraft was shot down and one damaged, but this was never confirmed.

After the cruisers had gone down, they left behind them a sea of human flotsam, over 1,200 men, many of them wounded, adrift in shark-infested waters 300 miles from the nearest land, and with very little to keep them afloat. Between them they had three whalers, two of which were damaged and leaking, a small skiff, a motor lifeboat and a few Carley floats. However, although the position looked hopeless for the survivors, the discipline – for which the Royal Navy is renowned – remained firm. They were gathered in two groups, some two miles apart, near where their ships had gone down. The wounded were put into the boats, while the others clung to the floats, or constructed makeshift rafts from pieces of wreckage. Sharks appeared, as they always will in these warm waters, but they did not attack the men.

Fortunately for the survivors, the *Cornwall*'s wireless operators had managed to get away a signal reporting the sinking of the two ships, and late that afternoon an Albacore torpedo bomber of the Fleet Air Arm appeared and flew low overhead. Shortly before the sun went down, a two-seater Fulmar circled them, flashing a message by lamp that help was on the way. With this reassurance buoying them up through the long, cold night that followed, they drifted in a sea that, mercifully, remained an oily calm.

The two groups of survivors drifted throughout the next day under a cloudless sky, from which the sun, like a huge ball of fire, blazed down on them. It was particularly hard for the wounded, crammed into the boats, which were so low in the water that any sudden movement threatened to swamp them. Many of them died, and were lowered over the side to the mercy of the sharks, who were becoming bolder by the hour. Both groups were short of food and water, but with strict rationing imposed, everyone received their fair share, little though it was.

It was late in the afternoon of that day, 6 April, before help arrived: first another Albacore flying over, followed shortly afterwards by the cruiser *Enterprise*, accompanied by the destroyers *Paladin* and *Panther*, appearing on the horizon to the south-west. An hour later, these three rescue ships had taken on board the 1,122 survivors, exhausted, burnt by the sun, dehydrated and hungry, but all overwhelmed with joy at their deliverance from death.

So ended another defeat for the Royal Navy at the hands of the Japanese. All for the want of air cover, another two fine ships had been lost, and 424 men were dead.

When Admiral Somerville withdrew his fleet to Adu Atoll, the threat of a large Japanese force, complete with aircraft carriers, at large in the Bay of Bengal, caused panic in Calcutta, even though the port lies almost 100 miles from the sea. All merchant ships able to leave were ordered to put to sea without delay. Some ships left in convoy, although without naval escort, others sailed alone. In retrospect, most of these ships would have been safer had they stayed in port.

The first merchantman to run into trouble was Harrison Line's London-registered *Harpasa*, a 5082-ton cargo steamer commanded by Captain Atkinson. The *Harpasa* had orders to proceed independently to Mombasa. After dropping his pilot at the Sandheads, at the entrance to the River Hooghly, Atkinson decided to stay close inshore on the east coast of the Bay of Bengal, hoping to slip clear before the Japanese ships came hunting. His plan was doomed to failure, for two days out of Calcutta, on Easter Sunday morning, a Japanese reconnaissance plane was sighted coming in from the east. The *Harpasa* was then off the port of Puri, some 160 miles south of the Sandheads, caught in open waters, and with no place to hide.

The enemy aircraft circled warily for a while, and then suddenly came roaring in to drop a single bomb, which landed in the after well deck of the fleeing steamer. The bomb turned out to be an incendiary, which set fire to the whole after end of the ship. The explosion damaged the *Harpasa*'s steering gear, and the flames were so fierce that no one was able to go aft to carry out repairs.

172

Captain Atkinson decided to abandon ship before the racing flames destroyed his lifeboats.

Mercifully, the *Harpasa*'s crew were not forced to spend long in their open boats. Within a few hours of their ship going down they were picked up by the 3471-ton *Taksang*, which arrived in answer to their radioed SOS. The *Taksang*, owned by the Indo-China Steamship Company, and commanded by Captain Costello, had been nearby in a small convoy bound from Calcutta to Colombo.

Unfortunately for Captain Atkinson and his crew, they had escaped with their lives from one sinking, only to be involved in another. Next day, the *Taksang*, which had a speed of 18 knots, was overhauled by two of Rear-Admiral Takeo Kurita's cruisers, the *Kumano* and *Suzuya*, accompanied by the destroyer *Shirakumo*. The *Taksang*, armed only with an ancient 4-inch mounted aft, was no match for the cruisers' 6-inch guns, which quickly pounded the small Hong Kong-registered ship to a halt. Her bridge took the full force of the shelling, Captain Costello being severely injured. Fifteen of his crew were killed, as was the *Harpasa*'s First Radio Officer. Many others on board were wounded by shrapnel.

Ten minutes after the first Japanese shell crashed into her bridge, the battered *Taksang* took on a heavy list, and then disappeared bow first in a cloud of steam and smoke. She had lasted just long enough to allow her survivors to clear the ship in two lifeboats and a life-raft. Those on the raft were picked up by a Catalina flying from Calcutta next day; the boats came ashore on the coast a day later.

Following their initial success, Admiral Kurita's ships moved south, and shortly after dawn on the next day, 6 April, found the 5686-ton *Selma City* near Vizagapatam. The New York-registered *Selma City*, owned by Isthmian Lines, and under the command of Captain John Griffin, was on a voyage from Colombia to Calcutta via Vizagapatam, and had left the latter port three hours earlier when she was sighted by an aircraft from one of Kurita's cruisers. The plane attacked, dropping two bombs, one of which missed, but the other crippled the American ship, exploding in her engine-room. The plane then made a second run and dropped a third bomb, causing major damage in her boiler-room. All the pumps were knocked out, but the *Selma City*'s crew formed a bucket-chain, and made a gallant effort to fight the many fires that had broken out. Finally, at 1130, with his ship burning fiercely and his engine spaces flooded, Captain Griffin ordered his men to take to the boats.

All thirty crew left the ship in four lifeboats. No sooner were they clear of the ship than two more aircraft arrived and subjected the helpless *Selma City* to a hail of bombs. But the old ship, solid-built in Chicksaw, Alabama in 1921, did not succumb easily. She finally sank at 1045 on the 7th. Griffin and his crew, who had escaped with only a few minor injuries, landed at Vizagapatam shortly before dark on the 6th.

Shortly after the *Selma City* came under attack, 80 miles to the south, aircraft from the Japanese carrier *Ryuju*, part of Rear-Admiral Kakujo Kakuta's air group, sighted Blue Funnel Line's 7857-ton *Dardanus*. Bound for Colombo, the *Dardanus* was sailing in company with the 5281-ton *Gandara* of the British India Line, both ships having been hurried out of Calcutta when the Japanese threat became evident. Third Engineer Alan Graham was on board the *Dardanus*:

It was 6 April, Easter Day. A single carrier-based aircraft made a dive bomb attack on us. We were not prepared for any attack and were hit by two bombs. One bomb hit the forward cargo space, the other hit the engine room. The engine room bomb entered through the skylight and passed between the two turbines. It did not explode until it passed through the lower hull and was underneath the ship. I was in the refrigeration area just off the engine room when this was happening. The engine room quickly filled with steam.

Most of the crew including the Captain abandoned ship, but the DEMS gunner, the 3rd radio operator and myself were left behind. We managed in the end to launch the ship's motor boat. During this operation the radio operator accidentally lost some fingers when he put his hand on the lifeboat launching runners. The motor boat had been damaged by part of the hatch cover blown up by the bomb hit on the forward part of the ship.

As we pulled away from the ship to join the others the motor

174

boat began to sink. The Captain's lifeboat rescued us just in time. Some time later it became apparent that the ship was showing no immediate sign of sinking, so we reboarded.

The *Gandara*, which somehow had escaped the attentions of the Japanese, now came to the rescue of the *Dardanus*. She passed a towline, and soon the two ships were under way and making slow but steady progress towards Vizagapatam, the nearest port where repairs could be carried out. However, they had not gone far when the masts and funnels of three ships came over the horizon from the north-east. As they came closer, the vague shapes hardened into the recognizable outlines of two cruisers and a destroyer, almost undoubtedly Japanese. The first reaction of the *Gandara* was to slip her towline and try to make a run for it, but the futility of the latter course was soon realized. As the Japanese ships came nearer, the crews of both merchantmen took to the boats. Third Radio Officer Roy Warwick of the *Dardanus* takes up the story:

> By the time the last lifeboat had pulled away from the ship, two Japanese cruisers and a destroyer had closed to within a mile of the *Dardanus*. They were modern looking streamlined vessels with upswept funnels and they opened up with their 6-inch or 8-inch guns and there was bedlam. Our lifeboat attempted to row round the stern of the *Dardanus* to get out of the line of fire, but by the time we had done so the cruisers had circled *Dardanus* and were headed straight towards us, their guns still pounding away. When it seemed inevitable that the lead cruiser would run us down, it altered course slightly and avoided doing so.
>
> All the shelling did not sink *Dardanus*, or even cause her to list. The destroyer had to sink her with torpedoes.
>
> All our lifeboats eventually made it to the Orissa coast. We suffered no loss of life or serious injuries, and upon reaching the coast survivors were greeted by curious local inhabitants who gave them refreshments and treated them very hospitably.

The *Gandara* did not fare as well as the *Dardanus*, thirteen of her crew being killed when her turn came to face the Japanese guns.

Both British ships were sunk by the enemy warships, which it was later learned were the light cruisers *Mikuma* and *Mogami* and the destroyer *Amagiri*. In the course of the action, which lasted for one to one and a half hours, they fired a total of 100 shells, approximately fifty of which were seen to hit the *Dardanus*. The Blue Funnel ship was finally sunk by a torpedo from the destroyer *Amagiri*.

Other merchant ships sunk by the Japanese cruisers on that day included a sister ship of the *Dardanus*, the 7621-ton *Autolycus*, commanded by Captain Neville, which lost sixteen of her crew, and British India's 9066-ton *Malda*, commanded by Captain Edmonson. Bombed and shelled, the *Malda* was consumed by flames, in which twenty-five men died. The 6622-ton *Indora*, another of British India's ships, picked up survivors from both the *Autolycus* and the *Malda*, but was then herself sunk by the guns of *Mikuma* and *Mogami*. There followed the 1279-ton Dutch steamer *Batavia*, the American ships *Bienville* and *Exmoor*, and the British ships *Silksworth*, *Shinkuang*, *Sinkiang* and *Ganges*, all sent to the bottom. In all, over Easter 1942 the Japanese cruisers and their destroyers sank twenty-one Allied merchantmen of 92,000 tons in the Bay of Bengal. At the same time, Japanese submarines had started operations off the west coast of India. They sank another five ships of 32,404 tons in that period. On top of all the other recent disasters suffered by British shipping in those waters, this was perhaps the final indignity. Winston Churchill was despondent. He wrote: 'This is only the beginning. Until we are able to fight a fleet action there is no reason why the Japanese should not become the dominating factor in the Western Indian Ocean. This would result in the collapse of our whole position in the Middle East.' And there *was* more to come.

In its heyday before Pearl Harbor, the Royal Navy's base at Trincomalee, on Ceylon's east coast, played host to the elite of the Empire's warships. Majestic battleships, white awnings spread and Marine bands playing, were regularly to be seen in the harbour, as were the sleek submarines and dashing destroyers of the Eastern Fleet. On the morning of 9 April 1942 Trincomalee was empty, except for a handful of unemployed cargo ships swinging disconsolately at their moorings. Twenty-four hours earlier, intelligence having been received warning of an impending attack by Japanese carrier-borne planes, Trincomalee had been cleared of the only naval vessels on station in the port, the light aircraft carrier HMS *Hermes*, which had no aircraft on board, the Australian destroyer *Vampire*, and the corvette HMS *Hollyhock*, and not a moment too soon, it transpired.

At 0700 on the morning of the 9th, wave after wave of 'Val' dive bombers, flown off from the carriers *Akagai*, *Hiryu* and *Soryu*, appeared over the port. Forewarned, the twenty-three Hurricanes based at Frederick Air Force Base in China Bay took off and climbed towards the enemy, while nine Blenheim light bombers were sent on a forlorn mission to attack the Japanese carriers, believed to be close to the south. The Hurricanes made a brave attempt to stave off the attacking force, but the 'Vals' were protected by a ring of Zeros said to be thirty-eight strong. Fierce dog-fights ensued, in which the Hurricanes shot down fifteen of the Japanese planes for the loss of eleven of their own. The damage done by the enemy bombers was not extensive, only one of the oil storage tanks, the main target, being set on fire. A number of civilian workers at the base were killed, and widespread panic caused most of the local population to flee the town. Meanwhile, the brave attempt by the Blenheims to bomb the Japanese carriers had proved to be a dismal failure. They scored no hits, and lost five of their number to the carriers' guns.

While the raid on Trincomalee was in progress, *Hermes* and her escorts were 100 miles to the south, and retracing their steps, having been recalled during the night. This order proved to be a very costly mistake, for at 0855 that morning the ships were sighted by a reconnaissance aircraft from the Japanese carrier force. At 1035, when 70 miles south of Trincomalee, they were attacked by seventy 'Vals' called up from the enemy carriers. *Hermes*, with no aircraft of her own to defend her, was hit forty times, and sank in ten minutes with the loss of 307 lives. Ironically, the *Hermes*, the first British ship to be designed and launched as an aircraft carrier, had now earned the distinction of being the first aircraft carrier to be sunk by air attack alone. *Vampire* and *Hollyhock* were similarly overwhelmed, the destroyer losing nine men. The hospital ship *Vita* later picked up 590 survivors and landed them in Colombo.

Following the havoc created by the Japanese fleet in the Indian Ocean in the first days of April 1942, it was decided to withdraw the remaining ships of Admiral Somerville's Eastern Fleet 2,500 miles eastwards to the safety of Mombasa, on the east coast of Africa. It was hoped that from there they would at least be able to keep open the vital shipping routes to India and the Persian Gulf. As for the Bay of Bengal and the rest of the Indian Ocean, for the time being that was abandoned to the Japanese.

Chapter Fourteen

Epilogue

The Third Geneva Convention of 1929, to which Japan was a signatory, plainly states that prisoners of war must at all times be treated humanely, adequately housed, fed and clothed, and should not be used as common labourers. Right from the outbreak of war in the Far East, the Japanese blatantly ignored this Convention. Prisoners were confined in the most disgusting conditions, were brutally beaten, starved, and forced to labour like beasts of the field.

When the Allies pulled out of Java in February 1942, they left behind them a beaten army of over 7,000 men, mostly British and Dutch, who became prisoners of the Japanese. These prisoners were subsequently distributed among the surrounding islands, where they were put to work building ports and airfields for Japan's rapidly expanding empire.

Emperor Hirohito's dream of vast conquests was short-lived. As 1943 drew to a close, the Americans, and to a lesser extent the British, had recovered from the humiliating defeats that followed Pearl Harbor. In fierce naval actions fought in the Coral Sea and at Midway, the Imperial Japanese Navy had tasted bitter defeat, American Marines were in possession of Guadalcanal, and the Australians steadily gaining ground in New Guinea. Further afield, in Burma, the British Fourteenth Army was about to go on the offensive, and Admiral Somerville's Eastern Fleet was back in control of the Indian Ocean. The tide of war was on the turn.

In November 1943, on completion of the airfield on the island of Ambon, which had been constructed by 4,000 prisoners of war shipped from Java, many of whom had died, the Japanese decided to return those now too sick to be of further use to Sourabaya. These men were in a very weak state, worn down by severe malnutrition, and most of them suffering from dysentery, beriberi or malaria, or a combination of all three. They were being moved to Sourabaya on the pretence that there they would be able to recover from their illnesses.

Ambon lies some 200 miles off the north-west corner of New Guinea, and 1000 miles east of Java, and the only transport available for the prisoners was Prison Ship No. 45, which sailed under the name of *Suez Maru*. The 6400 ton *Suez Maru*, a coal-burning steamer built in 1919, was one of fifty-six Japanese 'prison ships' used to house and transport prisoners of war, most of which closely resembled the slavers of the eighteenth century that criss-crossed the Atlantic between Africa and the Americas with their human cargoes crammed in below decks like so much cattle.

Boarding began early on the morning of 26 November, and with many of the prisoners too weak to negotiate the *Suez Maru*'s gangway, was an agonizingly slow operation. The guards screamed abuse and made free use of the bayonet and rifle butt, but to no avail. Their charges were walking skeletons, men drained of the will to live, and no amount of chivvying would hurry them. It was well after noon before the *Suez Maru* sailed from Ambon. The prisoners, 422 British and 127 Dutch, including twenty stretcher cases, were packed into the ship's after holds. In charge of their guards was Lieutenant Koshio Masaji, whose orders from the High Command were explicit. Should the ship be sunk, he was under no circumstances to allow any of the prisoners to fall into the hands of the enemy. The Japanese wanted no witnesses to their inhumanity.

Also on board the *Suez Maru*, housed in the forward holds, in rather better conditions than the prisoners, were 250 sick and wounded Japanese servicemen. The *Suez Maru* was, in effect, a hospital ship, and to comply with the Geneva Convention should have been painted white overall and marked with Red Crosses on her hull and funnel, these markings being illuminated at night. Showing no lights, and her hull and superstructure painted drab-grey, any hostile submarine commander might have been forgiven for mistaking her for a Japanese cargo ship or troop transport, both legitimate targets for his torpedoes. And with much of the Japanese fleet heavily engaged elsewhere, a number of Allied submarines were on the prowl in these waters. The Japanese Maritime Code had been broken by American Intelligence in March, and these submarines were regularly informed of the movements of any enemy ship in the area.

US Navy Submarine Squadron 16 had been transferred from Pearl Harbor in the previous August, and given the primary task of intercepting and sinking Japanese tankers carrying oil from Borneo and Sumatra to Admiral Mineichi Koga's fleet based on Truk in the Caroline Islands.

A relative newcomer to Squadron 16 was Lieutenant-Commander Tom Hogan's *Bonefish*. A Gato-class submarine of 1525 tons displacement, *Bonefish* had a top speed on the surface of 21 knots, and was armed with a 50 Cal. 3-inch gun and ten 21-inch torpedo tubes. She had already made her mark by sinking three ships totalling 24,000 tons in the China Sea. On 22 November, *Bonefish* sailed from Fremantle on her fourth patrol, with Tom Hogan proudly wearing the ribbon of the Navy Cross. Her destination was the Flores Sea, through which the Japanese tankers from Sumatra were known to be passing. Hogan estimated she was on station on the morning of the 29th.

The *Suez Maru* left Ambon on the afternoon of the 26th, and once clear of the anchorage was joined by her escort, the fleet minesweepers W11 and W12. These small 600-ton vessels were each armed with three 4.7-inch guns and two machine-guns, carried twenty-four depth charges, and were equipped with sonar. At first glance, this seemed a more than adequate escort for one ship, but the situation changed very quickly. No sooner was the land out of sight than W11 gave three blasts on her whistle and made off to the west at full speed. Her services were required elsewhere.

Now the future of the *Suez Maru* began to look less certain. At her maximum speed of 13½ knots, she had ahead of her a three-day passage through waters full of dangers. It was perhaps just as well that it was not known on board the Japanese ship that W12's sonar was not working. Her sole escort had no means of detecting and tracking an underwater enemy.

At daylight on the 29th, the *Suez Maru* and her escort were off the Kangean Islands, with less than 200 miles to go to their destination, Sourabaya. Unfortunately for them, and for the want of a working sonar, quite unknown to anyone on board the ships, the enemy was close by. During the night, USS *Bonefish* had slipped through the Bali Strait, and in the early hours of the morning of the 29th was on the surface near the Kangean Islands. Hogan's radar picked up the two targets at 17 miles, and when they were in sight he identified them as a medium-sized cargo ship escorted by a small destroyer. With no Allied ships reported in the area, he correctly assumed them to be Japanese. He began patiently stalking his quarry, going to periscope depth at daylight.

As *Bonefish* could manage only 9 knots underwater, and the enemy convoy was sailing at 13½ knots, the chase was a long one. It was 0800 before the gap had closed to 1,500 yards, and Hogan judged he was in position to attack. The two ships were then overlapping in his periscope, and he fired his Nos. 1 and 2 tubes simultaneously, hoping to get a double hit.

Captain Kawano Usumu, commanding W12, without the advantage of sonar, was completely unaware that his two-ship convoy was being stalked by the enemy. The first indication of danger came when a lookout aboard the *Suez Maru* saw the track of a torpedo heading directly for his ship, and gave the alarm.

The officer on the bridge of the transport took immediate evasive action, turning the ship under full helm to parallel the track of the torpedo. This was successful, and Hogan's two torpedoes passed clear, one on either side of the ship. But following hard on the heels of these came *Bonefish*'s second salvo. One torpedo exploded prematurely but the other went home, a direct hit in the *Suez Maru*'s No. 4 hold.

Hogan's torpedo dealt the *Suez Maru* a fatal blow, blasting a huge hole in her side below the waterline, fracturing her propeller shaft, and killing many of the helpless prisoners confined in the after hold. Water poured into the breached hull, and with her propellerless engines racing madly, she came slowly to a halt, listing heavily.

The shock of the exploding torpedo and the turmoil that followed caused panic to break out amongst the prisoners, few of whom had lifejackets to give them any reassurance against drowning. A semblance of order was restored by their officers, and those who had the strength to do so helped the injured up from below. Their efforts were wasted, for what few boats and rafts the *Suez Maru* carried were exclusively reserved for the Japanese on board.

At 0940, the *Suez Maru* gave one last shudder and went down stern first, taking with her the dead and those too badly injured, or just too weak, to throw themselves over the side. When she had gone, she left behind around 250 Allied prisoners of war and an equal number of Japanese in the water, some clinging to pieces of wreckage, but many floating face down.

A faint cheer was raised when, an hour or so later, the minesweeper reappeared, having gone off at full speed when the *Bonefish* struck. But Captain Kawano's initial rescue efforts were directed solely towards the Japanese survivors, all of whom were pulled from the water. By the time they were all on board W12, she was near to capsizing, having taken on board 205 Japanese sick and ninety-three guards and crew members. Kawano would take no more.

It was revealed, four years after the war, that Kawano had called all his officers to the bridge and asked their opinion on what should be done about the enemy prisoners. The officers were unanimously opposed to offering any help to an enemy that they despised, and agreed that the Army's standing order, 'Under no circumstances shall any Allied survivor fall into enemy hands' be adhered to. The honour of 'disposing of' the surviving prisoners was awarded to Lieutenant Koshio Masaji.

Koshio set up a machine-gun in the bows of the minesweeper and stationed six men on each side of the fore deck with rifles. Captain Kawano then took W12 in amongst the men in the water, her bow-wave gently nudging aside the living and the dead. The lifeless bodies remained face-down, bobbing on the wave, the living, thinking rescue was at hand, lifted their heads and cried out for help, but all they received was a fusillade of bullets that ripped into their wasted bodies. They joined the dead, face-down in a sea turned red with their blood.

With Lieutenant Koshio meticulously directing the shooting, it took almost two hours to complete the execution of the men in the water. Out of an estimated 250 Allied prisoners who survived the sinking of the *Suez Maru*, only one man was left alive, Kenneth

Thomas, a British soldier. He was picked up twenty-four hours later by the Australian minesweeper HMAS *Ballarat*, which was passing through the area.

Satisfied that all enemy prisoners had been disposed of, Captain Kawano set course for Tandjong Priok, having been advised that mines had been dropped in the approaches to Sourabaya by American aircraft. After the war, Captain Kawano Usumu and Lieutenant Koshio Masaji were brought to trial in Tokyo by the Allies, but no action was taken against them for the deliberate murder of prisoners of war.

USS *Bonefish*, unaware of the terrible slaughter she had initiated, carried on with her patrol. She was lost to enemy action on 18 June 1945 in the Japan Sea. Lieutenant-Commander Lawrence Edge was then in command. He died with all his eighty-seven crew. On her final patrol, *Bonefish* had earned herself the distinction of being the last submarine of any nationality to be lost in the Second World War.

A number of Japanese ships carrying prisoners of war were sunk before the war in the Far East ended, unfortunately most of them by friendly fire. It is on record that well over 4000 Allied prisoners of war were lost in Japanese transports sunk by American submarines. However, it must be said that none of these ships carried any distinguishing marks to warn submarine commanders of what they had on board. It might well be that the Japanese saw this as a convenient way of getting rid of the men they had already starved and worked near to the point of death in their camps.

One of the Japanese 'hell ships' which slipped through the Allied net was the *Maros Maru*, an ex-Dutch island steamer of 600 tons gross. She left Ambon, bound for Sourabaya, on 17 September 1944 with 500 British and Dutch prisoners of war on board, all of whom were weak from ill-treatment, malnutrition and various debilitating diseases. Flight Lieutenant W. Blackwood, a senior RAF officer who was on board the *Maros Maru*, wrote of the commencement of the voyage:

> The first night after setting sail was a terrifying ordeal for the men, worse than any conceivable nightmare. The rain continued, the wind got up and the sea was rough and choppy. The ship was constantly swamped with high seas, which swept

across the deck with every roll of the vessel, throwing exposed stretcher cases around the waterlogged deck causing them to smash into solid objects which had broken free and were crashing around in the storm. One man died before morning came . . .

Four days after leaving Ambon, the *Maros Maru* put into Raha Moena in the Celebes, where another 150 British and Dutch prisoners boarded. These men had already been through a traumatic experience when their transport was sunk by an American aircraft, and most were naked and racked by beriberi. Their arrival on board made a bad situation worse. There was now barely room for any prisoners to sit, let alone lie down.

The voyage continued, the ship calling at Macassar, where she lay at anchor for forty days, with all the while conditions on board deteriorating. Having been under water for a year before the Japanese decided to raise her, the *Maros Maru* was far from seaworthy when she set out and, not surprisingly, her engines broke down after leaving Macassar, thereby prolonging the voyage even further. The prisoners were dying like flies, the Japanese guards throwing their bodies overboard weighted down by sandbags.

A voyage of 900 miles that normally would have been completed in under four days eventually stretched out to sixty-seven days. Of the 650 prisoners on board, only 325 were still alive when the *Maros Maru* reached Sourabaya.

Japan's dream of carving out an Empire stretching from India in the west to New Guinea in the east came to an end on 6 June 1942 near a tiny island in mid-Pacific aptly named Midway. In an attempt to capture the island, to be used as a stepping stone to the Hawaiian Islands, the Japanese sent in a powerful fleet under Admiral Nagumo, consisting of seven battleships, six aircraft carriers, twelve cruisers, forty-six destroyers and sixteen submarines. Opposing them, the Americans had three aircraft carriers, eight cruisers, nineteen destroyers and nineteen submarines. But the battle, when it came, was fought out in the air by planes from the carriers. The fleets were never less than 100 miles apart, and at no time did the ships exchange fire. The result was decisive, Nagumo losing the four carriers *Akagi*, *Hiryu*, *Kaga* and *Soryu*, and the heavy cruiser *Mikuma* to the American bombers. *Mikuma*'s sister cruiser, *Mogami*, was also badly damaged, and 322 aircraft and 5,000 men were lost. The Americans, on the other hand, lost only one carrier, 150 aircraft and 300 men. The original exponents of air power at sea had been beaten at their own game; Pearl Harbor, Singapore, Java Sea, and all the other humiliating defeats inflicted on the Allies in the preceding six months were avenged, and the face of sea warfare had been changed forever. Churchill wrote: 'This American victory was of cardinal importance, not only to the United States, but to the whole Allied cause. The moral effect was tremendous and instantaneous. At one stroke the dominant position of Japan in the Pacific was reversed.'

Bibliography

Abend, Hallett, *Ramparts of the Pacific*, Bodley Head, 1942

Allen, Charles, *Tales from the South China Seas*, Andre Deutsch, 1983

Banks, Arthur, *Wings of the Dawning*, Images Publishing, 1996

Blair, Clay, *Silent Victory*, Bantam Books, 1975

Brooke, Geoffrey, *Singapore's Dunkirk*, Leo Cooper, 2003

Burchell, David, *The Bells of Sunda Strait*, Robert Hale, 1972

Churchill, Winston, *The Second World War*, Cassell, 1950

Collier, Richard, *1941: Armageddon*, Hamish Hamilton, 1981

Costello, John, *The Pacific War*, Collins, 1981

Firkins, Peter, *Of Nautilus and Eagles*, Hutchinson (Australia), 1983

Gibson, Walter, *The Boat*, W.H. Allen, 1974

Gough, Richard, *Escape from Singapore*, William Kimber, 1987

Gunther, John, *Inside Asia*, Hamish Hamilton, 1939

Haldane, R. A., *The Hidden War*, Robert Hale, 1978

Hara, Tameichi, *Japanese Destroyer Captain*, Ballantine Books (New York), 1961

Hashimoto, Mochitsura, *Sunk – The Story of the Japanese Submarine Fleet 1942–1945*, Cassell, 1954

Howarth, Stephen, *Morning Glory*, Hamish Hamilton, 1983

Humble, Richard, *Aircraft Carriers*, Michael Joseph, 1982

Ishimaru, Tota, *Japan Must Fight Britain*, Hurst & Blackett, 1936

Kennedy, Paul M., *The Sea War in the Pacific*, Marshall Cavendish, 1976

Martienssen, Anthony, *Hitler and his Admirals*, Secker & Warburg, 1948

Middlemiss, Norman L., *The British Tankers*, Shield Publications, 1989

Moffatt, Jonathan & Holmes McCormick, Audrey, *Moon Over Malaya*, Coombe Publishing, 1999

Montgomery, Michael, *Who Sank the Sydney?*, Leo Cooper, 1983

Rohwer, Jürgen, *Axis Submarine Successes 1939–1945*, Patrick Stephens, 1983
Roskill, S. W., *The War at Sea*, HMSO, 1954–61
Slader, John, *The Fourth Service*, Robert Hale, 1994
Thomas, David, *Battle of the Java Sea*, Deutsch, 1968
Whitehouse, Arch, *Subs and Submariners*, Doubleday, 1961

Index

189

190

Rogers, Chief Petty Officer Charles, 41, 45
Rogers, Leading Seaman Ronald, 135
Rogge, *Kapitän-zur-See* Bernhard, 5, 7
Rooks, Captain, 77
Rorup, Captain Adolph U., 151, 152
Ross, Vice Consul, 115
Rotterdam Lloyd Line, 121, 122, 124, 127
Royal Dutch Mail Line, 4, 110, 119, 121
Royal Engineers, 39
Royal Packet Navigation Company (KPM), 111, 129, 130, 139, 144
Rushton, Able Seaman W., 132
Ryan, Chief Stoker P., 134

Sanderson, Second Engineer, 146
Schokking, Lieutenant Colonel, 110, 121
Schultz, Captain Paul F., 155, 156
Scott Smith, Third Officer Alan, 65
Schoer, Captain Cor, 119–21
Searle, Ronald, 39
Simpson, Telegraphist C., 132

Ships, Merchant
Augustina, 98–104; *Autolycus*, 176; *Automedon*, 2–9; *Am Pang*, 37; *Batavia*, 176; *Benledi*, 167; *Bintoehan*, 129; *Boero*, 107, 124; *Bienville*, 176; *British Judge*, 104–8, 167; *British Loyalty*, 151; *British Motorist*, 61, 63, 64; *British Sergeant*, 167; *Capetown Castle*, 26; *Cecilia*, 138, 139; *Chicksaw City*, 156; *City of Manchester*, 111–15, 124; *Chilka*, 145–7; *Clan Murdoch*, 167; *Clifton Hall*, 152; *Coloradan*; 156; *Christos Markettos*, 152; *City of Canterbury*, 27, 28; *City of York*, 25; *Dardanus*, 174–6; *Devonshire*, 26–8; *De Weert*, 153; *Don Isidro*, 58, 65; *Dundrum Castle*, 154; *Duchess of Bedford*, 26; *Eidsvol*, 116–18, 141; *Eknaren*, 153; *Elmdale*, 157; *Empress of Asia*, 25–8, 30–3, 35, 36, 51; *Empress of Japan*, 25, 26; *Enggano*, 119–21;

Examelia, 156; *Exmoor*, 176; *Felix Roussel*, 26–8, 32, 33; *Firethorn*, 155–7; *Florence D.*, 57, 58, 65; *Francol*, 105, 129, 132, 135, 136; *Gandara*, 174, 175; *Ganges*, 176; *Garoet*, 127; *Goldenfels*, 4; *Goviken*, 152, 153; *Gulfstate*, 159; *Harpasa*, 172, 173; *Harrikuku Maru*, 144, 145; *Hector*, 167; *Hellenic Trader*, 152; *Indora*, 176; *Johnstown*, 151, 152; *Kamogawa Maru*, 92; *Kota Gede*, 111, 124; *Langkoeas*, 95–7, 106; *Mahronda*, 152; *Malda*, 176; *Maros Maru*, 184.185; *Marella*, 33, 51, 118; *Mauna Loa*, 56; *Maunganui*, 152; *Meigs*, 56; *Modjokerto*, 121, 122; *Mundra*, 153, 154; *Neil Maersk*, 151; *Neptuna*, 59–61, 64, 65; *Norden*, 155; *Ole Jacob*, 3, 7; *Parigi*, 130, 131, 136; *Pijnacker Hordijk*, 107; *Pipina*, 147; *Plancius*, 26–8; *Poelau Bras*, 147–50; *Poelau Tello*, 148; *Portman*, 56; *Prominent*, 116, 118; *Rooseboom*, 139–45; *St. Francis*, 58; *Sea Witch*, 83, 84; *Selma City*, 173, 174; *Shinkuang*, 176; *Silksworth*, 176; *Sing-Keng-Seng*, 35–8, 51; *Sinkiang*, 176; *Steaua Romana*, 152; *Suez Maru*, 180–3; *Swiftsure*, 156; *Tjimanoek*, 136; *Taksang*, 173; *Tasmania*, 152; *Tawali*, 110–12, 120, 121, 132, 136; *Tomohon*, 111; *Toradja*, 120; *Tulagi*, 56, 63, 64; *Van Waerwÿck*, 144; *War Sidar*, 105; *Zaandam*, 115, 116, 123, 127, 155–9; *Zealandia*, 63

Ships, Naval
Abukuma, 165; *Akagi*, 57, 87, 165, 177, 185; *Alden USS*, 69, 80, 81; *Amagiri*, 176; *Amatsukaze*, 76, 93; *Anking HMS*, 105, 121, 129, 132, 135, 136; *Arashi*, 91, 118, 120, 128, 129; *Arizona USS*, 13; *Asagumo*, 71; *Ashigara*, 79; *Atago*, 87, 118; *Atlantis*, 4–7; *Asheville USS*, 90, 91; *Ballarat HMAS*, 184;